The Elements of Small Business

A Lay Person's Guide to the Financial Terms, Marketing Concepts and Legal Forms that Every Entrepreneur Needs

John Thaler, Esq.

SILVER LAKE PUBLISHING
LOS ANGELES, CA   ABERDEEN, WA

The Elements of Small Business
A Lay Person's Guide to the Financial Terms, Marketing Concepts and Legal Forms that Every Entrepreneur Needs
First edition
Copyright © 2005 by John Thaler

Silver Lake Publishing
P.O. Box 29460
Los Angeles, CA 90029

•

111 East Wishkah Street
Aberdeen, WA 98520

For a list of other publications or for more information, please call 1.360.532.5758.

Library of Congress Catalogue Number: pending

The Elements ofSmall Business
A Lay Person's Guide to the Financial Terms, Marketing Concepts and Legal Forms that Every Entrepreneur Needs
Includes index.
Pages: 354

ISBN: 1-56343-784-8
Printed in Canada

Acknowledgments, Dedication & Disclaimer

This book would not have been possible without the aid and support of my research assistant, James Souvay, and my personal assistant, Alison Bock. Their tireless dedication to checking facts, locating information, searching out forms, and copyediting resulted in a reference guide that everyone can use.

Also, this book would not have been started without the simple words of Jeffrey Rose, accountant extraordinaire, who said, "John, I think you should write a book." Hey, Jeff, I finally took your advice. Don't let it go to your head.

This book is dedicated to my wife and best friend, Melinda, who put up with the long hours of work. And it is dedicated to my son, Matthew (a.k.a. "Mr. Matthew"), who continues to amaze me every day with his accomplishments. Someday soon he will snatch the pebble from my hand.

And now a word from our lawyers...

THIS BOOK IS INTENDED TO OFFER GENERAL INFORMATION ON MANY ISSUES PERTINENT TO SMALL BUSINESS OWNERS. NEITHER SILVER LAKE PUBLLISHING NOR THE AUTHOR IS ENGAGED IN OR ATTEMPTING TO RENDER LEGAL OR PROFESSIONAL ADVICE OR SERVICES. THOUGH GREAT CARE HAS BEEN TAKEN TO ASSURE ACCURACY,

In other words, if you want the best advice for your situation, spend the money to retain a good attorney or other competent professional. Come on, it's only a book.

—John Thaler

Table of Contents

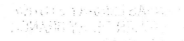

Chapter 1

Welcome, Bienvenue, Shalom...

*The two most engaging powers of an author
are to make new things familiar, familiar things
new.*

—William Makepeace Thackeray

Running a business is never simple. But it can be *simplified* if you invest the time to learn the basic elements. If you don't, owning and operating your own business will likely become a complex nightmare of unforeseen and unresolved problems. I know. As an attorney who specializes in dealing with business problems, I have a lot of experience with *complexity*. Let me start this chapter with one good example.

On a chilly November afternoon, a couple of guys sat in the office, the location from which they operated several small businesses. The older man rested comfortably in the black faux leather recliner. He leaned back slightly as he looked at his younger partner who was seated across the desk in a chair normally reserved for clients. They looked at each other for a few seconds, neither uttering a word.

Then: "The deal looks good," said the older man. "Make the call."

The younger man nodded his agreement. At long last, they would purchase the nightclub. These guys were not freshmen, they were not beginners and they were not neophytes to the intricate details of operating a small business. In fact, they owned other clubs and thought this one would be a great addition. And they were certain that the purchase price for the land, the improvement (a euphemism for the building) and the business fell far below their true value.

After telephoning the seller and arranging a meeting, they hopped in the car and drove to "escrow." Once there, they met with the purported owner. Actually, they met with the alleged sole shareholder of the corporation that owned the land, the building and the improvement. A nice enough guy. He had operated the club for more than a decade under the auspices of a corporation. During the course of the meeting, they agreed once again on the price and then shared the information with the escrow agent.

Everything about the deal seemed simple: the corporation would be sold in a stock share purchase. The buyers would pay partly in cash and partly through financing. The deal would close in 30 days. During that time the entertainment and dance permits along with the alcohol permit would be revised to reflect the names of the new shareholders. What could go wrong? Everything.

Remember: Escrow is not the place where agreements are written. No, that special place is located in your attorney's office. Escrow is like that neutral corner where a boxer stands when his opponent is being counted out. Most people associate it with buying and selling their home. Escrow is nothing more than trusted party ensuring that anything agreed to by the parties is carried out to the letter. That's all.

Do you know that in most states agreements for the purchase of real property or agreements that include real property, such as a lease with an option to buy, must be in writing? Neither the buyers nor the seller knew. Do you know that the allocation of the total purchase price to the land, the improvement, and the business triggers different tax ramifications and liabilities? Neither the buyers nor the seller knew. Do you know that there are different ramifications between an asset purchase versus a stock share purchase? Do you know about a "UCC 6" bulk sales announcement, when to use it, and how it removes potential creditor liabilities in an asset purchase? Do you know what permits are required to operate a club serving alcohol or to operate a club where dancing will take place.

We're not done yet.

Do you know whether any zoning ordinances changed that might result in the denial of a transfer of the permit? Do you know whether all tax returns been filed, whether payroll taxes been paid, whether all sales taxes been paid, especially in a stock share purchase? Do you know if a workers' compensation policy and liability policy (not to mention fire insurance policy) are in effect? Do you know how to get these policies?

How many employees are on the payroll? Are they doing a good job? Will they remain under new management? If not, who will manage the business? Are they trustworthy, especially in a business that sees a lot of cash. Are more employees needed? Do you know if there are any liens from lawsuits? Any community property issues?

Lots of Rude Surprises

Within a few weeks, the nightclub buyers discovered that the sole shareholder had not filed any federal tax returns or state tax returns in more than ten years—resulting in a suspension of the corporation many years previous. So the buyers hired an accountant. They spent $88,000 in back taxes and tax return preparation. The process took more than three months. The suspension was lifted and so the sale continued...or not.

Then the buyers discovered that the shareholder had been married and that, per the divorce judgment, the ex-wife held 50 percent interest in the shares. They also discovered that per the terms of the divorce, she had a right to review any purchase offers since she would be receiving one half of the sale proceeds. She had a lawyer. And he wanted to review everything. More delays.

Then the buyers discovered that the sales taxes had not been paid for at least five years when an investigator for the state taxing authority called to see about collecting the debt. With the suspension of the corporation, that resulted in the retail sales license and its liability being "transferred" to the seller. It also resulted in an audit and findings that more than $100,000 was owed. Not to be outdone and in going for that perfect record, the payroll tax payments were a bit lacking as was the worker's compensation insurance payments. More delays. And then there was the Labor Board lien from an employee who had won a judgment against the corporation or the individual or from somebody.

The buyers' financing company held on for a while but could not tie up hundreds of thousands of dollars waiting for the deal to finish. Every time the buyers reported that the deal was a "go," they had to call back telling the company that it was a "maybe." Ultimately, the financing company lost interest in this mess and pulled out. Almost one year of time and effort and $88,000 in damages later, no financing.

This 30-day escrow meandered into its eleventh month no closer to resolution that it was on that November afternoon a year earlier. The deal finally closed *16 months* after the initial handshake.

Any attorney who specializes in business transactions has agreement forms for asset purchases and for stock purchases. Those forms require the seller to guarantee that each of the above taxes has been paid. And they require the seller to guarantee that the business, including the stock, is not encumbered (like subjecting any deal to the approval of an ex-spouse). For less than $500, the buyers would have known that a problem existed or would have had a great fraud suit against the seller.

A good attorney would have provided a checklist to the buyers and made sure that they reviewed all necessary records and permits. Meanwhile, the attorney would have checked on zoning and permit transfers. And the attorney would have examined the insurance or made certain that liability and worker's compensation insurance was available and at a reasonable rate.

You might recall an episode of *I Love Lucy* where Lucy decides to write a book about her life with Ricky and the Mertz's. Her manuscript is rejected by everyone except one publisher. When the publisher's agent came to visit, naturally Lucy is very excited. That is until she learns that only a portion of the manuscript will be used in a textbook entitled, "Don't Let This Happen to You."

That is the theme of this book.

My Experience

I come from a long line of lawyers. My father is a lawyer. During my misguided youth (that which I can recall), I observed many small businesses. Some succeeded; others failed. I watched and I learned. And then I became a lawyer, much to my own chagrin.

What many people don't realize is that a law practice is a small business. In addition to the briefs that must be filed, the court hearings that require my presence, the filing deadlines for complaints and motions, the recycled paper requirement, and the stringent court-imposed deadlines on everything, I have to bill clients and hope that they pay. I have to hire and fire. I have to pay taxes. I have to manage and pay expenses and apportion my time. Sound familiar?

In the past 10 years, I have had three clients wipe out my bills by filing for bankruptcy. Recently, I was retained by a client who was a leading executive in the fashion industry. This woman had an annual income of over $500,000 without consideration of her bonus. She and several other parties were sued by a financial entity that had loaned money to a corporation in which they owned stock and to which they had pledged their stock shares as security for the loan. After only three months, I convinced the plaintiff's lawyer to dismiss my client voluntarily. A motion requesting dismissal would have cost at least $5,000.

You would think the client would have been grateful. Sure. On a total bill of less than $2,000 for all the services provided over the course of six months she sent $100 checks for a few months and then stopped. I wrote her several letters. Finally, she sent a check for one half of the remaining balance and a nasty letter telling me she would not pay any additional amounts since I screwed up her case. In truth, I saved her tens of thousands of dollars in litigation costs.

I have a saying: the practice of law would be great if it weren't for the clients.

Not all clients are like the fashion maven. Most of my clients pay on time, send me thank you letters and even refer their friends and relatives to me. Nonetheless, like you, I need a place of business and that means leasing office space. I need a billing system. I need a few employees including a secretary to handle everything from filing hundreds of pieces of paper each week to answering over thirty telephone calls per day. I need to purchase or lease certain equipment such as computers and copy machines. I need a constant stream of new business and I need (or pray for) payment of my bills.

For more than a decade, I have dispensed advice to clients who intend to create small businesses and to clients who already have them. Some listen to me; others don't. For the first and only time in this book, let me paraphrase self-help guru Anthony Robbins: *If you want to be successful, observe successful people and do what they do.* That sounds simple. For reasons only sociologists can explain, the practice of that adage is far more elusive.

People are far more emotional than logical. And when they become fixated on an idea, there is no technique or empathic dialogue that will permit me—or any advisor—to talk them out of a bad idea. But the marketplace is the ultimate judge of good and bad ideas. That's what's refreshing about business.

The fact is business requires hard work. But it is not just about hard work. While feeling passionate about your business helps you to get up every morning, having a narcissistic and narrow view that you can place a restaurant on a site where 10 others have failed defies all logic. Success is about observation. What products or services are needed? How will you fill that need? Are other businesses doing what you want to do? Are they successful? If so, what you can discern from their success? If they are not successful, can you really do it better? How will you do it better?

> There are 24 million businesses in the United Stated defined as "small." You can bet that the proprietor works 18 hour days for the privilege of not having a boss. And by the way, being on your own means you will receive none of the customary benefits big companies provide—such as cheap medical insurance, cheap life insurance and employer contributions to your retirement plan.

Instead you get long hours, the agony of decision making, the expense of health insurance or the thrill of belonging to an HMO, and a crash course in employer-employee relations when the secretary you hand picked after countless interviews (all of which interfered with the time you needed to develop new business) thinks that the work day begins at 10:00 A.M. and ends at 3:45 P.M. Also, if you can make the time for a vacation, it's not a *paid* vacation since you are not at your desk cultivating clients or accounts (and neither is that new secretary).

Owning and operating a small business is not for everyone and probably is not for most people. But, if you are tired of making millions for someone else—if you have the strength, the passion, the discipline and dedication required—owning your business can be quite satisfying. You answer to no one. You set the hours, you hire the employees, you choose the direction the business will travel and you make it happen. The spoils are yours to enjoy.

Consider this book to be a vocational testing device. If it all makes sense when you get to the end, then operating your own business might be right for you.

This Book Is Your Starter

This book is not the only one of its kind. So what distinguishes this one from the others? That's easy. Many authors and publishers claim that with the author's instruction you do not need an attorney or an accountant or other professionals and specialists. Even if attorneys have evolved only to one step below garden slugs, attorneys and other professionals are absolutely essential components of operating a successful business.

In fact, you cannot be successful in small business without the advice and assistance of a smart lawyer and a deft accountant. Anyone who tells you different probably has some swampland in Florida or a bridge somewhere in the Brooklyn area of New York that he wants to sell.

The fact is you don't know what you don't know. No "how-to" book in the world can make up for three years of law school, two years of MBA study or years of testing and work credits leading to a CPA credential. And nothing, really nothing, can ever substitute for the years of experience these experts possess.

There is no crime in ignorance. But there is stupidity in stubbornly refusing to seek out those who have the knowledge and experience.

In our system of laws, rules and regulations, there are many loopholes and ambiguities. It took me three years of law school and many years of practice to get to know them. I specialize in this stuff. You don't. You need the help of lawyers and accountants and other experienced professionals to avoid situations that may hurt you. If you don't believe me, ask anyone you know who operates a successful small business. And ask anyone who found himself or herself or their business in litigation.

My lawyer friends and I have a saying: It doesn't take 100 clients to build a successful law practice. It takes five who never listen. Don't be one of those five.

Chapter 1: Welcome, Bienvenue, Shalom...

Our journey begins with the issues of choosing to buy an existing business or building your own from the ground up, including an examination of the different business entities available, including their pros and cons. We'll tell you how to go about making a partnership agreement, should you decide to open that tack and feed store with your Cousin Barry. One of your possible business choices is franchising.

We will then discuss how to determine if franchising is right for you, including how they operate and the requirements for buying one. Next, you'll need to get some money for start-up capital, and we'll tell you where to look and give you some ideas on how to get it.

Once you've got the money, you'll want to tackle the infamous business plan and think about marketing your product or service. More than likely, an office or other space for your operation is needed. We'll tell you how to deal with commercial leases and the landlords that inadvertently go with them. A tour through financing and operations is discussed along with insurance and those dreaded taxes.

> While almost every business is different, small business generally falls into two categories: sale of goods from manufacturing to retail or services from plant maintenance to business consulting. Most of the topics in this book relate to both. Where little difference exists, little or no distinction is made. However, where significant differences exist, I will point them out to you.

Starting a business can be a most exciting and rewarding experience. However, you may have to deal with some unpleasant situations. Some of the most common unpleasant situations arise between partnerships in business. And although there are good times to be had running your business, there may be other unfortunate incidents to deal with, like divorce or bankruptcy.

After all your hard work starting and running a successful business, you will also want to look into retirement planning for yourself and your employees, if you have any.

The Elements of Small Business

While the task at hand may seem overwhelming, the point here is not to make you memorize a lot of information. Rather, this book will provide you with the background necessary to understand the issues you face. Business is a process of responding to changing conditions. You don't know what you don't know. This is not a book for dummies. After reading this book, when an issue arises you won't panic; you will know what to do or who to call. That alone will increase your chances for success.

We have provided some forms for you to review. Unlike other books that leave you with hundreds of forms or a CD-Rom, we have chosen to include a sampling of what you can expect— because the fact is you must learn to rely on the expertise of others if you want to succeed in your own business.

So go to it and good luck.

References

Attard, Jane. *The Home Office and Small Business Answer Book: Solutions to the Most Frequently Asked Questions about Starting and Running Your Business*. Henry Holt & Company (July 2000).

Bossidy, Larry, et al. *Execution: The Discipline of Getting Things Done*. Crown Publishing Group (June 2002).

Koch, Richard. *The 80/20 Individual: How to Accomplish More by Doing Less*. Doubleday & Co., Inc. (August 2003).

Zimmerer, Thomas W., and Norman M. Scarborough. *Essentials of Entrepreneurship and Small Business Management* (3rd Ed.). Pearson Education (June 2001).

The Elements of Small Business

Chapter 2

Economics 101

If all economists were laid end to end, they would not reach a conclusion.

—Anonymous

Anyone in business needs to have sharp understanding of business elements. But this doesn't have much to do with all the chattering about the stock markets or economic trends that you see on cable television, hear on the radio or read in most newspapers.

Sure, economic trends affect business. In a recession, everyone has less money to spend and small businesses are more likely to fail. But these things happen in many steps. Most business journalism simply tries to locate trends.

Check out the headlines of any major newspaper: "The recession will not subside until next year, economists say." Or: "Economists predict greater sales in the high tech sector but a slowdown in durable goods this holiday season." Or: "Housing Starts will continue to grow, economists conclude. What is a *housing start*? How does it finish? Who are these economists and why are they so important?

Most Americans are uneducated when it comes to economics. Maybe they took a class in college…or maybe not.

How will the trade deficit affect your business venture? How will the federal deficit affect interest rates and borrowing? What are durable goods and who orders them? And what about the strength of the Yen as compared to the dollar as compared to the Euro?

This book is not a dissertation on economics. However, before you decide to take the plunge and take it with your life savings, you must consider the economic environment that faces you. This is especially important if you rely on parts or supplies from overseas where the economy of foreign countries and the currency exchange rates affect you're your operating costs.

Paying attention to the changing economic climate and knowing how it will affect your business is important. So let's examine a few key terms and conditions and how they might relate to you. But remember: this is not a treatise. It is meant to assist you in recognizing the effects of external economic conditions on your new business venture.

Recession

A recession occurs when too many goods have been produced versus the number of buyers. Why is this a problem? Because if warehouses are filled with goods no one is purchasing, then manufacturers have no reason to manufacture. Profits decline as the retail prices decline. Businesses lay off workers. In turn, the workers apply for government benefits and pay little or no taxes back to the government. That causes increased deficits. Depending on the party in power, higher deficits, especially at the state level may result in higher taxes. That places additional burdens on new businesses.

But a recession also creates certain advantages. It is an employer's market when so many skilled workers are unemployed. If manufacturers have built too many widgets and your business depends on widgets, then your purchase costs will be greatly reduced. And for consumers, the final product, sitting in the warehouse, will go on sale long before the after-Christmas sale.

In fact, a recession can be one of the best times to create a business and to hire employees. As the economy recovers, your business is ready to go.

Futurist Alvin Toffler wrote a well known book entitled *Futureshock*. Among his many observations was the analysis that technology is developing faster than the average person can adjust to using it. Do your parents have a computer? If so, do they think that if they hit the wrong button the planets will collide? Mine do. Actually, a recent example of this problem involves Personal Digital Assistants (PDAs).

The people who build PDAs spent most of the late 1990s building new and improved PDAs with more and more features no one could understand and would never use. The manufacturers did not consider that they were creating technology at a pace the average consumer could not understand. If they could not understand it, then they were not going to buy it. And they didn't. As a result the early 2000s saw a glut of PDAs in the marketplace—and a recession for PDA makers and their suppliers.

> Building the better mousetrap does not always result in a sale. In business, a warehouse full of the best mousetraps is the worst possible scenario.

Inflation

Inflation occurs when the cost of goods rises faster than the income of those who have to pay for them. Sometimes this happens because consumers are purchasing goods and services at a rate faster than companies can manufacture or provide them. Or this results from external factors such as shortages in raw materials which in turn create higher prices. Or this results from increased requirements (i.e., taxes) by the state or federal governments to cover employee benefits such as health care or family leave—with the added cost being passed on to you.

In the early 2000s, people in the United States have seen inflation result from changes in oil prices. Wide fluctuations have caused unleaded gasoline to range from $1.35 to more than $2.00 per gallon. Think about it. If your company depends on shipping or if your business involves pizza delivery, gas prices make a difference.

> Higher costs to manufacturers and service providers mean higher prices to consumers. So do increases in the minimum wage or increases in insurance costs, workers' compensation costs or employee benefits. If California passes a law requiring employers to cover medical expenses for employees, that cost often results in job cuts or higher prices for the goods and services—or both.

Then we have the minimum wage. When I was a child, I asked my mother why the government could not just give everyone a million dollars. Everyone would be a millionaire. My mother gave the only answer she could: "I don't know. Go ask your father."

The fact is most of our inflation gets exported. That is, companies beat inflation and increases in the minimum wage by building factories overseas and paying far less labor costs. In the past few years, service industry jobs have traveled overseas. Check out the Microsoft annual report with respect to the number of high tech jobs performed in India.

Or people get laid off. Several years ago while on vacation, I met a man who owned a Baskin Robbins franchise in Lemon Grove, California, a suburb of San Diego. The state had just raised the minimum wage from $5.85 to $6.25. Between the higher hourly wage and the various payroll taxes (a subject I will discuss in detail later), he was left with two choices:

raise the price of the ice cream or hire one less high school student during summer vacation.

But sometimes, like with increased gasoline prices or increased raw material prices, there are no alternatives for businesses except to raise prices. Hence inflation.

Gross Domestic Product (GDP)

In measuring the state of the economy, economists often discuss the GDP figures. GDP does nothing other than measure the number of transactions in the economy regardless as to whether the transactions are positive or negative. It is measured on a quarterly basis.

What constitutes a *transaction*? Basically, any exchange of money for a product or service. For example, if you go to the supermarket and purchase a Hostess Cupcake, that is one transaction. If you tip the bag boy and he uses that tip to purchase a cheeseburger at McDonald's, then you have another transaction. And so forth.

Why is this figure so significant? Three reasons: firstly, a recession is defined as two or more straight quarters of negative GDP; secondly, the more transactions in the economy, the more people who have to be involved in the transactions. So a high "GDP" figure often equates with higher employment or at least the need to hire more people.

Projections of higher GDP in the future mean more people working. The third reason: the greater number of transactions, the more taxable events. When you purchased the cupcake, you paid sales tax. When the bag boy bought the cheeseburger, he paid a sales tax. And so on.

Economist Arthur Laffer, famous for the "Laffer Curve," opined in the 1980s that the country could grow its way out of deficits by lowering tax rates. Less taxes would mean more spending and more spending would result in more taxable events via higher GDP. Many economists laughed at him. But his curve reflected the dynamic nature of the GDP.

In the late 1990s when the country ran budget surpluses, it was due primarily to a strong GDP. The increase in taxable transactions actually eliminated the deficit. In fairness, many economists do not believe that a reduction of taxes on the rich stimulates the economy; they'd prefer reductions that focused on middle class households. But no one can deny that, for a short time, the budget was balanced as a result of growth.

Federal Funds Rate

Unlike many European countries, the United States does not have a central bank. Instead, it has a Treasury Department (those nice folks who print the money) and an independent Federal Reserve Board. The Board members set monetary policy. The Federal or "Fed" Funds Rate is the rate of interest the government charges banks for borrowing money. This rate is set by the Federal Reserve Board.

Lower interest should result in more borrowing because the rate ultimately affects the interest you pay on a loan or line of credit from your neighborhood bank. More borrowing means more spending and more spending means higher GDP.

Periodically, the Federal Reserve Board meets to discuss and determine the interest rates. The Board also states its future intentions. If you intend to apply for a bank loan or a line of credit, interest rates may play a significant role. If you have reason to believe that rates will increase in the future and you have plans for expansion or for start-up, you might want to obtain a loan *before* the rates increase. Also, if you plan to buy large quantities of supplies from manufacturers, you can bet that their higher borrowing costs will result in higher costs to you; so, if you know you'll need a million widgets, you should get them sooner later rather than later.

Exchange Rates & More Information

As we discussed previously, the rate of exchange can have a significant effect on your business. Are you buying raw materials from afar or are you importing goods from foreign countries to sell in this country? Fluctuations in currencies can have a significant impact.

When this book was being written, the Japanese Yen is trading at 110 Yen to the Dollar. But a year earlier, the Yen was trading at 124 Yen to the Dollar. If your raw materials or finished goods come from Japan, a ten percent change just raised the costs of your goods. And that means either a lower profit margin for you or an increase in prices to cover the difference.

While the number of daily newspaper subscribers has decreased with the advent of cable television and cable news, there is no substitute for in-depth coverage. The *Wall Street Journal* (like its main competitor, *Investor's Business Daily*) provides a wealth of information on the goings on of business, current trends and future trends. To understand recessions, inflation, Fed Funds rates and exchange rates along with business trends and the strategies of your competitors, read these daily newspapers.

 Unless you majored in business or have received an MBA, a lot of the material in these periodicals may seem like a foreign language. But hang in there. As issues arise in your business, you will be surprised how many abstract terms have a direct affect on what you do...and how many other small business owners are having the same experience.

Conclusion

As you will see in the next chapter, you don't have to be a genius to operate a successful business. However, knowledge is the key to success and the most important element in operating any small business. Don't skimp on studying economics and reading business papers and magazines. You would be surprised at how far a little knowledge will take you.

References

Clason, George S. *Richest Man in Babylon* (reissue). Signet Classics (January 2002).

Heilbroner, Robert L., and Lester Thurow. *Economics Explained: Everything You Need to Know About the Economy Works and Where It's Going.* Simon & Schuster Trade Paperbacks (April 1998).

Slavin, Stephen L. *Economics.* The McGraw-Hill Companies (July 2001).

Sowell, Thomas. *Basic Economics.* Basic Books (January 2001).

Sutton, Walt. *Leap of Strength: A Personal Tour Through the Months Before and Years After You Start Your Own Business.* Silver Lake Publishing (November, 2000)

Wessels, Walter. *Economics.* Barron's Educational Series, Inc. (September 2000).

Chapter 3

Business Formation

Most are engaged in business the greater part of their lives, because the soul abhors a vacuum and they have not discovered any employment for man's nobler faculties.

—Henry David Thoreau

If there is one place where impulse buying is the most dangerous, it is the purchase of a business. Many small businesses fail. Not because of bad economic times and not because of bad management, but because of a failure to do the homework in advance of the purchase.

In this case, *homework* involves questions. Lots of questions.

Is this the right location? Is there local competition? Do the demographics of the marketplace support the business in the mid- and long-term? What *are* demographics of the marketplace? How do the channels to market (distributors, wholesalers, resellers) work?

Does the business have seasonal highs and lows? How quickly do clients or customers pay? How quickly do vendors or suppliers expect to *be* paid? Does the business need employees? How many? What kind?

And so the journey begins…

Research, Research, Research

Whether your talent is law or advertising or computer programming, chances are someone already operates the business of your dreams. That's okay. You don't need to monopolize the marketplace.

 Business experts say that controlling ten percent of the market is all you need. Think about it. How many companies build cars or produce laundry detergent or canned coffee? How many gas stations do you find at any given intersection?

One client who informed me that she wanted to open a business. She had driven around her neighborhood and noticed that the area had many fast food restaurants but lacked a *certain kind* of food. Based on her knowledge of the neighborhood, she believed that this type of food would sell well. So she contacted the parent company that sells franchises for that type of food and is currently looking for space to lease.

With the expansion of the Internet, researching successful businesses and why they are successful is easier than ever. If your business is local, such as a fast food restaurant, then you will want to examine the neighborhood. Is your area expanding or has everyone been laid off from the widget factory and leaving town? Does your area have a lot of couples in their twenties? Does it have a lot of children?

Children love to eat fast food and parents love to avoid cooking, especially when both parents work.

If you will be providing a service, such as dry cleaning, you may want to review the number of clothing or department stores in the area and the percentage of adults whose income is above the median (higher than the average). High-scale clothing stores or department stores or even stores featuring big and tall suits for men mean more clothes sold that require dry cleaning. And those clothes are more likely to be purchased by adults with higher than average incomes.

28

Location, Location, Location

In purchasing residential real estate, this is the only rule and it simply means that where the house is situated makes all the differences to its current value and any increases in future value. For a business, location has more to do with these issues:

- foot traffic;
- vehicle traffic;
- lease costs per square foot;
- property taxes;
- property purchase costs;
- available labor pool;
- signage and zoning restrictions; and
- parking.

Most people understand that no matter what the business, taxes will be paid to the Internal Revenue Service. And most people are aware that many states grab their share of the tax pie. But what about local city and county government? In the City of Los Angeles, a business tax is levied based on the revenue of the company; while, in nearby Beverly Hills, taxes are computed based on a set-fee structure derived from the number of employees.

> These differences in abutting areas can make a huge differences to your bottom line. If you have few employees but a high income, Beverly Hills may be a better location than Los Angeles. On the other hand, a business with many employees will want to pay taxes based on revenue, not head count.

The Elements of Small Business

And let's not forget property taxes. If you buy, you pay; if you rent, the landlord likely will require that you pay or at least pay a proportional share if other businesses exist at the same location.

High volume foot traffic and vehicle traffic also can be crucial for retail sales—but they're less important to manufacturing or servicing where the local community is not the customer. For example, an intersection that receives a lot of traffic is likely to have a higher volume of fast food sales than an area of light volume. On the other hand, if you are intending to manufacture or provide services outside of the local community, then you may wish to place an office or build a plant where the rent and related costs are cheaper—the outskirts of town.

This is where signage comes in. Those golden arches mean something. If you can see them from the street or freeway, you might stop in; if you don't know the business is there, then you won't.

> If your business will rely on traffic, you may wish to check the zoning ordinances in the community you intend to place your business. Many towns have banned signs and billboards or strictly reduced their height and size.

That leads us to lease costs and property purchase costs. If you are building a factory, then you want to go where the land is cheap. Beverly Hills is out of the question. If you drive from Los Angeles to Phoenix, approximately 25 miles west of Phoenix is the town of Goodyear. You get three guesses as to how the town got its name.

Many manufacturers build their plants on the outskirts of the city or even a little farther away because the land and its taxes are cheaper to purchase or to lease. In fact, outlying areas or small suburbs may provide certain incentives such as tax breaks so as to encourage you to establish your business in that town.

One of the least considered danger zones is labor force. If you purchase a Baskin Robbins franchise, your labor force will consist of minimum wage workers—that is if you intend to make a profit. So building the ice cream parlor near a high school may be the best location for business and for employees. You get instant customers and you get teenagers who need jobs.

If you are manufacturing, consider this: Is the area large enough to provide for a number of skilled and unskilled workers needed now and in the future should you wish to expand? If not, or if you find a shortage, will potential employees move to your town?

UCLA has a great deal of difficulty recruiting professors from the East Coast because the cost of living and the cost of housing in the East is significantly less than the West. So UCLA must either subsidize the housing or increase salaries. A difficult choice, at best.

What the Heck Is It?

One of the most confusing aspects of small business is trying to understand the different types and the ramifications of choosing one type over another. To confuse you more, state legislatures have been adding to the list. Prior to 1990 hardly anyone had ever heard of limited liability companies or limited liability partnerships. Yet, they are almost as widely used in many states as corporations.

Before we explore how to start our new business, we need to understand structure. The most common business structures are:

1) Sole Proprietorship
2) Closed Corporation
3) Limited Liability Company/Limited Liability Partnership
4) Limited Partnership

Sole Proprietorship

A sole proprietorship is simply a business often owned by an individual or a family. It is likely that the owners have used their first or last name or initials in the title such as "Jane's Flower Shop" and that they have registered the name as a fictitious business name, also known as a "dba" (for *doing business as*), in the county where the business is located.

There are no shares of stock or bylaws or board members or officers. The income (and expenses) belongs to the owner(s).

Unless your name is part of the business name (e.g., Joe Smith Accounting), most states or counties require that you register any fictitious business name. It is a good idea to register the name of the business with the county where it is located. Usually, this consists of filling out a simple form and paying a few dollars to a county registrar. [Form 3-1] Even corporations can operate under a fictitious name.

For example, Green Corporation might be in entertainment. So it might have a dba called "Green Television" and another called "Green Records." If it were in the greeting card business, it might have a dba called "Green Cards."

As these businesses develop clients, the names become assets and may have value if they are known to the public. If you purchase the stock shares, these names will come with the package. If you purchase the assets, make sure that the names are included.

The advantage of the sole proprietorship is simplicity. You go to work every day. Hopefully you make more than you spend and you pay taxes on the difference. Most lawyers who practice without partners are sole proprietors. Just make sure to purchase adequate insurance.

The *dis*advantage of this business type is that any lawsuits, whether for a slip and fall on your premises or for the cut received by a customer

32

from the thorn on the rose your assistant failed to snip off, falls on your shoulders.

Closed Corporation

Often referred to as "C" corporations, most corporations are *closed corporations*. The term "closed" comes from limitations on the number of shareholders. In most states, that number is one hundred or less.

It also refers to the fact that the shares are not publicly traded on an open market such as the New York Stock Exchange or the NASDAQ. Those companies are known as "public" companies and are subject to complex rules and regulations by the state where they are headquartered and by the Federal government.

If you ever grow to the point that your corporation could move from private to public, you will need the services of multiple accountants, lawyers and investment bankers. And the fact is, they will likely find you. Few closed corporations ever make the move, so it is not a topic covered by this book. Just note that the preliminary steps often used to go public, such as private placement offerings, are not steps you can accomplish without experts.

Take note that in the event a closed corporation intends to have more than the maximum number of shareholders permitted in its home state but is not intending to be publicly traded, states have developed an intermediate category. Often it requires filling out and filing a form with the office of the Secretary of State in the state of incorporation.

A corporation has shareholders, but does not have "owners" because a corporation is an independent entity. The corporation begins with filing "Articles of Incorporation" along with paying a fee to the office of the Secretary of State in the state where the incorporation occurs. [Form 3-

The Elements of Small Business

2] The Articles contain the corporation's name and the maximum number of shares it can to sell or distribute. The incorporator determines the number of shares that are available for distribution.

Choosing to have one million shares does not mean that you need to distribute them. Many businesses anticipate future expansion through sales of shares— to friends and relatives or in private placement offerings made to the general public. So at the time of filing, the incorporator will provide for a high number of shares in the Articles of Incorporation but only issue one share to himself at the time of start-up. That will leave the corporation with plenty of shares to sell later on.

Figuring the number of shares you wish to create in the business depends on what you want to do with the business. If you are in a "partnership" or have investors, they may want to own a certain percentage of the business. You can fulfill their dreams by issuing more shares. Each time you issue shares, they need to be so designated on a shareholder's certificate. [Form 3-3]

The certificate is really nothing more than a fancy looking piece of parchment containing the name of the company, the certificate number (as they are sequentially numbered) and the number of shares the certificate represents.

If a party purchases one hundred at one time, the certificate will indicate that. If that party purchases more shares in the future, you issue another certificate for the new purchase. You note the distribution of shares in any certificate in the corporate records.

Tip: Where an investor purchases a certain number of shares and then later purchases more shares, you may be tempted to take back the first certificate and issue a new one for the totality of the shares. Don't. While no rules or laws would be broken, this "simplification" can cause accounting nightmares, especially if the purchases occur in different calendar or fiscal years. That is because the certificate will imply a single purchase. Yet, the revenue received by the company will reflect the lesser total amount paid from that second purchase. In figuring out all of this, your accountant will

have an anxiety attack forcing hospitalization and when his
disability runs out, he and his children likely will starve—all
because you wanted to make things simple.

The Articles of Incorporation also states the corporation's purpose
for its existence and provides for an "agent for service of process" who
can accept official documents including lawsuits. Anyone over 18 years
old can be the accepting agent for the company—the main shareholder,
the president, the attorney or a partner.

 **Tip: Some states require that you specify the nature of the
business. Other states have no such requirement. If your state
has no such requirement, then you should make the broad-
est statement possible such as "Any and all business that
may be legally conducted in the State of California." That
way if you change direction, you do not have to amend the
articles or form a new corporation.**

Also, If you need to change the number of shares available in the
future, you can file an amendment to the Articles of Incorporation and pay
a fee to the state of incorporation. But why bother to do this? If you
consider future expansion at the time of filing, you can avoid the time effort
and expense in the future.

The comprehensive operating rules are contained in bylaws. This
document contains when and where meetings are to take place. Usually,
notice of an annual meeting or special meeting must be provided. It states
how many directors and officers will be elected by the shareholders, what
their term of office will be and their responsibilities. It is approved at the
first or initial meeting of the shareholders. Many states require that certain
positions be designated with a named individual. For example, you may
be required to provide for a president, a secretary and a treasurer.

However, this does not prohibit you from having other officers with other titles and designations. To determine the requirements that apply to you, check with the Secretary of State's Office in the state you will be operating your business and in which you will be incorporating, if it is different. Often, that information is readily available over the Internet.

I know what you're thinking: what is the difference between a *director* and an *officer*? Plenty, though the degree of difference likely depends on the size of the company. Members of the Board of Directors are responsible for the overall direction of the company while officers run the joint on a day-to-day basis.

> In a small company or one that really comprises a partnership between two or three people, the officers and the directors are likely to be one and the same.

In larger companies, and especially publicly traded corporations, the board of directors might consist of as many as 20 to 30 people; but the company may not have 20 to 30 officers. And, while officers traditionally are also members of the board of directors, they do not have to be.

Directors who are not officers and have no other daily connection with the corporation are called "outside" directors. The reason for having outside directors is to obtain feedback from time to time regarding the direction of the company from those who are not so intimately familiar that they have little objectivity or are potentially biased. "Outside" directors can provided a fresh perspective. Also, they can ward off trouble by preventing financial shenanigans such as Enron-style "creative" accounting. In larger corporations directors often are paid for their services; in smaller or charitable corporations, board members normally serve free of charge.

Meanwhile, in small businesses, the incorporator, the agent, the shareholder, the officers and directors can be and often are one and the same as well. This is especially true if the business is family operated or beneficially owned by one or two persons, such as a husband and wife.

The advantage of a corporation is the separation between you as beneficial owner of the company and the company itself. If mom and pop own a taco stand by way of a corporation and a customer suffers from food poisoning, the suit likely will be limited to the corporation as defendant and not to mom and pop as shareholders.

A danger zone does exist where liability can be placed on the shareholders or on the officers or directors of the corporation, not just on the corporation. This is called "alter ego" liability or "piercing the corporate veil." Certain conditions can result in the ability of a suing party to break through the separateness of the corporation. In Chapter 16, we will discuss this topic in greater detail including where and when a party can pierce the veil and the steps you can take to avoid the problem.

Tip: Many large corporations are incorporated in Delaware because that state's laws governing corporations are considered more favorable to corporations than to individual shareholders or third parties. Also, as a result of so many large corporations choosing to incorporate businesses in Delaware, the law is considered to be more settled in Delaware than in other states.

But location of the corporation—its *domicile* in legal terms—is more an issue for large businesses than small ones. Don't be fooled by radio or television commercials that advertise incorporating a new business in another state. While you can incorporate anywhere, you still have to *register* your corporation in any state where it conducts business. And you have to pay taxes in that state.

For example, if you incorporate your business in Nevada but the business is actually operating in California, you will have to file for "foreign" corporation status in California and then pay California taxes. So what did you get out of having a Nevada corporation? Nothing unless you consider the expense of paying some company to act as the corporation's agent for service of complaints or other official documents.

The "S" Turn

You may have heard of the term "S Corporation." Actually, there is no such entity. However, under a certain subchapter of the Internal Revenue Code—the "S" subchapter, of course—individual shareholders can have the income after expenses pass through the corporation and filter down to the shareholders.

Each shareholder must receive an amount equal to the percentage of shares they have in the corporation. Also, all shareholders must be individuals. Another corporation can't be a shareholder in an "S" corp.

If you plan to raise capital through a private placement offering or if you think you may go public in a few years, designating the corporation as an "S" is *not* for you. In those cases, you will want file the business as a "C" corporation.

Traditionally, the standard "C" permitted deductions for certain expenses not available to the "S." However, the leftover income was usually taxed at a rate of approximately 35 percent. Though a smaller range of deductions was permitted for the "S," the remaining income to the owner was often taxed at that person's rate, usually far below 35 percent.

> More recently, many of the advantages of the "C" have been eliminated by tax laws that permit "S" corporations or the individual shareholders to use alternative methods to obtain the same deductions.

These changes have underscored the fact that the significant difference in the two types of filing is whether you intend to seek investors—especially corporate investors—or go public.

Limited Liability Companies

For those who want the liability protection of a corporation but do not want or need the formalities, many states now permit Limited Liability Companies (LLCs) and/or Partnerships (LLPs). [Forms 3-4, 3-5]

Prior to the acceptance of LLCs, some states created LLPs for certain business types that traditionally had more than one owner. This allowed multiple owners to have the protections of a corporation without all the fuss.

Today there is essentially no difference between the LLC and the LLP in most states—except that the LLP still requires a partnership, such as lawyers in a firm.

An LLC or LLP runs like an "S" corporation. The income after expenses passes through the business and down to the partners in proportion to their partnership interest. When LLC's and LLP's first were approved by states, lawyers and accountants often shied away from them and did not recommend them to clients.

Despite the removal of formalities attendant to corporations, LLCs and LLPs are still required to make filings with the state. So, rather than Articles of Incorporation, you now have articles of company or articles of partnership. Also, most states require some form of operating document such as a partnership agreement in place of bylaws. (I discuss the mechanics of *partnership agreements* in detail in the next chapter.)

In the event of litigation, the company assets or partnership assets are on the line. If the veil of the company is pierced, liability runs only to the partner who screwed up. For example, in a malpractice case, the claimant might sue the partnership or company. If the claimant successfully pierces the veil, the partner who made the error may be liable. In an LLP, if other partners participated in the bad act the veil could be pierced to all of them—no different than had the company incorporated.

The Elements of Small Business

Type	Management	Owners	Transfer of Interest	Profits/Losses	Taxes	Liability
Sole Proprietorship	By the owner(s) or by anyone so designated	One or more individuals	A simple sale of assets.	Individual or partners (per agreement) share in the profits or losses	Profits are taxed as income to the individuals who received them	Individual or partners are liable
"C" Corporation	Officers who are elected by the Board of Directors	Individual shareholders including corporations (most states have a maximum number	Sale of assets or sale of stock	Corporation makes or loses money	Corporation files federal tax return an may be required to file state tax return; pays payroll taxes on salaries	Corporation is liable; individual shareholders can be held liable for unpaid taxes
"C" Corporation-with Subchapter "S" election	Officers who are elected by the Board of Directors	Individual shareholders; no corporations permitted to own shares (most states have a maximum number)	Sale of assets or sale of stock	Remaining income after expense distributed to shareholders in proportion to stock ownership	Corporation files a return listing income less expenses and distribution to all shareholders	Corporation is liable; individual shareholders can be held liable for unpaid taxes
LLC	Individual or partners or persons designated	One or more individuals (some states have limits)	Sale of assets	Individual or partners divide the income less expenses per their respective interests	LLC files a return lisitng income and expenses and distribution to individual/p-artners	Company and individual who committed act is liable; individuals can be liable for unpaid taxes
LLP	Partners or persons designated by them	Two or more individuals (LLP's only available in some states and only for certain businessed)	Sale of assets	Partners divide the income less expenses per their respective interests	LLP files a return lisitng income and expenses and distribution to partners	Company and individual who committed act is liable; individuals can be liable for unpaid taxes
Limited Partnership	One or more general partners	General and limited partners	Sale of assets	Distribution of profits per limited partnership agreement	Limited partnership files return listing income less expenses and distribution of profits; General partner(s) and limited partners pay taxes based on their type of entity; limited partners	General partner(s) is liable; limited partners can be liable for tax deductions subsequently disallowed.

40

Limited Partnership

This type of entity grew out of a desire by investors to invest collectively in a business but without liability as officers, directors or shareholders. At the top sits a "general partner," who operates the limited partnership. The general partner can be a person or persons or it can be a corporation or an LLC or LLP. Often, the general partner is a corporation, thus shielding the individual from liability.

 Limited partners are part owners of the business but they have little or no say in the operations of the business. They are passive investors. In return they enjoy immunity from liability for the acts of the general partner.

The limited partnership operates under a lengthy agreement similar to a corporation's bylaws, only longer and more detailed. The limited partners have detailed information on the duties and responsibilities of the general partner and, more importantly, when the limited partners will get paid. The general partner receives a fee for managing the affairs of the business. But the general partner cannot be fired or removed unless there is a violation of the agreement or some illegal act.

> If you wanted to purchase a car wash but were short on cash, you might create a limited partnership. You would then form a corporation that would serve as the general partner and would manage the business. Friends and family could provide you with the operating capital you need and in return be limited partners. In that way, they own a piece of the action. Meanwhile, Aunt Edna has no power to show up one day and tell you that you are cleaning the windshield all wrong.

Once the target income less expense has been reached, similar to an "S" corporation, that money is distributed to the limited partners based on each partner's percentage of ownership.

Limited partnerships can be quite helpful to small business and are especially common in the restaurant industry.

Limited partnerships do require registration in most states with either the Secretary of State or other designated agency. The reason for the registration is that limited partnerships often raise money from outsiders (non-relatives, non-friends or others whom you do not have a prior business relationship). Most states like to ensure that offeror is not a convicted felon before solicitations are made.

Purchasing an Existing Business

Let's face it: There are a lot of businesses. Regional newspapers or the local paper will carry advertisements for the sale of companies, some big, some small. Other resources include the Internet. But best of all is the business broker. Whether you are buying or selling, business brokers constantly look for opportunities to put buyers and sellers in touch with each other— for a commission.

A good broker knows the marketplace and, like a real estate broker, may have key knowledge about the business, its history and its level of success along with the success of similar businesses in the same area. If you do not know what to research or review or what documents to request from the seller for review, the broker can help. Also, he can draw up sales documents and select an escrow company to handle the transfer of money in exchange for stock or assets.

> Never start a business all on your own. Most people think of accountants as those old men that tend to their 1040 forms every April. But accountants, especially those who specialize in small businesses, are crucial to the purchasing process.

And that is because businesses do not fall into the format of one size fits all. There are many types of businesses and many types of business structures. These structures affect many aspects of your purchase and may affect the structure that you decide will be the best for you, especially with respect to taxes you might owe or taxes you might pay in the future.

All businesses file taxes with the Internal Revenue Service. Most states also charge an income tax to businesses and to individuals. Fortunately, if your business operates in two states or if your state of incorporation is not the state where you conduct business, you do not pay taxes twice. Instead, you attribute the proportion of revenue received by the state in which it was received. Who would know something obscure like that? Your accountant, that's who.

If the seller is an individual who owns the business as a sole proprietorship, the most relevant tax information will appear on a "Schedule C" of the tax return. You might also examine other schedules that show depreciation of business equipment and use of vehicles for the business. If the business is a corporation, the entirety of the return will be helpful.

In addition, many businesses maintain monthly or quarterly profit and loss statements and income and expense statements along with a balance sheet. We will discuss these documents and other financial statements in greater detail in the accounting chapter. For now, you should know that these documents indicate the revenue received and the bills paid.

Tip: Don't be surprised by a tax return that shows the company is losing money or barely breaking even. "C" corporations generally show losses or minimal gains. This is a structural phenomenon set up by accountants to avoid the high corporate tax rate. Should you choose a "C" corporation as your structure, your accountant will help you create a financial environment where most of the revenue is spent on business related expenses. These might include your vehicle, your cellular telephone, your health insurance and other expenses. When your accountant reviews the financial documents, he will recognize those expenses created in whole or in part to reduce income.

The Elements of Small Business

If the business of your dreams is losing money, this doesn't necessarily mean that you shouldn't buy it. But you need to be very careful to see that the losses are not coming from situations you will not be able to change.

> For example, you would like to buy a restaurant, but it has been incurring losses. The previous owners also incurred losses and you think the reasons for the losses are operational—too high of a cost of food or personnel or gas and electric or all of the above. So ask yourself why your management will make a profit for the business. Chances are if several different owners incur losses doing business at the facility, you will, too.

The value of the business is key to any purchase. In addition to a traditional accountant, some accountants do nothing but perform business valuations on small and medium revenue companies. These accountants examine assets, liabilities and "going concern" value. The term *going concern* is also known as *goodwill*. When the liabilities are subtracted from the assets, we have the "book value."

But there is more: going concern value measures the effect of a business's name and reputation in the community. It measures the business's client base, which aids in predicting future revenue, and it measures the possibility of product licensing to other companies.

Because going concern value measures the intangibles, and is a subjective assessment of the company's worth, this figure is often in dispute. The seller will claim a relatively high value and the buyer will claim a lower value. Like the relationship you have with a car salesman, this is where you get to use your negotiating skills.

So with that in mind, these are the most significant issues to examine for each business entity.

• *For the sole proprietor*: A sole proprietorship is a business that is owned by an individual. There is no corporation; there is no limited liability company; there is no limited partnership. Rather, there is simply a person and his or her business. To make this purchase, you may want to purchase the name of the company, its assets and possibly its location. So you will request a copy of the lease and speak to the landlord about taking over the monthly payments. And you will want to ensure that the seller cannot go down the street and start anew taking all of his clients and their loyalty with him.

Sole proprietorships using a trade name (e.g., Jane's Flowers) are required to file a dba. You will want to make sure that it was actually filed. Since a sole proprietorship has no shareholders, by definition the purchase of a sole proprietorship would be a purchase of the assets only including, in some instances, the name of the business. You are not required to buy the name or keep the name. However, if the business has been around for a long time, if the community is familiar with the name, and if the business has a great reputation, you will most likely want to keep the name.

- *For the corporation*: As we will discuss in more detail later on, there are two methods by which a corporation is purchased: an asset purchase or a stock purchase. In a stock purchase, the buyer is purchasing all of the shares of the corporation. In so doing, the buyer gets all the assets, including everything the corporation owns. But he also receives all of the liabilities— all the debts or other negatives.

In an asset purchase, the buyer is not purchasing the stock. Rather, he is buying the stuff that makes the corporation valuable including its inventory and its clients. More often than not, the asset purchase is the better method. But the sales price can be less in a stock purchase since the buyer is taking on all the assets and all the liabilities. Also, if the buyer plans to capitalize on the name or location, continuity can be important. So purchasing all the assets may not be the best bet.

If you choose an asset purchase, then you will want to do three things:
1. Make certain that the corporation owns what it says it owns and that none of the assets has been pledged as security for a loan;

2. When available, remove the ability of the corporation's creditors to make any claim against the assets by purchasing through a specialized escrow under section 6 of the Uniform Commercial Code. Section 6 provides that if notice is given to creditors by way of publishing the sales transaction, and none of the creditors lodges a complaint against the sale, they must forever hold their peace. And you don't have to worry about creditors attempting to collect their monies through the stuff you just bought;

3. Include in the sales agreement a representation by the seller that seller will indemnify you for any undisclosed liens, debts or taxes.

Whether you're buying stock or assets, you will want to obtain the tax returns, the income and expense statements and any other related financial documents. And, as with buying a sole proprietorship, you will want to obtain a copy of the lease and confirm that the landlord will allow you to continue in the space if you plan to use that facility.

If you're buying assets, make sure that the assets you're purchasing are owned by the seller and that none is the subject of a security agreement. A security agreement occurs when a vendor or seller of equipment for the business (for example) still retains a vested interest in that equipment. In other words, it hasn't been paid off yet. So whoever sold the equipment will be breaking your kneecaps instead of the previous owner's!

If you're buying stock, make sure the shares are free and clear of any encumbrances and that the seller has provided all information concerning debts, if any.

Encumbrances come in several forms. For example, there may be a number of restrictions placed on any sale that need to be met before the shares are sold. This could arise if the shares have been used to secure a loan. Or the corporation may have a right to first refusal—meaning that the corporation would have to be provided with the chance to repurchase the shares for the same amount as the bid made by the other purchaser. In other words, the corporation gets first dibs on buying the shares back.

Presumably, a stock purchase of all the outstanding shares will not come with any objection regarding restrictions as the corporation and its board or officers can eliminate the restriction for purposes of the sale. But: if the shares have been pledged against a loan taken by the corporation then you will want to obtain the permission of the loaning party. Often, it will permit the purchase to proceed so long as the buyer takes the shares subject to the loan, and of course makes payment on that loan.

Tip: In the confusion of all the paperwork required to buy a corporation, one of the most overlooked liabilities is taxes. Be sure that the all taxes to the federal, state and local governments have been paid. More important, make sure that all payroll taxes and sales taxes have been paid. We will discuss these taxes in detail later. Payroll taxes are the monies withheld, the social security withheld, and the unemployment and disability withheld from employees' paychecks. Since the tax returns and the income and expense statements may not indicate that these taxes have been paid and are up to date, you need to ensure that you or your accountant do it.

Since a corporation operates under its own name, it does not require or need a fictitious name. However, corporations can use fictitious names the same way a sole proprietor uses a name. If the name known to the public is a DBA and not the corporation name, you will want to confirm that the DBA papers were properly filed. If you are making a stock purchase, you should check to be sure that the corporation filed taxes as they claim, under "C" or "S." With corporations, you are buying either the shares or the assets. When purchasing the assets, you do not assume the liabilities. If you buy the shares and become the main shareholder, you become liable to all creditors. This can become very complicated.

So why would you *ever* buy shares? If you are purchasing a liquor store or some other business subject to a state or local permit, it may be easier to take over the existing license by obtaining approval with you as the new sole or majority shareholder than to start the whole process again. If you by the assets only, you may have to provide a new application. This process could be more expensive and more time consuming.

Conversely, if you are purchasing a rental car company, one which has been run into the ground and is debt ridden, you would only want to purchase the assets (i.e., the cars) so as not to assume responsibility for all of the debts and other problems the seller has incurred.

- *For the LLC or LLP*: For all practical purposes the purchase of an LLC or LLP is an asset purchase unless you are intending to become a partner. Remember, although LLC or LLPs don't have stock shares, they operate in a manner similar to corporations. Though in most jurisdictions individuals can form LLCs, most of the time a group comes together to be partners in a venture with profits distributed per the percentages of ownership in a manner similar to a subchapter "S" corporation. But without stock there can be no stock purchase and therefore an asset purchase is the only vehicle available.

  Before purchasing the assets of an LLC or LLP, you absolutely must consult with your professionals because of the various complications that each entity ensues. And of course, every case is different, so your lawyer will be able to sift through the garbage and tell you exactly how to make the purchase.

- *For Limited Partnerships*: Purchases of limited partnerships can be a little tricky. While technically considered an asset purchase, since limited partnerships are often created to conduct a specific business, it has the look of a stock purchase. For example, some years ago, I represented a limited partnership. Its asset was a car wash in an obscure California town. After operating the car wash for a number of years, the general partner received an offer to lease the business to a small group of individuals with an option for the group to buy the business at a later date. Before the sale, the limited partners divided the profits based on the percentage of ownership as delineated in the

Limited Partnership Agreement. Once leased, the profit was the monthly rent and would have been the purchase monies had the group chosen to exercise the option.

Similar to the LLC or LLP, you and your attorney will want to be sure that none of the assets are encumbered.

- *For the franchise*: While you can start your own franchise, it is also possible to purchase a franchise. Normally, the franchisor will have to approve the sale. So be prepared to show your credentials such as your income, your credit and your business acumen. The franchise most likely has a predetermined method of operation with its own set of restrictions pertaining to the products or services that you sell.

When you purchase a franchise, you will sign a franchise agreement, which could simply replace the previous owner's name with yours. However, the franchise owner may draft, at his discretion, a new agreement, which can change certain aspects of how the business is to be run. You will still want to get a hold of the Profit and Loss and Balance Statements of the franchise to review with your accountant.

Tip: A successful franchise organization, such as McDonald's or Subway or Las Vegas Golf and Tennis, does not necessarily mean your specific outlet is or will be successful. Also consider that the success of a franchise may depend on intangible factors. For example, if you start up or purchase a Las Vegas Golf and Tennis franchise in Bozeman, Montana, sales during the winter months will be weak due to the weather. We will delve into the wild world of franchising in Chapter 5.

Forms and the Corporate Kit

When you form the corporation or the limited liability company/partnership, you or your attorney should also obtain a "corporate kit." The kit is usually in notebook form with a hard cover that fits in a box. The kit contains a number of useful documents.

If you have formed a corporation, those documents will include by-laws, minutes of the first meeting of the board of directors, an IRS Form SS-4 and an IRS Form 2553. [Forms 3-6, 3-7] If you have formed an LLC or LLP, the forms will include rules of governance or some other form of agreement between the partners as to the operational rules for the company in place of bylaws, minutes of the first meeting, and an IRS Form SS-4.

First the bylaws or rules of governance. Many states seem to feel that one size fits all. That does not mean that the document must be accepted in its entirety. You can modify the provisions or even eliminate clauses or sections that do not apply to your situation.

Also, if you are the sole shareholder or owner of the LLC (or you have only two or three partners in the LLP), you do not have to stand on ceremony. You only need a document that sets forth the basic rules of operations for the business.

This document begins with the address of the principal office. Then it provides for the duties of management and how management personnel will be chosen. It includes rules for when and how meetings of the partners or principals or shareholders will occur. And if the business is a corporation, it provides for how officers and directors will be chosen. At the conclusion, the document should be signed by the Secretary of the corporation or the individual in the LLC or LLP designated to act as a secretary for purposes of maintaining the minutes and other records.

> Minutes of the organizational meeting are intended to solidify the actual process of choosing leaders and provide for the names of those chosen or elected to lead. It also provides for the approval of the bylaws or other operational documents. If you have formed a corporation, the distribution of shares is noted along with any consideration (i.e. money) paid for the shares. If the business is an LLC or LLP, then the minutes will provide for the ownership percentages of the parties.

Other information such as bank, bank accounts and who has the power to sign checks is traditionally included. It might also include the name of the attorney and the name of the accountant retained by the business. Finally, any other related issues such as employee benefit plans and retirement plans can be included. At the end, the document should be signed by the secretary as well as the person charged with leading the business such as a Chief Executive Officer or managing partner.

Tip: Though many states do not require mom and pop businesses to maintain formal records such as bylaws and minutes of annual meetings or special meetings, you should pay attention to these issues. The maintenance of corporate documents aids in the prevention of casting liability on the individual shareholders or owners/partners of the business in the event of a lawsuit.

Don't become so complacent that you don't issue the stock share certificates to yourself and to other shareholders. It is the issuance of shares that marks the start of the corporation. Even though many states have relaxed the rules and formalities for corporations with few shareholders, the failure to distribute the share certificates can result in a determination that the protections granted normally to individual shareholders from lawsuits are suspended.

At or before the time of the initial meeting, you will need to obtain from the IRS an identification number. As an individual you are often identified, especially with the IRS or state taxing authority, by your Social Security number. As a business entity, the company is identified by its EIN—employer identification number. The SS-4 form should be completed with name, address, name of principal officer or partner, type of business, when it started, and the current number of employees. The principal party executes the document and then faxes it to the nearest designated IRS office. Yep, with all of the high tech methods of communication, the IRS has chosen the fax machine for receiving your request and then returning to you the document with a number in the upper square.

Tip: the IRS continually experiments with the method by which one can obtain an identification number. As of this writing, you can fax a request or call the IRS. If you call, you will need to fax the SS-4 form to the agent with whom you are speaking.

With respect to corporations only, for an "S" election, all shareholders have to agree and all must be individuals. Form 2553 must be completed and filed with the IRS. In addition to providing the same information as that contained in the SS-4 form, the name of each shareholder, his or her signature, Social Security number, the number of shares and the date they were acquired must be provided. The form is then filed with the IRS. Be sure to check with the Secretary of State's office in your state or with your accountant as to whether your state requires the filing of that form or a similar form.

Zoning and Permits

If you acquire a space from which to run your business or even if you acquire a business through a stock or asset purchase, the local officials may not be generous about extending existing permits to you or supplying you with new ones. In these cases, you may have to get creative.

Tip: If your new venture consists of an office or two in a high rise, then zoning issues likely will not apply to you. But if you operate from a stand-alone facility or in a strip mall or near residences, Mr. Zoning Guy will be your best or worst friend.

There is nothing logical about the ways of zoning. For example: One of clients recently leased a warehouse that he intended to turn into a restaurant. The property had fifty parking spaces. But because of the size of the building, the maximum occupancy was approximately 500 people. Assuming two persons per vehicle, "full" would translate into 250 cars, far more than the property could handle.

In fact, the problem wasn't really a problem. The locale was surrounded by light industry where everyone went home at night. The result was plentiful street parking after 5:00 p.m. The local zoning office did not care. It would not permit the restaurant to open until it solved the dilemma. So, my client was forced to lease parking space at a nearby building. No one ever used the second lot. But my client still had to pay the monthly lease fees to the nearby building.

I have another, even more personal experience with bizarre zoning issues.

In 1995, a large law firm wanted to lease all of the space on the floor where my office was located. The firm agreed to provide office space with a separate entrance for me. Until this time, for the previous 30 years, the names of the business or those in business had been posted on the main entrance door to each office. Because of the extensive renovations necessary for the new firm, all new codes—local, state and federal—had to be implemented.

One of the codes prohibited any names or information on doors.

The code was based on the disability needs of nearsighted people. There was a nearsighted persons' interest group that had lobbied against names on doors. It was concerned that any near sighted person might get so close to the door in order to read the names on it that he or she could be struck in the face if the door were opened at the same time. No, I am not kidding...that was reason for the zoning.

The getting struck in the face story might at least have some marginal merit except: All of the doors in the building, including all of the doors on that floor, opened *in*. So it would not have been possible for some nearsighted person to be hit in the face. Did that matter to anyone? No. The names came off the doors in favor of a little sign on the walls next to the doors. Your tax dollars and bureaucrats at work— making the world safe for...well, no one.

> You may have certain zoning requirements or necessary permits in order to operate legally the business you want. And you may be subject to certain restrictions including hours of operation. You can check with the local zoning department office to see what your property is zoned for or talk with a qualified broker. If you hired a broker who found the business, he or she should know the zoning designation of the business and any other operating restrictions.

Permits are another issue. Did you know that in many states you must have a permit if you want to put a pool table in your establishment? Did you know that you also must have a permit if you want to have karaoke or have an open microphone night at your coffee house? Your trusty lawyer can help you when it comes to the plethora of permits you may need to obtain. Your broker should also know this information. Make sure you ask and get any response confirmed in writing.

Conclusion

Most of the difficulties—tax structures, partnership agreements, leases, zoning and permit problems—that plague my clients after they start or buy a business are issues that could have been avoided if they had visited me *before* completing the transaction. It's not a good idea to try to save money in the closing stages of the purchase by foregoing expert advice. It will come back to haunt you. And the cost will be ten or twenty times more than the bill for advice and for reviewing all of the documents attendant to buying a business.

The last thing you want to do is get shut down simply because $35 wasn't paid for a certain permit you didn't know you needed.

References

Browning, Robert. *Setting Up and Running a Limited Company: A Comprehensive Guide to Forming and Operating a Company as a Director and Shareholder*. How To Books (March, 2003).

Cooke, Robert A. *How to Start Your Own 'S' Corporation* (2nd Edition). HCM Publishing (March, 2003)

Edwards, Paul, et al. *Home Businesses You Can Buy: The Definitive Guide to Exploring Franchises, Multi-Level Marketing, and Business Opportunities*. J. P. Tarcher (June, 1997).

Gumpert, David E. *How to Really Start Your Own Business* (4th Edition). Lauson Publishing Co. (April, 2003)

Haines, Lionel. *How to Buy a Good Business With Little or None of Your Own Money*. Times Books (September, 1987)

Hupalo, Peter I. *How To Start And Run Your Own Corporation: S-Corporations For Small Business Owners*. HCM Publishing (March, 2003).

Joseph, Richard A., et al. *How to Buy a Business: Entrepreneurship Through Acquisition*. Dearborn Trade Publishing (December, 1992)

Mancuso, Anthony. *The Corporate Minutes Book: The Legal Guide to Taking Care of Corporate Business* (2nd edition). Nolo Press (June, 2002).

Mancuso, Anthony and Beth Lawrence. *Form Your Own Limited Liability Company* (3rd edition). Nolo Press (January, 2002).

The Elements of Small Business

McQuown, Judith H. *Inc. Yourself: How to Profit by Setting Up Your Own*. Corporation (9th edition). Broadway Books (February, 2000).

Shenkman, Martin M., et al. *Starting a Limited Liability Company*. John Wiley & Sons (April, 1996).

Silver Lake Editors. *Family Money: Using Wills, Trusts, Life Insurance and Other Financial Planning Tools to Leave the Things You Own to the People You Love*. Silver Lake Publishing (September, 2002).

Sniffen, Carl R.J., et al. *The Essential Corporation Handbook* (3rd edition). Oasis Press (September, 2001).

Sutton, Garrett. *How to Use Limited Liability Companies & Limited Partnerships*. Success DNA, Inc. (October, 2001)

Sutton, Garrett and Robert T. Kiyosaki. *How to Buy & Sell a Business: How You Can Win in the Business Quadrant* (Rich Dad's Advisors). Warner Books (April, 2003).

Chapter 4

Partnership Agreements

It is more shameful to distrust our friends than
to be deceived by them.

—Honore de Balzac

Yeah, but did Balzac ever have to dissolve a business partnership?

In a sole proprietorship, you have all of the control. In a limited partnership, the general partner has the control. But when you and partners form a corporation or form an LLC or LLP, certain agreements must be created to ensure the stability and governance of the business. At a minimum, two agreements should be considered:

1) an agreement regarding the duties and responsibilities of each partner; and

2) an agreement providing for an exit strategy when circumstances result in one partner being unable or unwilling to participate in the business.

Since most small businesses—especially in the services and *professional* services sectors—are some form of partnership or partnership LLC, I'll spend this chapter discussing the mechanics of and strategies behind different sorts of partnership agreements.

Partnership/Employment Agreements

Let's start with a simple situation. Suppose you and your partner buy a liquor store. Who opens the store in the morning? Who closes the store late at night? Who is in charge of ordering product? Who hires the employees? Who handles the bookkeeping? If one party will be in charge of daily operations while the other partner supplies the capital but otherwise manages another unrelated business, how much should the working partner get paid?

Even simpler issues—such as where to bank, whom to hire for legal expertise, and whom to hire to perform the accounting and tax return preparation functions—could lead to conflict if not addressed.

> And then there are more profound issues. What if one partner simply decides to leave? Or what if one partner dies or is disabled?

The lack of any agreement in writing as to the duties and responsibilities of the parties almost always results in disputes and possibly lawsuits. At the beginning of the relationship, things always seem so rosy and no one wants to rock the boat. In my experience, efforts to convince clients that they need a piece of paper with a list of duties and obligations often fall on deaf ears.

And then your partner fails to show up at the office for a few weeks…or takes vacations every month…or leaves the work to you while he takes the Porsche for a spin. Without a written agreement, how can you—and the other partners, if any—exercise discipline over him? What if he just doesn't want to be involved in the business anymore? Can he sell his interest to someone else? *Anyone* else? Do you have a right to first refusal or a right to object to the sale of his interest to some third party?

You get the problem. The solution is easy and not very expensive. You need an agreement. Whether it is called a "Partnership" Agreement or "Shareholder" Agreement or "Employment" Agreement, you need an agreement between you and the other principals so that everyone knows what is expected of you. [Form 4-1] And you need a "Buy-Sell" agreement to provide continuity and solutions when a partner or partner-shareholder is unwilling or unable to continue. [Form 4-2]

The Key Point: Define Partners' Duties

If the partnership is a proprietorship or if you have formed an LLC or LLP, then the agreement is simply called a "Partnership Agreement." If you and your friends have formed a corporation, then the document is commonly called a "Shareholder Agreement." For our purposes, these agreements are virtually identical. For purposes of this chapter and in an ode to simplicity, we will discuss the agreement from a partnership perspective.

What are the duties of each partner? Since few businesses intend to have the partners performing the same tasks and since each partner often has certain unique skills he or she brings to the table, an agreement as to the duties, responsibilities and salary, if any, should be spelled out in writing advance.

What are the duties and responsibilities of each partner? What if a partner fails to carry out his or her duties? Does the non-performing partner have the right to any notice and time to correct the situation? Along with detailing the duties and responsibilities, the bases for firing a partner should be included.

In very small businesses, the failure of a partner to perform may result in the termination of the business. This occurs because the failing partner cannot be replaced without financial hardship to the business. However, larger businesses with greater cash flow and a significant number of employees do not have to fold. Instead, another partner or a non-partner employee might take over the tasks previously assigned to the partner.

The Buy-Sell Agreement

While the shareholder agreement covers the duties and responsibilities of the partners, the Buy-Sell agreement covers three additional topics: death, disability and "Please stop the ride, I wanna get off!"

With respect to the death of a partner, in the absence of an agreement his shares go to his spouse or other heirs.

The easiest way to resolve this issue is through the use of an insurance policy. We will discuss insurance issues in more detail later. For now, you should know that "Key Man" policies provide benefits to the company by paying the company the monies needed to buy out the spouse.

> For example: Your business has three partners with evenly divided shares. The partners decide that the value of one interest is $500,000. So, they purchase a life insurance policy in that amount, which pays to the company that sum upon the death of the first partner. When a partner dies, the $500,000 is paid to the company and then to the surviving spouse or to any other beneficiary chosen—ahead of time—by the dead partner.

The disability of a partner creates certain complicated issues, too. A serious disability such as a stroke or cancer or even the loss of a limb clearly disrupts a partnership.

One solution is for the business to provide for a disability insurance policy for all partners. In the event of the disability, payment is made directly to the disabled member. Such a policy covers about 75 percent of the salary the partner was making for the length of the disability.

Beyond those payments, the partnership agreement would describe how the remaining partners would treat the disabled partner's equity while he or she is out of the picture.

If the disability is permanent, the agreement might also provide for additional payments over time in exchange for the return and cancellation of that partner's shares thus terminating his or her interest.

60

A partner leaving the business creates far more trouble than an incapacitated or deceased partner. Since you won't have the benefit of the insurance policy, some other formula must be created for buying him or her out of their interest.

When I draft a Buy-Sell agreement, the most common solution is to provide for an accountant who specializes in business valuations. He or she would be retained for that purpose. If the accountant declares that the business has a value of $1.5 million, then (assuming three equal partner/shareholders) a formula is provided that permits the other two partner/shareholders to pay the $500,000.00 usually over a specified period of time to avoid financial hardship.

Why Buy-Sell Agreements Matter

A client called to inform me that her partner, an equal shareholder of the corporation they used to operate their business, wanted out of their business. Rather than sit down with my client and discuss a buy out, the partner sent in the lawyer. (Imagine *Dragnet* theme music playing here.) He stated that the business was worth $300,000 and that his client wanted $150,000 paid within 10 days. Sure.

My client replied with a request to know how the lawyer arrived at such a high figure. He stated that an unnamed business appraiser had reviewed some financial information for the company and that the appraiser came to the conclusion that the business was worth $300,000.

There's nothing like the omission of details to spark my ire.

Next, this self-styled hardball player stated that, if the matter were not resolved, his client would sue to have the business dissolved. Nothing like a threat to motivate me to write a letter.

In my letter, I informed the lawyer that since no Buy-Sell agreement had ever been created or executed, his client was free to walk away from the business and forgo her salary—but she had no right to force a buyout of her interest from my client. She was a shareholder. Nothing more. I suggested that the parties agree on a neutral business evaluator and mediate a final price by which my client would purchase her partner's shares.

> Without a Buy-Sell agreement, you may not have an automatic right to dissolve the business unless there's been gross misman-agement or criminal activity. Simply put, you can't just walk away and expect that the other principals will buy out your interest in the operation. Moreover, any value the business may have could be destroyed in a dissolution, especially if the business is a service provider with no tangible assets.

In this case, my client was willing to purchase the other half of the business for its fair market value. As a result, a court would have no reason to dissolve the company. Instead, at best the court would order an appraisal and for my client to pay the other shareholder—just as I had suggested in the first place.

As I was writing this book, the relationship between the two partners remained unresolved. Because my client's partner wanted her name (and all of the responsibility that goes with it) removed from the loans and lines of credit—and because banks don't like doing that—the buyout remained pending. And it might remain so for years.

A Buy-Sell agreement or a Shareholder Agreement with provisions for one partner to jump ship would have resolved this problem simply and easily. Chances are the agreement would have required a business appraiser to be hired that the parties both accepted. He or she would have provided a value with an explanation as to how the value was derived. My client would have paid one-half and that would have been that.

No lawyers. No lawyer letters.

Families, Spouses and Significant Others

One issue that comes up frequently in partnership agreements—but gets little attention in most business books—is family matters. At the beginning of this chapter, I mentioned briefly that a partner's death can mean partnership with a spouse, child or significant other that you don't know…or don't like.

Chapter 4: Partnership Agreements

Like Paul McCartney, you too could get stuck doing business with your own Yoko Ono. Or you could wind up in a partnership with the idiot son who thinks that watching every episode of *The Apprentice* makes him the next Donald Trump.

 Tip: While not a requirement, it is a good idea to have the spouses of partners execute the Buy-Sell agreement, especially if you reside in a community property state. While most courts will reject any circumvention of the agreement, especially if the consideration (payment) for the decedent's shares is adequate, the shares held by your partner are also "owned" by his or her spouse. If the compensation appears to be inadequate, the spouse may refuse to return the shares or may sue for additional compensation.

The key point here is that, if things are going well in your business, you don't want the death of a partner to derail the form of the partnership that the business has taken. An interruption of even a few weeks during a pivotal contract negotiation or sales season can do damage that lasts months and even years.

On a related note, you shouldn't enter into a partnership with anyone who refuses to pay an attorney for advice or who refuses to execute the appropriate Buy-Sell agreement or similar Partnership Agreement reviewed by that attorney—and, separately, by *your* attorney.

If you think the divorce rate is high, you should examine the partnership dissolution rate. The breakups are almost as ugly (and I have seen a few that are *uglier*).

> Following this marital metaphor, it's often useful to think of the Buy-Sell agreement as a pre-nup for your partnership.

The absence of an agreement will cost you far more than its creation and adherence to its terms. A refusal to enter into written agreements is a red flag. Don't let it fly too long.

Conclusion

You cannot prepare for every contingency. But you can take all reasonable steps to keep the business in operation regardless of the disasters that often occur. Being prepared really will help you and your partner to sleep better at night. Remember: it isn't just 50 percent of marriages that end in divorce. Partnerships fail every day. Lawsuits are filed and the lawyers make out while your dreams are erased. Don't let this happen to you.

References

Clifford, Denis, et al. *The Partnership Book: How to Write A Partnership Agreement* (6th edition, with CD-ROM). Nolo Press (May, 2001).

Clifford, Denis, and Ralph E. Warner. *The Partnership Book: How to Write a Partnership Agreement*. Nolo Press (May, 2001).

Haman, Edward. *How to Form Your Own Partnership*. Sourcebooks, Inc. (May, 2002)

Kleinberger, Daniel S. *Agency, Partnerships and LLCs* (The Examples and Explanations Series). Aspen Law & Business Publishing (September, 2002).

Jaffe, Azriela, et al. *Let's Go into Business Together: 8 Secrets to Successful Business Partnering*. Career Press (December, 2000).

Chapter 5

Franchises

…we can be as separate as the fingers, yet one as the hand in all things essential to mutual progress.

—Booker T. Washington

Name recognition can be a very significant factor in establishing a successful business, especially in the service industry. A franchise provides this opportunity. From *McDonald's* to *7-Eleven* to *Las Vegas Golf & Tennis*, these names are recognized and trusted.

A franchise is a business operation where a complex relationship exists between the creator (the franchisor) and the purchaser (franchisee) by way of an agreement.

Franchising offers people a business alternative to inventing the wheel or reinventing the wheel, so to speak. Franchised businesses distribute products and services related to every industry from sales of tools to income tax preparation to restaurants and exercise centers.

The Elements of Small Business

Few days pass by without my using an expression coined by me to describe many of my clients. When the task or tasks at hand appear to be so taxing, I say they are "overwhelmed by the task." For many, the prospect of work involved in starting a business from scratch and then advertising can be quite daunting. And let's face it: If you have read this far, you may already feel overwhelmed. Instead of taking the risks to reap the rewards, the daunted end up sitting on the couch eating Bon-Bons, frozen by the monumental task before them.

> To avoid the work and risk involved with starting a new and independent business with no customers or name recognition, many potential small business owners look to franchising—the chance to buy into a recognized brand name—as the best choice for them.

The person or company that controls a franchise is called a *franchisor*; the person or company that pays for its use is the *franchisee*. Generally, the franchisee sells goods or services that are supplied by the franchisor. The franchisor oversees the method or system of conducting business between the two parties.

Think of your franchisor as your entrepreneurial governor. For a piece of the action—often a substantial piece—franchisors provide:

- business expertise, such as marketing plans;

- management guidance;

- financing assistance;

- training and support services for both management and staff;

- product suggestions; and

- collective advertising.

This method of conducting business is tried and true; franchises have been tested and proven successful for decades. Some forms of the franchise have even been in use since the Civil War! Although each franchise offers a unique system of operation, it is up to you to determine which one will best satisfy your needs as a budding entrepreneur.

 Even though the success rate for franchise-owned businesses is significantly higher than many independently run businesses, your success as a franchisee is never guaranteed, and there will always be a risk when involved in a business venture. Franchising is not for everyone, so it is important to research thoroughly before entering into an agreement.

Is Franchising Right for You?

There are four preliminary questions that you need to ask yourself before you get started in a franchise business:

1) How much money do you have to invest in the venture—including marketing and advertising, once the business is ready to operate?

2) What are your abilities as an entrepreneur in the industry you have chosen?

3) What knowledge do you have about operating a small business? and

4) What are your professional and personal goals?

The answers to these questions will contribute to the type of franchise you choose. This is also a good thing to do at the very beginning because these few questions will quickly narrow the scope of your efforts, making the rest of the process more manageable and therefore, enjoyable. Getting it down on paper is a good idea as well, so you can easily see the project in front of you.

The Elements of Small Business

1. Initial Contact	*Write or call the franchise and request a Franchise Application. Complete and return.*
2. Initial Interview	*Once the franchise has received and reviewed your application, they will follow up with a telephone interview.*
3. First Personal Meeting	*During this first meeting you will be presented with their federal disclosure document (UFOC) and a detailed description of the franchise system.*
4. Second Personal Meeting	*Select your desired store of those available and receive a business plan outline to be completed by you.*
5. Presentation of the franchise agreement	*You will meet with management and discuss your business plan.*
6. Signing of the Franchise agreement	*The agreement is prepared and you are given five days minimum to review it before signing.*
7. Franchise system training	*The training program is scheduled and completed.*
8. Transfer of operation	*You fly solo. You made it! You are now the proud parent of a franchise!*

Qualifications

The step-by-step flowchart that appears on the opposite page follows the process of qualifying for and buying a franchise. The amount of time it takes to complete each phase will vary from franchise to franchise.

Beyond these steps, you should consider several other factors:

Investment Capabilities

Your investment capabilities can easily determine what happens as you begin your franchising venture. Or shall we say AD-venture? There are many start-up costs that need to be paid before your grand opening. You can refer to the "Capital Formation" chapter for additional ideas for gathering dollars. Also, financing is often available for franchise newbies, but the level of investment required can vary greatly, from $10,000 to $250,000 or more.

Even within the same franchise there may be different start-up packages available based on the amount of money you wish to invest. How much money you have to invest can also be determined by how much money you can afford to lose. If your franchise fails, you may be left with loan payments for years following the demise of your efforts. If you need to refer to the Bankruptcy chapter, do so now.

Finally, your credit rating will affect the amount of money you will be able to dig up. Obtaining your franchise with one or more partners can lower your investment requirements, but will most likely lower your income as well. With or without partners, you should have additional income or money set aside to live on during the start of your franchise, as money will only come after you have opened your business.

Knowledge of the Industry

If you were a Literature major in college, chances are you may not know the first thing about repairing an automobile or preparing taxes. One of the biggest mistakes made in the creation of a small business and in purchasing a franchise is the desire to start a business that the franchisee knows nothing about. It is never a good idea to create, operate or even invest in a business or franchise without knowledge of the product or service it provides. Makes sense, right?

Yet, this may be the most common error committed by would-be entrepreneurs.

Additionally, you need to check out the franchise's requirements regarding technical or other experience because you may need training or education. Take note that although many franchisors offer training, the training may delay your start date. And consider this: what knowledge or training can you bring to a business? Have you ever managed a business? Even with the support usually provide, you need to make a preliminary assessment.

Your Goals

Putting your goals on paper is also a good preliminary assessment, not just for your franchise research. Outlining where you want to be, both personally and professionally, gives you a sort of written statement to which you can respond and accomplish those goals you set for yourself.

- What kind of income do you require or desire?

- What field do you want to pursue?

- Would you rather go into retail sales, or perform a service?

- How many hours can you work and do you want or need to hire a manager?

- Will this business be your primary source of income?

Most franchise agreements last anywhere from 10-20 years. So if you can see yourself operating the business in two decades, you have probably found a match.

Many franchisees enjoy their business so much and are so successful that they may want to operate more than one outlet. In fact, many franchises are bought by existing franchisees in the company, which can be a clue to the business' success and level of franchisee satisfaction. In some instances you may be required to buy more than one outlet. For example, Del Taco requires franchisees to purchase three to five outlets.

Selecting a Franchise

Name recognition is often the primary reason to purchase a franchise, because then you can use a name that is already well-known. This is important because it is hard to build a loyal client base in any field. Franchising with a company that already has a name recognizable by the largest demographic possible will most likely draw customers who are familiar with your business.

If the franchise is not well-known to you, find out how long the franchise has been in operation and what the reputation is. You can contact the Better Business Bureau at www.BBB.com for information regarding the franchise organization. The bureau keeps records of complaints against local businesses and gives a rating of the business.

Since franchising requires capital and that creates a risk, you should consider certain factors when deciding on which franchise is right for you and which will most likely be successful in the location you choose:

- Is there a demand for the products or service you offer?

- What is the competition like now?

- What will be the competition in the future?

- How much distance is there or will there be between your franchise or sales territory and that of existing or future franchisees?

Ask questions. Investigate the franchisor's history, growth, and level of support by contacting its franchisees. The franchisor's history can show what kind of relationship you may have with your entrepreneurial governors. Remember, what they say goes. So, even though the company's name itself may be known far and wide, the inner-workings are important to consider.

The good thing about franchises is that many of them have been operated very successfully and have years of experience under their belts. Some franchises began with the average person operating one small shop that grew.

> The Subway sandwich shop chain is one such franchise. It was founded by Fred DeLuca and several family members as a way to raise money for college for Fred. What was first started in 1965 with a plan to open 32 stores in the first ten years (*that* goal was actually reached in the first year) has since grown into an empire with over 17,000 stores in 75 countries.

It is important to consider how much experience your franchisor has so you can gauge their assurance of support and have trust in the system they have created for the franchise.

The Ratings

A fast-growing franchise could mean a successful business. Subway has been named number one 10 times in the Franchise 500 rating by *Entrepreneur* magazine. The Franchise 500 rating is determined by the company's growth rate and size, financial strength, and stability. If the franchise you've selected is growing, which it should, this increases the chances of customers available to you. However, a successful franchisor doesn't always mean a successful franchisee. Check out the financial assets of the company and also their staff. A company that grows too quickly can collapse for lack of internal support.

Even though the franchise fee includes assistance above and beyond the name rights and format or system developed by the company, the support that you get from your franchisor will vary.

> 7-Eleven, the largest convenience chain in the world, offers its franchisees training, counseling, bookkeeping, auditing, financial reports, advertising, and merchandise assistance. Aside from regular consultant visits to maximize business performance, 7-Eleven even has a 90-day trial period! Some franchises may have a weekend of training and an operating manual, or provide you with advice on hiring employees, marketing, and management.

Some franchisors include support continuing beyond your grand opening, such as toll-free assistance numbers, periodic seminars and workshops, and monthly newsletters. Find out the kind of training required to operate your franchise, the quality of training from them as opposed to other places, and how that compares to other franchisees in the same company. If you have previous or formal training in the area it can help tremendously when you start your franchise

Site selection

One of the services a franchisor will most likely provide is site selection. You may be offered a franchise opportunity in an existing outlet, or one in an existing building, or one that hasn't been built yet. Depending on the franchise you choose, you may also have architecture or interior design requirements.

Ever notice how all Del Tacos look alike? It is important, then, to consider the demand for products or services in that particular area. Consider also the fact that your franchise's products or services may have a seasonal or temporary demand as many new products become obsolete within several years.

Once you have determined the demand for the franchise's offerings in the community in question, you should assess your competition. Are there other competing companies that offer the same business, and do they get their inventory and equipment for a cheaper price?

If you open a dry-cleaning franchise but the mom-and-pop shop down the street charges half of your prices because they live in the apartment upstairs and own their building, you might be out of luck. What about competition from franchises in the same company *and* in the same area? On the other hand, you may have wider name-recognition and have access to the advertising needed to be successful.

The more you consider when deciding which franchise is right for you, the happier you'll be when you finally sit down to sign the franchise agreement. Even if you come to the conclusion that franchising isn't your thing, you will have at least done your preliminary research for an independent business venture and outlined some of your life goals in the process.

Franchise Expositions

Franchise expositions are like job fairs and car shows. Lots of booths in really big rooms. Actually, you have myriad franchise details, proposals and networking possibilities right in front of your eyes. But you must be careful to filter the information you are receiving, because exhibitors are there to sell their franchise systems. Some will do so aggressively. Then again, don't reject a hard sell automatically. Everyone's gotta make a buck; that's why you're going into business in the first place.

 Doing your homework before an exposition will make the whole experience most rewarding. You can find out about expositions in your area by accessing the Franchise Info Web site (www.franchiseinfosite.com) and clicking on *Upcoming Franchise Expos.*

There are many expositions held all over the country and around the world which you may attend throughout the year. You will want to decide ahead of time what your investment capabilities are, along with your goals and your abilities assessment. It is easy to get caught up in the excitement of everything, and you want to make sure you have some definite figures and ideas in your head before you jump in the shark pen.

The advantages of attending an exposition are comparison shopping and pooling your information. You can visit many exhibitors and ask necessary questions during their presentations or in discussion. Find out:

- how long they've been in business,

- how many outlets exist and their locations,

- what controls the franchise imposes upon its franchisees,

- what kind of assistance they provide and if it's ongoing and,

- of course, you'll want to talk about money. What are the initial start-up costs and what are the ongoing costs?

Because franchises are based around using a trademark or symbol, there is almost always a royalty fee that you must pay to the franchisor. I'll explain more later as to what types of costs you can expect to incur.

> Some franchisors may tell you that you can earn a specific amount of income by investing in their company. Take such claims with extreme caution. You can bet they are telling you about their top-performing franchises. The Federal Trade Commission, an agency that regulates interstate commerce, requires franchisors who make claims regarding income and/or profits to "substantiate" their claims in writing. Make sure they do that.

Requesting information and start-up packages from separate companies can be costly and time-consuming; but attending a franchise exposition can relieve a lot of that stress. Do not feel pressured in any way when speaking with an exhibitor. Just get your information so you can take it home and study further. But taking notes is essential, because there is no possible way you will remember the answers to all of the questions you asked. Plus, you will have spoken directly with a number of people, thereby establishing a personal relationship with a representative of your franchise of interest.

Disclosure Documents and Other Fun Things

The Federal Trade Commission (www.ftc.com) has a lovely little concept which goes by the name of *Franchise Rule*. The Franchise Rule imposes six requirements concerning "advertising, offering, licensing, contracting, sale or other promotion" of a franchise in or affecting commerce. Under this, a franchisor must provide you with a Franchise Offering Circular (FOC). This is fancy government talk for a disclosure document.

The FOC contains a number of "disclosures" which are of significant value to you and any other investors you may carry.

Most franchisors are legitimate business; but, as in any field, some are scams. The bad ones are designed to grab money from eager franchisees, while offering little or nothing in return—and bad ones often flood the marketplace with *too many* franchisees.

The FOC is particularly helpful in avoiding scams by disclosing information about the *people* involved in a franchisor. In the document, you can find a number of provisions cluing you in about the backgrounds of the franchisors. You can see what experience they have with the company as well as other information—whether they have criminal records, bankruptcies, been involved in lawsuits, etc. If you're considering a franchise, make sure you review the FOC.

Typical items in the FOC also include detail issues such as franchise fees and other fees you will incur. You have certain rights under the FTC's franchise rule in case of misrepresentation on the part of your franchisor. You will also learn what the obligations are of each party with respect to territory, trademarks, restrictions on sources of products and services, restrictions on what you may sell, and how renewals and terminations of agreements will be handled.

FOC Required Items of Disclosure

- the full legal name of the franchisor, its predecessors and affiliates;
- any bankruptcies of the principals or any previous franchises under their control;
- current litigation involving principals;
- business experience of principals;
- initial franchise fee;
- total initial investment;
- franchisee's obligations;
- restrictions on sources of products and services;
- restrictions on what the franchisee may sell;
- financing offered to franchisees;
- territories;
- trademarks, patents, copyrights and proprietary information;
- any obligations or requirements that franchisees participate directly in the actual operation of the franchise business;
- renewal, termination, transfer and dispute resolution;
- list of outlets;
- substantiation of any earnings claims;
- franchisor financial statements;
- standard operating agreements and contracts.

The FTC requires that you receive this information at least 10 business days prior to signing any contract. Though you should not have to ask for it, don't be afraid to do so. Get to know this document. Get clarification of anything that is vague.

Read the FOC yourself. Good ones are written in plain English. If you need help, the Franchise Profiles International Web site (www.franchise411.com) has a page outlining the best way to read and interpret the FOC. If you don't understand what the document says, get your lawyer to help you. Do this before you sign any franchise agreement.

Comfort Zone

Once you review and understand the sections of the FOC, you should write down your concerns and questions of each section. Pay attention to the different provisions of the document, and then compare these with your franchise's competitors, even if they aren't franchised companies. Then you can look at the difference between your company and the competition to see if you feel comfortable with your company's policies.

The next thing you should do is to contact other franchisees of your company. Interview them. Find out what they like. Find out what they would like to change. Find out if there was anything they found out about *after* they had signed the agreement. Visit their stores.

Be aware of franchisees that have been recommended for contact by the franchisor. Some franchisees may be compensated to say good things; so, call franchisees of the company that aren't on the recommended list. In fact, try to find at least one franchisee who's not happy with the company (even good franchisors have a *few* of these at any given time) and try to understand his or her complaints.

This helps you to see through any hype or exaggerations there may be regarding the franchise.

Red Flags of Franchising

Below is a list of things to consider when weighing the advantages and disadvantages of the system you are considering, taken from the Franchise411 Web page, for use in studying the Franchise Offering Circular:

Red Flag	Yes/No
1. Low job satisfaction or lack of challenge	_____
2. High employee count or turnover	_____
3. Long or unpredictable work or store hours	_____
4. Complicated or lengthy paperwork	_____
5. Saturated or Highly Competitive Industries	_____
6. High or unpredictable real estate or store costs	_____
7. Product obsolescence or possible technology change	_____
8. Existing or imminent industry regulation or red tape	_____
9. Large minimum inventory or equipment purchases required	_____
10. Physically demanding or skilled employee requirements	_____
11. High insurance costs or liability exposures	_____
12. Lack of outlet for personal talents or skills	_____
13. Poor socio-economic/educational traits of employees	_____
14. Restrictions on growth or expansion or relocation	_____
15. Political or social scrutiny of product or service	_____
16. High volume sales required for break-even	_____
17. Salesmanship or high advertising/marketing costs	_____
18. High maintenance or perishable or shrinkage costs	_____
19. High capitalization of equipment or real estate	_____
20. High initial financial exposure/high downside risk	_____

If you answer "Yes" to any of these Red Flags, you should proceed carefully. If you answer "Yes" to several, you should reconsider the franchise opportunity you're seeking.

Don't Rush

Aggressive franchisors may pressure you to make a quick decision about buying in. Their representatives might talk about how quickly prime locations are being taken, etc. This doesn't necessarily mean that the franchisor is crooked; it just means it's...aggressive.

Don't cave to sales tactics. A legitimate franchise opportunity won't vanish in a few weeks.

And the FOC isn't the only place to find information about your franchisor. Additional financial information on any company can be found— for a fee—through commercial reporting agencies such as Dun & Bradstreet.

You can also check with the local or state Better Business Bureau to see if any complaints have been filed by consumers, and if and how they were resolved.

Your lawyer or accountant may be able to give you good advice regarding the integrity of the franchisor and the franchise. And they may have clients with experience regarding a particular company. And make sure to have them go over your franchise agreement to point out any clauses that are of interest to you or are confusing.

 In addition to all of the other issues presented here, don't forget the advice I offered in the introduction: The economic climate— local, state and national—can have a big influence on the success of any business, including a franchise. Certain businesses do quite well in hard economic times, while others fail. If you do not pay attention to these conditions, you might have the nicest store no one ever visits.

Responsibilities of a Franchisee

It is good to know the answers to every discrepancy you might find in the FOC and learn what your duties are as franchisee. This will help eliminate any future dissatisfaction once you sign the agreement. Keep in mind that, although the investment risk is lower when starting a franchise than an independent business, you may have to give up control of many aspects of your business in order to operate within the agreement.

Depending on the type of franchise you buy, you may or may not incur the following costs or be subject to specific business controls.

For example, if your franchise of interest is a home-based Internet consulting firm, you probably won't be paying for building an outlet or certain types of insurance. You probably will, however, pay for the domain name on the Web.

Costs

The first thing you will most likely need to pay is the franchise fee. The franchise fee gives you a format or system developed by the franchisor, rights to use the name for a limited time, and assistance in various ways, as stated before. The franchise fee can range from a few thousand dollars to a few *hundred* thousand dollars, depending on these factors and what type of franchise you are buying.

You may have to pay to rent, lease, or build your own outlet. Depending on the type of business, you may need to purchase the initial inventory, and all or part of the operating licenses and insurance. After your grand opening, you may have to pay ongoing royalties to the franchisor for the right to use their name. This could be any given percentage of your revenues, even if you don't earn a profit for some months.

Some franchises will provide your advertising for you, in which case you will pay ongoing advertising fees, or place a certain percentage of your revenue into a type of advertising fund that contributes to national advertising. An extra contribution may supply you and other franchises in your area with promotions and marketing for your specific community.

The Elements of Small Business

Sometimes it is optional and sometimes it is required. Know the difference before the bill comes.

The following is an example of the financial preview for a 7-Eleven franchise. Note that income is received only once the gross profits have been paid to the company, and you have used your share to cover necessary expenses.

Fifty-two percent (52%) of the store's gross revenue goes to 7-Eleven's corporate parent for:

- Property and building rent

- Equipment rent

- Property taxes

- Some utilities (heat/cooling/lights/water)

- National advertising

- Bookkeeping and audits

- Financial reports

- Merchandising

- Product selection/price recommendations

- Point-of-sale materials

- General business advisory assistance

- Local and national franchisee advisory counsels

The Franchisee keeps the rest (48%) of the store's gross revenue to pay for:

- Payroll and payroll taxes

- Employee group insurance

- Equipment repair

- Laundry

- Business taxes and licenses
- Janitorial services
- Landscaping
- Security
- Extra advertising for the store
- Cash variation
- Bad merchandise
- Store supplies
- Inventory variation
- General maintenance
- Telephone
- Miscellaneous store expenses

The franchisee keeps anything left from the 48 percent cut. While it seems that there would be little or nothing to keep, note how many 7-Eleven stores (or Circle K stores) are in your area. Someone's making money somehow.

Business Controls

Because franchises are territorial by nature, it is possible that the only available site is on the other side of town. Or maybe in another town altogether. Or maybe you would have to move to a different state because the franchisor's needs have been met in your state. Are you willing to do this? Weigh out the advantages and disadvantages of a career move such as this and a personal move.

When a site has been approved for you, chances are that research has been done to maximize customer attraction. However, you may be limited to this area only because of other franchisees. So you may be out of luck if you want to purchase more than one outlet in the same area. Your area may also be restricted to limit the competition between you and another franchisee nearby. That could limit your growth potential.

If you set up shop at one location but, later, want to move to another location, approval must be obtained by the franchisor.

Make sure to review the clause addressing territorial rights in your agreement. This is definitely one of the larger chunks of field research you should do when exploring your franchising options, especially if it isn't addressed in your Franchise Offering Circular.

There may be certain design or architecture requirements for your franchise to ensure the same *identifiable look* for each location. You also may be required to keep up with design changes and the renovations that go with it. This may not be too often, but if your franchise does seasonal display changes, the costs can add up.

The franchisor may place restrictions on the sale and purchase of specific goods and services pertaining to your business. Those who are looking for structure in their businesses may like this aspect. But if you notice in your restaurant, for example, that customers never buy a certain menu item, you may still have to carry that item in stock.

If you are operating a fitness establishment and would like to add a specific service, like massage, you may not be allowed to per your franchise agreement, even though you know it would bring in more new clients or better satisfy your current clients. Some franchisees feel that some of the creative management or marketing opportunities are curbed by these restrictions.

And if you think that is control, you may be surprised to learn that you must operate during specific business hours, wear certain uniforms (*a la* the Hot Dog on a Stick fast-food chain), use predetermined book-keeping procedures and advertise in a specific manner or with only approved signage. These requirements will vary from one establishment to the next.

If you sign a franchise agreement and then fail to pay royalties or operate by the standards required, you could be held in breach of contract. Remember, agreements can run anywhere from 10 to 20 years, and if you break this you will most likely lose your investment. Even if your franchise experience is all that you hoped it would be and you want to renew the agreement, those entrepreneurial dictators can raise your royalty payments and/or enforce new standards and restrictions.

Recently, an acquaintance of mine sought a license from a well-known manufacturer to create stores selling the manufacturer's products to the general public. After obtaining the license, he decided that selling franchises would be the fastest way to grow.

All states require that a franchiser register its information and obtain state approval before proceeding. The acquaintance had missed that class and began selling franchises anyway. Bad idea.

When one state agency regulating the sale of franchises discovered this, it issued a cease-and-desist order. Simply, my acquaintance was ordered to stop. "Aren't I allowed to make a living?" he whined.

Not without the approval of the state.

Make sure that any franchise opportunity includes proof that the state has approved of the offering. And if you plan to franchise your business, seek the assistance of a qualified attorney before you begin.

Conclusion

Owning a franchise means you have marketing, market research, advertising and name value immediately. But you have to pay for that. So pay attention to the fine print. The franchisors are your landlords and you're their proverbial tenants. This is the lease of your life. Be good. Franchise responsibly.

References

Dixon, Edward. *The 2003 Franchise Annual*. Info Press (January 2003).

Keup, Erwin J. *Franchise Bible : How to Buy a Franchise or Franchise Your Own* (fourth edition). PSI Research/Oasis Press (June 2000).

Seid, Michael, and Dave Thomas. *Franchising For Dummies*. IDG/For Dummies (July 2000).

Sherman, Andrew J. *Franchising & Licensing: Two Ways to Build Your Business* (2nd edition). AMACOM (March 1999).

Tomzack, Mary E. *Tips & Traps When Buying a Franchise* (2nd edition). Sourcebooks, Inc. (April 1999).

Chapter 6

Capital Formation

The business of government is to keep out of business—that is, unless business needs government aid.

—Will Rogers

When Marx and Engels wrote *The Communist Manifesto*, they concluded that socialism was a natural outgrowth of capitalism. The implication was that a society could not get to socialism without a capital base—MONEY!

Okay, so now I can write off that college education. But the fact is capital is necessary to achieve and be successful in business. In the real world, Hong Kong remains a mecca of capitalism even under Chinese control because the Chinese understand that they make money from the sale of goods and services. That income allows them the luxury of ruling all others with an iron fist.

Every business needs money. But how you get it could mean the difference between success and failure. Some people go to friends or family to raise money for their business. This may include a "gift" up to $10,000 per person, a method originally devised for parents to provide down payment funds for an adult child's first home purchase. At the time this book was published this amount was current, but tax laws change so rapidly that it is a good idea to ask your beloved accountant.

Assuming that Aunt Edna did not leave you a small fortune or Uncle Ralph just could not find anything else he could do with his lottery winnings, outside sources will be required. The methods available depend on the type of business formation you have chosen. In fact, the type of formation you choose may come as a result of how you intend to raise capital. Loans from a variety of sources, as well as capital contribution and selling of shares as ways to raise money for your business are discussed in this chapter.

First, you must assess the amount you will need—*really* need—to make the business work.

There are many things to consider when figuring the capital needed for start-up. If you are incorporating, you will need to factor in the cost of the fees, taxes, and government filings. You will likely need to lease equipment in advance, rent a space, and purchase insurance. Make sure you make a start-up list alongside of your budget. And don't forget to factor in the costs of retaining that accountant and attorney to advise you on the formation of your business and the tax ramifications.

 One of the most common mistakes is to set the amount needed to get the business started—but not have enough money set aside to advertise the product or service. It's great to have the best widgets in town. But what if no one knows you have them? You should project up to six months of expenses, including advertising or giveaways or other promotions, while counting on only a little income to offset the expenses.

Several years ago, a client of mine decided to open a sports bar and restaurant. To sell alcoholic beverages, he had to obtain a license from the state's Department of Alcoholic Beverage Control. He never bothered to discuss the matter with me—and proceeded, anyway. He was a successful real estate guy with plenty of access to money; but he knew nothing of the rules and regulations regarding alcohol permits. And he didn't realize that the department could reject his application for reasons that had nothing to do with him.

> He agreed to purchase an alcohol license from a private party who'd run a local bar but was getting out of the business. This kind of transfer was allowed, under certain conditions. Per the instructions of the state, my client set up an escrow account and submitted the transfer application. All of this was done during the construction and equipment leasing—the business matters my client considered most important.

Soon, my client had spent more than $500,000 on a business without having secured the essential permit. That's a lot of speculation, even for a successful guy with good banking relationships.

Then it came: The rejection letter. The vice squad of the local police department had to sign off on all alcohol permit transfers—and it wasn't going to approve this one. The police claimed that the crime rate in the neighborhood was too high (including some gang activity) and that the area already had too many bars.

And so began a two-year odyssey of appeals and hearings. Ultimately, we prevailed and got the permit transferred. But the victory was Pyrrhic.

During the period from the rejection to the reversal and transfer, my client couldn't open the doors to a business he'd spent heavily to start. He covered all of his debts; but, ultimately, the financial burden on the business was so high that the restaurant lasted only three years—struggling the whole time to service its larger-than-originally-expected debt.

My client hadn't contacted me until after the rejection of the permit application, so his capital structure wasn't what he needed to make the business a success. He was a smart, experienced guy; but he didn't know how much money his business *really* needed.

Bank Loans

Your bank can give you a loan. Often, it comes in the form of a line of credit. That means the bank makes available to you a maximum sum that you can use as necessary. You pay back what you use. Of course, you will pay interest on what you borrow while you borrow it.

On occasion, the interest rate for the loan is fixed—meaning that it will not change through the repayment. However, many banks prefer to offer a variable rate. These rates are tied to changes in a particular index.

The most common variable is the *prime interest rate*. This is a rate set by the Federal Reserve Board and represents the lowest rate banks charge their best customers. A common loan rate might be "prime plus 2.5 percent."

Tip: If you choose a variable rate, make sure you understand the index upon which your rate is set and that the rate has a cap so that it can never be higher than a certain percentage or raised in any period, often quarterly, more than one-half of a point. Certain indices tend to move faster to the upside and down side, while others, such as the 11th District Cost of Funds Index moves very slowly in either direction.

Another Tip: When loan percentages are provided, you will see two numbers. The first is the interest rate and the other, referred to as the Annual Percentage Rate (APR) is the actual rate you pay. Why the difference? Ask yourself : How is the interest accruing? Monthly? Quarterly? Annually? The faster the interest accrues, the higher the APR. When the rate and the APR are close, then that is a good deal. But be wary of very low rates.

I have seen rates on car loans advertised as 1.9 percent but with an APR of 3.5 percent. The real rate you will be paying will be that 3.5 percent. So maybe it was not such a bargain in the first place.

Your credit rating will determine the amount of your line of credit. If you have formed a corporation or LLC and you have been in business for more than five years, the business' tax returns and profit and loss statements may be adequate.

If the money is for a new business venture, then your personal tax returns will be requested regardless of whether you have formed a corporation. Also, the bank may wish to review a formal business plan (which we will discuss a little later) and your credentials.

SBA Loans and Other Options

Just about all types of businesses can obtain loans from the federal agency known as the Small Business Administration. These loans are made by banks, secured by the federal government, and come with an interest rate as low as three percent.

"Secured by the federal government" simply means that if you default on the loan the bank can be reimbursed by the Federal government. You can obtain an application from bank personnel. The bank will supply you with an SBA loan with a much lower interest rate than their own because they will most likely get other business from you as well.

> **For more information on SBA loans and financing options, you can visit www.SBA.gov.**

If you're a member or are eligible to be a member of a credit union, you might use its services. A credit union operates in a manner similar to a bank. Generally, credit unions are owned and operated by their members; membership generally consists of belonging to a union, trade group or other organization.

If you attended a major college or university, you may have the right to belong to a credit union. Recently, the federal government changed the membership requirement so that the general public could receive the services of credit unions. Thus many credit unions are openly soliciting the public.

The advantage of seeking loans from credit unions is that they tend to have lower rates of interest and can be less stringent in their requirements for providing loans to their members. Also, you often receive a higher rate of interest on your savings accounts and certificates of deposit (CDs).

Tip: if you borrow money from friends or family, the IRS requires a minimum interest rate for the loan. So Uncle Hank's offer to loan you "a few grand" really is a loan and if Uncle Hank fails to declare the interest as income, the IRS will do it for him at the next audit—along with its charges for penalties and interest on the unpaid taxes. However, parents and other family members can give up to $10,000.00 each to a child as a gift. This rule was set up to assist parents in providing a down payment for their adult child's first home but can be applied for just about anything including the creation of a business.

Capital Contributions and Loans

If your business is set up as a corporation or LLC or LLP, you or other shareholders or partners are permitted to provide funds to the corporation. The funds fall into two categories: Capital contribution or loan.

A capital contribution is monies provided to the company that are not intended to be repaid. This money is not considered income and therefore is not taxable. It also does not provide a tax write-off to you.

A loan from a shareholder or officer works in the same manner as if the money had been borrowed from a bank. While there is no tax consequence to a loan, if the money is ever repaid, the minimal IRS interest rate must be declared by the loaning party as income.

Security Agreement

If the amount of the loan is substantial, the loaning party may want something of value to secure the loan—something that the loaning party can sell off to cover the debt you failed to pay.

Think of it this way: When you buy a home, the bank lends you money. In exchange, it holds the deed to your nice new home. A mortgage is born.

In the world of securities, a stock pledge agreement or a security agreement uses shares of stock as collateral for the loan. If you default (fail to pay), the lending party gets the shares. If the number of shares pledged is substantial, that party may be able to take over the business. If not, maybe he or she can sell them.

Bottom line: Unless the company becomes worthless, don't default.

Several years ago, a client retained me to defend her in a suit filed by a creditor. She and other major shareholders had pledged their shares as security (something tangible the creditor can take and sell if you don't pay) in order to raise capital for investment. When it came time to make payments on the loan, the corporation did not have the money. Rather than selling the shares right then and there, the creditor inexplicably chose to wait.

Several months later, the company failed. That eliminated the option of the creditor selling the shares. So, it sued the individuals who had pledged their stock. Since the loan was provided to the corporation and since the only collateral was pledge of the shares of stock, in the absence of fraud or other intentional mismanagement, the creditor was out of luck. Case dismissed.

Selling Shares

Selling stock in your company is another option. Friends or relatives may take a liking to you or your cause and want to invest their money. After all, there is a chance that you really know what you are doing and that they can go along for the ride. For these purchasers, they give you money, you give them some stock. In most cases, the stock or "security" and its sale does not require approval by any state agency.

If your business is small and intended to be family operated with a handful of employees with friends and family owning the business or the shares, then this next section doesn't apply to you—directly. (But think big. Read it, anyway.)

For situations where hundreds of thousands of dollars or even a few million dollars will be needed, another set of rules applies.

To begin, you will want to develop a "prospectus." Similar to a business plan, it explains to investors who you are and what you are trying to do. You must file or register the prospectus and other related information with every state in which sales of shares may take place.

Don't attempt this on your own or the planets will collide. In fact, failure to use an attorney may result in serious consequences. Nonetheless, you should know the tenets of raising money this way. So we continue...

For these investors, you will create and provide to them the prospectus and a "subscription agreement." This agreement basically states that the investment is not guaranteed and that you could lose all of your money. Often, a section of the agreement or a separate document requests that the investor declare that he or she is a "qualified" investor—that the individual has participated in similar investments, is able to lose the money investment, and knows what he or she is doing.

Do not take any money from investors without obtaining their signature on the subscription agreement prepared by an experienced attorney. In the event the company fails, that agreement may be the only thing that protects you from a lawsuit. Nothing breeds lawsuits like a good business failure.

Depending on how much money you intend to raise, you may have different kinds or classifications of investors. For businesses requiring a lot of capital, "angel" investors may be necessary. These are the first big money folks (sometimes referred to as "venture capitalists").

Since their contribution has just paid your bills for the next year, the term "Angel" is fitting. In exchange for making your dreams come true, the angels receive a number of benefits such as stock, stock options and buyouts of their shares at a certain strike price—meaning that if the stock develops a certain value, they can require the company to purchase their shares.

> In short, angels provide the bulk of the start-up capital. However, they are arms-length investors. Selling shares to them or to the general public triggers a set of rules and requirements far more stringent that the rules for sales to people whom you know. This is a good time to retain a securities attorney.

Depending on the type of investment and its status, if you want to sell shares to the public you will have to register the investment prospectus with the "Department of Corporations" and/or the office of the Secretary of State in each state where you will be soliciting potential investors.

The prospectus is a fascinating collection of information about you, the company, what it does and why one would want to invest in it. It also has a multi-page disclaimer which when broken down really informs the investor that he or she could lose all of his or her investment and it ain't your fault.

If you sell shares to random investors in multiple states, you may also need to register the investment with the SEC (www.sec.gov). The Securities and Exchange Commission regulates the sales of anything defined as a "security." And the fact is any investment sold through interstate commerce is a security. Even if you live in Phoenix and call a potential investor in Tucson, this activity is considered to be "interstate" since you used interstate telephone lines to make the call. Again, time for that securities lawyer. Just think: if it all goes wrong, at least you can sue him or her for malpractice.

Types of Shares

Most small businesses will have one type of stock—common stock. In certain cases, you may wish to consider different classes of common stock or different series of common stock. The rules and restrictions of issuing separate classes or series very from state to state. Often, a corporation will use different classes or series of stock at different intervals of sales. For example, if at start-up the corporation sells shares for $1.00, that might be termed Class "A."

The following year, the stock offering might be set at $2.00 per share and be termed Class "B." The corporation might have rules granting it a right of first refusal to purchase Class A shares at a certain set price before those shares can be sold to the general public. Or the different classifications may result in different distributions of proceeds from a sale of the company. Before you create separate categories you should seek advice from a competent professional.

In addition to separate categories for common stock, businesses can have separate types of stock. The most common of these is "preferred stock." These shares often come with certain rights that common stock does not have:

- priority on the assets in case the corporation is dissolved;

- special voting rights on certain specified issues;

- priority over dividends, if paid by the corporation;

- possible right to convert to common stock at a discount;

- other rights that protect the shareholder's interests.

You don't have to have a completed product in order to solicit investors. A client wanted to develop an animated television show for children. The only problem was that he knew nothing about television shows for children especially animated shows. Always a good start. Knowing what he did not know, he found those who did. One of those he found had already developed on paper a concept for a superhero style of show. The cost of producing an entire episode would run as high as $600,000. A three-minute trailer would cost on tenth of that amount.

So, my client decided to produce the trailer after the client raised the money necessary. With trailer in hand, the client could show others who might invest enough money to pay for the first episode and maybe more.

By creating a prototype and by working through a realistic process of raising enough money to create a viable product to be used to make more money, the client was able to meet his goal of creating an animated show. Had he attempted at the beginning to raise all of the money without the benefit of a trailer, it is likely he would not have been successful or if so, he would have worked for months without knowing whether in the end he would be able to raise all the money needed.

Factoring

If you have a small business but receive really big orders, you may have the ability to borrow enough money to cover the raw material and packaging costs of a 100,000 unit order but waiting for thirty to sixty days for payment will grind the business to a halt. Maybe you can rely on a line of credit. Maybe not. So now what?

A *factor* or factoring company will lend you money based on purchase orders you've gotten from customers or your accounts receivable—for a fee. Usually the fee is a percentage of the purchase orders or receivables. In exchange, you assign collection of the receivable to the factor. Your profit will not be as high, but at least you have operating capital.

Tip: Ever buy that king size jar of grape jelly because it was cheaper per ounce than the smaller size? Is it still sitting in the refrigerator half full? Unless you fear a shortfall of certain raw materials, don't stock too much of anything. Years ago when the price of gold was over $400.00 an ounce, a client in

the jewelry manufacturing business simply never figured that the price would go lower. So he bought a lot of gold. The price then dipped to $300 and has ranged between $268 and $420 for the past five years. Ouch. Since the company could not raise prices in a competitive market, the company could not recoup such a loss and has since folded.

Another Tip: While we have not included a chapter on shipping, beware that shipping prices are bizarre, illogical, and can vary by five times from company to company. Fluctuations in gasoline or diesel fuel prices can result in fuel surcharges. If you are in the manufacturing business or retail sales that include shipping, make sure to shop around and to negotiate rates. Find out if increases in the cost of fuel will result in price increases. If possible, check with your competitors to see what they are paying. There are a lot of shipping companies and many will work out deals for the exclusive rights to ship your goods.

Conclusion

The fact is capital comes in a plethora of forms—from banks, individuals, venture capitalists and from family and friends. The best method for you will depend on the amount you wish to raise and the type of business you are starting.

But be forewarned: Don't try to raise money from anyone without consulting any attorney or an expert in raising capital. Once again, the few hundred dollars you spend at this stage could be the difference between fulfilling your dreams and law suits costing tens of thousands of dollars or even criminal charges.

References

Bartlett, Joseph W. *Fundamentals of Venture Capital*. Rowman & Littlefield Publishers, Inc. (August, 1999).

Chandler, Linda. *Winning Strategies for Capital Formation: Secrets of Funding Start-Ups and Emerging Growth Firms Without Losing Control of Your Idea, Project or Company*. McGraw-Hill Trade (August, 1996).

Gladstone, David, and Linda Gladstone. *Venture Capital Handbook: An Entrepreneur's Guide to Raising Venture Capital*. Pearson Education (October 2001).

Gompers, Paul A., and Josh Lerner. *The Venture Capital Cycle*. MIT Press (January, 2002).

Van Osnabrugge, Mark, and Robert J. Robinson. *Angel Investing: Matching Startup Funds with Startup Companies: A Guide for Entrepreneurs and Individual Investors*. John Wiley & Sons, Inc. (May, 2000).

The Elements of Small Business

Chapter 7

Business Plans

To be a success in business, be daring, be first, be different.
—Marchant

If you want others to understand what you do and why, the creation of a business plan is key. In fact, a business plan provides three benefits:

- A road map for your business to which you can review at any time to keep focused.

- A format by which others can understand what you are doing or trying to do, especially if you intend to convince potential investors that you "have a plan" for making the big bucks.

- A *brochure* for bidding on certain jobs.

If you are not intending to raise money from investors, then a business plan is not a necessity. However, one of the biggest mistakes small businesses make is expanding into areas where the owner or management has little knowledge and experience, or expanding before ironing out all of the bugs in the primary area of the business. A plan assists you in staying focused on your goals, so it may be a good idea to get one on paper even if you don't seek financial help.

If you are considering investment from outside sources a business plan is essential.

Other than you speaking directly, the plan is the best tool for describing what you do, why you do it and how much money can be made. Investors take more seriously those who have spent the time to put their ideas on paper in detail. Consider this: the fewer questions investors have to ask, the more they will believe that you are educated about the business.

It is very difficult to operate a company without capital. As I discussed in the "Capital Formation" chapter, the sale of shares of stock or other company interest is the sale of a "security." Most states require that the sale be registered and that the state approve the company's plan to sell shares or interests prior to conducting any sale. Failure to do so can lead to civil and criminal penalties.

As I mentioned before, the exception to this rule involves sales to friends, family, or others with whom you or the company have done business in the past. However, it is always a good idea to have these individuals or entities execute a waiver. A *waiver* is a simple lawyer term for a document that states roughly, "If I invest in a company that has not started yet and remains untested, I cannot sue when my money is lost."

Business plans also provide those operating a business guidelines to prevent them from losing focus on the big picture.

While no one format fits all, remember that others will be reading the plan. If they do not understand it, then how can you expect them to invest? Also, this may be your only opportunity to impress people who are considering signing their name to a really big check. So don't blow it.

Business plans have no set rules except for having the capacity to inform the reader as to the nature of the business, who will be in charge, what qualifications those in charge have, and why this particular business has a *revenue model* (a fancy term for how the business intends to make money). Think of the plan as a newspaper article. You are answering to the "who, what, when, where, how and why."

The Business Plan

While no rules exist, over the years business plans have taken on a certain format that is generally accepted and expected by investors. Below is a common arrangement for a fictitious company. While one size does not fit all, it provides a good template for you. If all of this seems a bit overwhelming, and it should, you can hire a professional to write your business plan.

Expect the cost to run from $2,500 to $5,000 depending on the sophistication of the business structure and complexities of the proposed financing scheme. We will use the fictitious company name "Hotronix, Inc." to illustrate the issues. Note that a good cover sheet states the name of the company and what the product or service is— in ten words or less. [Form 7-1]

Executive Summary

It is always helpful to tell the reader what he or she will be reading. This can be executed by attaching a summary at the beginning. Just think of it as "Mini-Me." This way, the reader knows what to expect and whether your concept is a good one—at least from his or her perspective.

In addition to explaining the revenue model, or how on earth you think you are going to make a fortune selling a rock resting on a bed of straw in a small cardboard box (remember the Pet Rock?), the summary includes basic information about strategy, key personnel, market research, and other factors that you believe make the business valuable. The executive summary should not be longer than two pages.

The Elements of Small Business

Environmental Analysis

No, we are not saving the rain forest here. Rather, this section provides valuable information regarding the current economic environment.

> Consider this: In a recession, why would anyone buy your product when they have less disposable income? Or maybe your product is less expensive than a similar product thus making it more affordable in tougher economic times. Or you may declare why your product is necessary and why you think people will buy it. You should include historical data regarding income and the economic climate.

If your product has certain markets that are overseas or purchases raw material from overseas, you should discuss the current political situation in that region of the world. And if your markets are foreign, don't forget to discuss geopolitical issues including treaties. For example, the North American Free Trade Agreement, passed in 1994, removed many of the tariffs and barriers to selling goods manufactured in Canada, the United States, and Mexico in the other's country.

"Most Favored Nation" trading status, a designation given to foreign countries where most, if not all, tariffs have been eliminated, may also be significant. Countries not so designated may have significant tariffs and other barriers for products coming from or going to the United States, and in turn the United States may be imposing certain tariffs or barriers on that country's products.

Assuming that it is not your goal to develop the business and then sell it, you may wish to examine the future economic climate. While no one has a crystal ball (or a good psychic), if you intend to borrow money, the direction of interest rates will matter. If you manufacture goods and any raw materials come from overseas, you had better make sure the origin of those materials is not subject to civil unrest or that you have an alternate supplier just in case. Or if you have a product or service that you believe will be immune to negative changes in the economy, then you should discuss that issue.

The more you show investors that you understand the issues that can derail your business ventures and that you have planned for such contingencies, the better off you are and the more likely investors will trust you. Let's face it: Anything that makes you look smart and thoughtful can't be bad.

Industry Profile

Unless you really believe you have invented something that has never been invented before, you will need to research every aspect of your competitors' tactics, including manufacturing, marketing and sales. Many small businesses assume that they need to be the first on the block to do whatever it is they do or that they have built the better mousetrap. Not only is this a bad idea, it's irrelevant.

Sometimes the better mousetrap doesn't prevail. Remember the Sony Beta videocassette player/recorders? Sony introduced home video with the Beta format around 1980. But it refused to license its technology to others. So a number of other companies consulted and came up with a VCR using the "VHS" format. Sony showed the VHS developers that a market existed for the product. The VHS developers did it better.

Why do you find more than one gas station on the corner? Because there is enough business to go around. And that is the key. Who are the major competitors and what do they do? Financial wizards will often tell you that you do not need one hundred percent of the market, but rather ten percent. So, how much business revolves around your type of product and what are you going to do to capture the market?

One way to show your genius is to discuss the industry. For those of you who saw the movie *Other People's Money*, you might recall that, during the proxy fight, Danny DeVito's character talks to the shareholders about buggy whips. He points out that the last buggy whip manufacturer must have been rather pleased knowing he had no competition...except: "The easiest way to go out of business is to obtain an increasing share of a decreasing market."

Simply put, you are better off having a small share of an increasing market than having one hundred percent of a decreasing market. Showing your potential investors that your product will become a "household" item and why may just be the key your success in gaining investors.

And then there are the competitors. While intuitive reasoning may hold that having the market place all to yourself is a good thing, the fact is an analysis of competitors and even having competitors shows that other companies see the marketplace in the same way you do. Yes, that strength in numbers thing is a valuable tool and can work to your advantage since investors will be impressed if you can show how your thingamabobber is better than the other thingamabobbers currently available to consumers. Simply, a product type already selling in the marketplace can be more impressive than trying to explain why people will purchase something unknown in their universe.

Also, the advertising and marketing efforts that your competitors have already put forth served to educate the public about the functionality of the product. Consider the personal digital assistant (PDA). How would you like to be the inventor of the Palm Pilot? Consider the fun in explaining how the darn thing works and the cost in doing that. Then, after years of advertising and explaining why you can't live without one, BlackBerry comes along with a better and more sophisticated product capable of more functions and more practical business functions. It provides a full keyboard, albeit for the fingers of children and simpler access to e-mail. Now, you can get a PDA or BlackBerry as part of your cellular telephone. What will they think of next?

Internal Analysis

This section usually includes:

- company background (introduction of the major players),

- financial overview,

- operations overview,

- value chain analysis, and

- resource-based view analysis.

So who are you and why are you qualified to create this business and make it work? A little bit about each major player in the company should be included along with an ORG or organizational chart—a chart indicating the names of the officers and those who will work for them.

And how about them earnings? If you have been in business for any reasonable length of time, you should discuss the company's revenues from existing products and future products in development. Even if you are just starting up, you can base your (projected) revenues from those of similar businesses and any other relevant factors. This can be arranged in a table format for easy viewing.

Don't forget an overview of the operations. When I interviewed for a job with the District Attorney's office just after graduating from law school, another D.A. said I should ask about a typical day—what would I be doing. I asked and got a good answer. I didn't get the job so take that for what its worth. But don't ignore the question. If you are entering the interior plantscape business, then a diatribe about watering plants probably is not interesting. But other business situations require more in depth information, especially if your product or service is not unique.

The example I've provided for you contains a "value chain analysis" or an analysis of the value of the product or products within the product and distribution chain. This section is not a requirement unless you believe that the investors will not understand what value your products or services might have and how your product or services fits into the industry.

You might consider this as a flowchart or diagram to depict pictorially how the product fits in the "food chain" for the particular industry.

SWOT Analysis

SWOT stands for *Strengths, Weaknesses, Opportunities, and Threats*. The most human of traits is to paint the rosiest picture of anything. In the wacky world of business plans, this is a bad idea. Anyone who has business experience knows that any venture comes with positives and negatives. Your ability to recognize both is crucial to your credibility. That is why most businesses use the SWOT method of analysis to assess the company's performance and the factors that will affect it.

The first half of the SWOT anagram (SW) concerns interior aspects of your business, or what we could call "in-house" factors. These are the things your business can control. In the Hotronix example, the plan author noted the following positives, or *strengths*, in the company:

- Hotronix(tm) brand name and reputation

- production of high quality products

- new management team

- sales representative training program

The author then notes the negatives, or *weaknesses*:
- poor inventory management

- limited strategic planning process

- limited emphasis on innovation

- lack of investment in advertising/promotion activities

The "out-of-house" or exterior factors affecting your business, are addressed by the second half (OT)—the opportunities and threats. These issues are normally outside of your direct control.

In our example, the author listed these *opportunities*:

- reduction in trade barriers (i.e., NAFTA pending)

- Internet popularity

- alternative distribution channels

- low labor costs in foreign territories (i.e., Asia, Mexico)

- increased number of households globally

- growing environmental concerns

And finally, the *threats*:

- international importers

- slow market growth

- shift in consumer trends

- growing environmental concerns

I have a friend who is an investment advisor. On speculative investments such as start-up companies, he calls clients and says, "Hey George, how would you like to lose $10,000?" No painting of the rosy picture there.

Your ability to recognize the pluses and minuses of your venture and to discuss how you intend to address both will impress investors. Don't get me wrong. You should be optimistic and excited and your plan should be positive and enthusiastic. You can accomplish all that while reminding the potential investor that nothing in business is certain.

You would be amazed at how far honesty gets you.

The Strategic Plan

So, now you have laid out the pros and the cons about your business and provided a comprehensive background. To paraphrase the crazy Carpenter kids, you've only just begun. Now it is time to share your vision by way of a strategic plan. The strategic plan methodically addresses all aspects of your company, from marketing strategies to labor disputes. It is also extremely beneficial to iron the bugs out of your system, preparing yourself for possible situations.

The Mission Statement

Your strategic plan starts with the mission statement or what do you intend to accomplish and how you intend to make it happen. You may want to think of this as your thesis statement for the entire business. Most businesses like to feel that their products or services are bettering the community in some way or another.

A fine-tuned mission statement can help you when performing valuations of your company. (I'll talk more about valuations in the upcoming Accounting chapter.)

The Marketing Plan and Strategy

Your plan should provide for a strategy on how you will inform others of your product or service—not to mention the fact that you need such a strategy. The first step with your product or service is to establish a goal. So, in our example, an overview with goals (*realistic* goals) begins this section. It is very nice that the company intends to increase sales by leaps and bounds. But remember that you will have to include specific information later.

After the overview, it is time to get to the specifics starting with market research, to packaging to store placement to advertising on radio or television or billboard. If you have strategic partners, the plan should discuss ways in which the other companies will be assisting you in enhancing your product. Just think of McDonald's and the Olympic Games or children's movies and any fast food chain.

If you have or intend to have retail outlets or service centers, the issue is how many, where they will be located and why they will be located in those locations. If there is a sales force, who are they and where are they going to be located?

There ain't no use in building the better mousetrap if no one knows it exists. It is not enough to set aside investment dollars. Since funds will be limited, you have to consider the best resources that will reach the most potential customers.

Unless your venture is unique, you should take every opportunity to observe what your competitors are doing—right and wrong. Note the customers they appear to have. Are they advertising? If so, where? If you think they're competent, let them do your research for you.

> **For example:** The sports sections of most newspapers contain ads for business equipment. It should occur to you that these companies have spent millions of dollars on advertising and have determined that the readers of the sports pages are their customers.

It is important to realize that advertising is but one step. For retail sales packaging matters. Certain colors matter. The inclusion of real life pictures matters. Displays matter. Endorsements, especially celebrity endorsements matter.

So, once you have considered all of these possibilities, assemble a game plan. Show the investors that you have a strategy and that it has been well thought out.

Tip: Newspapers and magazines need advertising to make money. Their internal advertising departments have a great deal of knowledge and want you to succeed. If you succeed, they succeed. They will be happy to prepare your ads and tell you where they should be placed to get the maximum exposure for your market.

The Financial Plan and Strategy

All of this planning leads to the denotation of a financial strategy. After an overview, the specifics provide potential investors with that which you will do with the hard earned cash of the investors.

> Knowledgeable investors will ask questions about the strategy and will expect answers. For example, how did the company decide to issue dividends and how did you arrive at the amount of the dividend. Even if you don't have such demanding investors, it's god to think this way yourself.

When I was in college, a longtime friend began a mail order business. One of his products was a "breast enhancer." This brilliant invention looked like the "Thigh Master" except that is was for use with the hands and arms, not the thighs. By squeezing the device, muscles around the breasts were supposed to gain mass giving the illusion that the breasts themselves had enlarged.

It may not surprise you that a quarter page ad in the *National Enquirer* turned out to be the best resource for cultivating sales.

After a few months of running ads, collecting checks and shipping the enhancers, my friend asked me to "chart the demographics"—a fancy term for "Where am I receiving the bulk of my sales?" It turned out that Florida and Georgia were high on the breast enhancer. I dared not ask why.

Armed with that information, my friend concentrated his advertising to that region of the country. Because the targeting brought in more money, he could afford to run ads in newspapers of higher circulation and thus his profits increased along with the breasts of many satisfied customers.

Operations

Maybe one of the greatest errors a young business can make is paying such close attention to sales of its products and services that it forgets about the operations of the company. For example, an attorney spends thirty percent (30 percent) less on his secretary's salary than other more highly trained secretaries. His theory is he saves money. But does he?

 A highly qualified legal secretary costs more. But if she is more efficient in handling her job duties, the difference in billable hours will surpass the cost. Think about it. At $300 per hour, an extra billable hour or two per week exceeds the costs of the more efficient and qualified secretary. It is not just the adage that cheaper is not always better, the lesson here is that increasing spending in one area, especially in operations, can result is significant profit increases.

Another operational issue concerns inventory and supply. The business plan should explain how you intend to get products from your plants (or your vendors' plants) to your customers. And it should include some thoughts about alternate plans—in case you have problems with vendors or transport. Or if business is either better or worse than you project.

> Either extreme can be difficult. There's an old saying among seasoned entrepreneurs: The worst problem is no business; the second worst problem is a lot of business.

You might have seen the commercial for the company that goes online. As the employees gather around the computer, they see a few purchases coming in. They smile as an additional few hundred more orders come in. But then the orders just keep coming and coming and coming. And as they do, their faces move from smiles to looks of shear terror. Buyers just are not too happy when it takes four to six weeks for their stuff to arrive. Plan for this happy problem.

Appendicies

The supporting data and documentation should be included in an appendix. This may include research information, sales forecasts and analysis, and the dreaded *pro forma*—the projected financial information including income and expenses. It might also contain the resumes or curricula vitae of the principals.

If you or your partners have special qualifications, then do tell. Investors want to know they are entrusting their money to people who have a history of success or a history in the same or similar business.

Conclusion

A good business plan will serve several purposes at once. It will give potential investors confidence in your venture. It will act as a sort of marketing tool—promoting your venture to people, whether or not they invest. And, finally, it can be a management tool, a map for making sure the company stays on track.

Remember that a plan is only a plan. The brilliant—in more than just court—U.S. federal Judge Learned Hand once noted that the worst reason for following a rule was that it was laid down in the time of Henry VIII.

The purpose of the plan is to help others to understand what you are doing not to determine how well you can copy that which has come before you. Don't be so rigid in following your plan that you cannot adapt to changing economic conditions. Be aware of trends and be aware of economic forecasts. They may be boring but they are required for the survival of any business.

References

Abrams, Rhonda M., and Eugene Kleiner. *The Successful Business Plan: Secrets and Strategies*. Rhonda, Inc. (June, 2003).

Covello, Joseph, et al. *Your First Business Plan: Learn the Critical Steps to Writing a Winning Business Plan*. Sourcebooks, Inc. (October, 1997).

Horna, James T., et al. *The One Page Business Plan: Start With a Vision, Build a Company!* One Page Business Plan Co. (May, 1998)

Patsula, Peter J. *Successful Business Planning in 30 Days: A Step-by-Step Guide for Writing a Business Plan and Starting Your Own Business*. Patsula Media (December, 2002).

Peterson, Steven D., and Peter E. Jaret. *Business Plans Kit for Dummies* (with CD-ROM). IDG/For Dummies (January, 2001).

Chapter 8

Marketing

Nothing's so apt to undermine your confidence in a product as knowing that the commercial selling it has been approved by the company that makes it.

—Franklin P. Jones

So you built the better mousetrap...

For many years, I have represented a marketing company. It serves as the middleman between creator/manufacturers of products and the retailers who sell the products to the public.

The main challenge to this client's business: Inventors usually lack a realistic perspective on the value of the things they create. Because everyone who "invents" the next product consumers can't live without *believes* that consumers can't live without their invention, I assisted the marketer in adding an introduction to its presentation. It was titled, *So You Think You Built the Better Mousetrap*.

While this book is not intended to be a primer on marketing strategies and techniques, we should pay some attention to the issues. And we have done so throughout this book. Nonetheless, it struck me that those of you who are creating a product and even those of you providing a service will need to bring home the bacon. If no one knows what you do or what you make, then it doesn't matter that you do it or make it.

What Exactly Is *Marketing*?

Marketing is the art of convincing someone that he or she cannot live without your product or service. Think it can't be done? Remember Cabbage Patch Kids, Beanie Babies or Furbies? Remember all of those screaming shoppers racing through the store just to nab one? Remember those teary-eyed parents who failed on their mission? It's all in the marketing.

 Effective marketing starts with knowing who buys your product or who retains your services. For example, if you choose to open a coffee bar with jazz music performances on the weekends you will need to consider the age group of your potential patrons—you will want to put the business in a location where people of that demographic reside.

If your likely patrons are singles between the ages of 25 to 40, then opening the business in a planned community of families with young children probably is not a slick business move. The older couple will be so busy taking care of the kids that they will not have the time to patronize the business on weeknights and probably seldom on weekends unless a cheap babysitter is available. Even if the adults get out of the house, they may have little remaining disposable income.

Assuming you locate your business in a beneficial location, then you have to consider where and how to advertise. The mistake many new businesses make is that all of their monies go to building and operations and employees without any monies reserved to tell people about the new business.

120

A few years ago, a friend decided to purchase a barely existing bar and renovate it into a quality restaurant.

Well, actually, the bar existed with a crowd that looked like something out of *Star Wars*.

Renovations took three times longer than expected and cost five times the amount estimated in the budget. By the time the restaurant opened, the owner had no money for advertising. For the three people (not counting my friend's family) who knew about the place, they were treated to scrumptious mouth watering delights. For the rest of the population, which did not discover the restaurant during its six months of operation, well...they missed out. The business filed for bankruptcy protection and that was that—$150,000 later.

Selling the Better Mousetrap

For service providers, few rules apply. If the service is needed and you can explain clearly why it is necessary, then you have a good shot at success. But for manufacturers, the picture is much different.

The American model of retailers is not only counterintuitive, it is also designed to prevent the better products from reaching the consumer. Yes, the picture is *that* bleak. Most major chain stores have buyers who meet with sales representatives from product manufacturers or sales and marketing to examine their products. Small companies have a difficult time arranging for such meetings because the buyers believe small businesses do not have the cash flow or the production capacity to meet the needs of the chain.

> Even if you get lucky, the worst thing that can happen is having a major chain order 100,000 units with an expected delivery in forty-five days when you have no cash or facility for fulfilling the order. Ouch. That's a good time to consider factoring and to have a company in place to factor your orders before you receive them.

So how do we solve these problems? Actors have agents who represent them to studios. Writers have agents who represent their works to publishers. Manufacturers and inventors have their own version of this. Sales and marketing companies make their money representing your blood, sweat and tears to retailers. They have reputations with the stores and their buyers.

 Marketing companies charge a commission on sales or charge a monthly retainer—or both. They know what each retailer wants and how to package and present your product in the most favorable manner. Using a network of independent sales representatives who have developed long-standing relationships with retailers, you can improve you product's chances of having its day in the retail sun.

Whether you hire a marketing firm or not, issues you will confront even before your product is presented include packaging, price point and advertising and the advertising budget.

Packaging

Strangely, it's the little things that consumers see that give them the impetus to buy a product. How many times have you bought the crayons in the yellow and green box because you know they are Crayolas and therefore the "best" crayons? What about the pink tub of Knudsen's cottage cheese because it also is the "best"? What makes most people buy white eggs instead of brown? Welcome to the psychology of advertising.

Once upon a time, the inventor of the binocular microscope attempted to sell his invention. But he found no customers. He was surprised, since he had created better optics and focus and the price was only a little more than monocular microscopes. And he had made it lighter for easier movement around the laboratory.

122

After having no success for many months, the inventor showed the thing to a friend who specialized in marketing. The man examined the microscope. He picked it up and set it down several times. Finally, he said, "I know what the problem is and I can fix it." Surprised, the inventor handed off the microscope to his friend and anxiously awaited its return.

A few days later, the microscope and the friend returned. The inventor looked at the microscope noticing that it looked exactly the same as when it had left. Then he picked it up. It was heavy, really heavy—several pounds heavier from dead weight added to the base of the unit. When the inventor asked why, the friend said, "It was so light that no one was taking your invention seriously."

> At first the inventor did not believe his friend. However, when he took the microscope to the same naysayers to whom he had seen previously, they were very anxious to buy. And they did.

So the answer to all of your marketing concerns is dead weight. Okay, not exactly. But you get the point: People buy a product (or service) when they *perceive value* in it. And perceptions of value are not always the same thing as actual value.

When it comes to product (and, to some degree, service) packaging, the color scheme you choose, the design elements and pictures or illustrations all can make a tremendous difference in perceived value.

Store buyers and merchandise managers are happy to tell you that they hate your color scheme or your design or other stuff related to the packaging of your product—before they even consider its actual merits. They judge books by covers. The key point for you: Don't take this personally. The comments don't have anything to do with the quality of your product. They're strictly marketing concerns. Listen...and apply as many as you can.

The Price Point

Every once in awhile someone invents a totally new product. But more likely you will be improving an existing product. So your mission is to convince the buyer that in addition to being a better product more units of your product will sell than the other five similar products. Another consideration will be the proposed price. When the retailer has five similar products, the issue is whether the profit margin will be greater than those already for sale.

Why would a retailer want to displace a product with predictable sales and profits in favor of your unknown product? If you think your protests that your invention is better will help, you're WRONG!

Welcome to the American business model. No one cares whether you have built the better mousetrap. Rather, they are concerned about profits. Period. If the buyer is interested, he will "suggest" a price point at which the store(s) would receive the profit in its model.

You're trying to sell your excellent widgets to a store for $5 per widget—and expect it to charge customers $8 per. The store believes that widgets can't be priced above $7; so, it rejects your widgets, even though they really are excellent. The store would rather sell an ordinary widget for $6.95, even if that means keeping a little less profit on each sale. Your best bet: Adjourn to a room with a calculator and cell phone and try to reduce the cost of your excellent widgets to meet the store's target. If you don't meet the price point, you won't get the purchase order.

Advertising

One way to beat the system is to provide for an advertising budget on your own and inform the store buyer. The buyers love radio and television advertising. But that is only one portion of the story. Buyers are even more excited by displays. Whether designed for the floor or pop up boxes on shelves, colorful displays attract consumers and increase sales. Also, floor displays do not take up shelf space and therefore do not displace other products.

You might have noticed all of those two or three page flyers stuck in your mailbox or included in your daily newspapers. Many retailers include this form of advertising, known as a *circular*, with daily or Sunday newspapers. The buyers will ask whether you are willing to pay a portion of expenses for the inclusion of you product in the circular. This is not a good place to say "no."

Some retailers may place your product in the circular anyway and then withhold your share of the proceeds as payment. When you raise a fuss, they simply return your product to you with a rather terse letter stating that you have not fulfilled the terms of their marketing program.

Complain all you want. But they have the gold and they make the rules... which also means they can break them. Certain chain stores are known for providing a forty-five day pay period under which they pay you in ninety days. Others are notorious for "deciding" without consulting you that you will be paying to advertise your product in the newspaper circular coming out next week. Well, you don't really pay them. Instead, they remove the money from your payment.

Don't like that? Who cares? The store is more than happy to pack up your product and ship it to you C.O.D.

Factoring....Again

As we have discussed in the chapter on finance, the last time you heard the terms "factor" or "factoring," you were probably falling asleep in math class. I know I was. That's why I became a lawyer and not a nuclear scientist. In business, factoring is a process whereby a company with little capital can borrow against its receivable accounts. Simply, when the chain of hardware stores buys one hundred thousand units and you don't have the money, a factoring agent will loan you the money secured by the purchase order from the stores.

Because the issue of cash on hand is so universal to small businesses, every major city and even a few minor ones have companies that factor purchase orders or accounts receivable. If you use a marketing firm or independent agents to represent your products, they likely will know of companies that factor orders.

Even the retailer who orders your product may be a good source of information since they have a vested interest in your ability to fulfill orders.

The Bottom Line

As we have discussed previously, building the better mousetrap does not guarantee sales. In the United States, retailers look at profit margins more than they seek out the best product. If you are creating a retail product, hiring a marketing company to represent your invention at meetings of the major chains may be crucial.

One of my clients has such a marketing company and a love/hate relationship with clients, especially those who are entering the market place for the first time. The inventor-manufacturers all think they have created the better mousetrap and believe that if only their product is seen by the right people, they will make millions.

Despite all the warnings to the contrary, manufacturers often blame the marketing company when it turns out that Home Depot does not want the new garage floor stain remover because it has five similar products all with a better than turnkey profit, a euphemistic expression meaning profits of more than double the cost to the retailer.

Sometimes the retailers are polite and suggest new packaging or price structure. But the inventor/manufacturers often don't care. Unfortunately, these people spend more time on calls to the Better Business Bureau complaining about those requesting the changes than they do listening the experts.

The bottom line (for real this time) is that you should consult and quite possibly retain a professional in marketing and have to be prepared to make changes in your product to meet with the needs of retailers. Don't scoff and don't laugh. The retail buyers will make or break your product. So they get what they want.

Isn't There Anything Else I Can Do?

There still is one option, other than the late night infomercial. You might consider licensing your product to another larger company that already has distribution channels.

Private labeling, as it is known, is quite common and a decent way to make money without a celebrity spokesmodel for that late night infomercial and without spending a fortune on a sales and marketing firm.

> Visit any larger retail store. Next to most of the brand name products are ones bearing the name of the store. Yes, it's often actually the same product. Really. It says so on the box: Compare to the brand name.

You can negotiate for an annual fee with unlimited use of your formula or for a royalty paid to you from the sale of each unit, or both. Many manufacturers enjoy licensing their products since they avoid retailers and store buyers.

The difficulty here is that you need to take steps to protect your rights to your product or formula such as patenting your formula, if available, or at least requiring the execution of the nondisclosure and non-competition agreement so that the licensee can't steal your product.

 And you need to have accounting rights if you are expecting to receive a fee for each unit sold. A standard licensing agreement provides that in the event you believe the licensee has not paid all that is owed, you have the right to bring in Uncle Bernie, your mother's brother and your accountant to review the licensee's books and records.

One of my clients is an inventor of colloid based cleaners. Not colon, colloid. Don't know what a colloid is? Think of it as super soap. It has a density greater than most oils and grease. As a result, when mixed with grease and grime, it breaks apart the molecules of the yuck and thereby cleans up the mess. The client makes everything from oven cleaners to products that clean army tanks. Moreover, the cleaners are nontoxic and biodegradable, making them safe to have around the house.

But the client does not have any desire to package and market the products he created. So he licenses formulae to various companies, sometimes on an exclusive basis and sometimes on a nonexclusive basis. Payment is made on delivery to the licensee. So, he gets paid whether the retail products are sold or not.

Marketing Magic

As I said at the beginning of this chapter, if your business consists of providing a service, then you will need to market yourself or your company in a manner where consumers think they cannot live without you.

When I was in college, a neighbor started a "plantscape maintenance" business. He had aprons and buckets and dusters and watering cans. For all practical purposes, he watered indoor plants.

In the beginning, he had three accounts, one of which was the office of a neighbor. Not exactly an auspicious start. However, within three years, the company grew from revenues of $3,500 per year to $350,000. I'll bet you never thought watering plants could be so lucrative.

In his case, my neighbor realized that soliciting a single business at a time would create an impossible situation. It could take years to make his millions. In fact, flyers placed at businesses and on cars netted about three calls for every one thousand fliers. So he targeted chains and franchises, including Denny's restaurants. After one year, my neighbor and his new employees serviced more than forty-five Denny's restaurant over a fifty-mile radius.

As you can see, my buddy created for himself an empire by showing his clients that his services were unparalleled and absolutely necessary. Could they have had their custodial engineers water the plants? Well, okay. But he convinced them that only he could ensure growth and beauty (just like Hugh Hefner)...with a guarantee of replacement if he failed.

They bought it. And so his enterprise became successful by focusing on a specific target market to maximize business potential. Twenty years later, the business still exists and is still successful.

Catalogue Sheets

If you sell a product, you will want to have a *catalogue sheet*. Also called a *sell sheet*, this device is usually an 8.5" x 11" sheet of card stock paper. On the front is the name of the company, a description of the product and a picture of the product. The back contains the product's specifications. That might include ingredients, material safety data (especially if chemicals are involved) and sales information such as minimum order quantities and pricing.

Also, the back page will include the UPC (Uniform Product Code) or bar code. The necessity of bar codes will be discussed later. These sheets are like enlarged business cards. They can be provided to potential buyers at meetings or trade shows. [Form 8-1]

Larger companies print these sheets at excerpts from their big catalogues, because most customers—especially new customers—are only interested in one or two products. Many aggressive smaller companies use catalogue sheets to promote their products long before they have an actual catalogue.

Tip: When possible, place color images in the front only. In printing lingo, this is referred to as a four-over-one (4/1)—meaning that, in order to reproduce the color, the sheet has to pass through the printer four times on the front side but only once on the back side. The absence of color and four passes on the back page can save you a lot of money.

Level One Literature

When introducing your business to a potential customer or client, you'll need some kind of written material. A business card is probably not enough; a business plan is probably overkill.

Instead, you should use what marketing professionals call *level one literature*—or what the rest of us call *a brochure*.

Like a miniature business plan, the brochure should provide the company's name and contact information. And it should state that which the company does. If you or another individual is well known in your industry, then by all means you should say so. Also, you should provide any information that distinguishes you from your competitors. [Form 8-2]

Most current word processing programs provide templates for a *three panel brochure*—an 8.5" x 11" paper folded into three sections. This actually gives you six sections (front and back) for text and images. While that sounds like a lot of space, it isn't. So, be sure to include only the essential information.

Some companies spend a lot on designers to develop brochures. But, if you have a computer and even crude design skills, this isn't necessary. Or you can do what my publisher does: Hire a professional designer to set up a template for a generic brochure—and then design each specific version yourself.

 As with any marketing piece, make your brochure vivid. If there are colors that go with your industry, use them. If not, use vibrant colors that stand out. Show the prototype to your friends and clients. Get their feedback. After all, sometimes we are not the best judge of our own work.

As to printing, in some instances you can print your own brochures. This option only works when you have a high resolution color printer. Otherwise, most major chain office supply stores or print shops can do the job. Also, professional print shops can do the job. Shop around for the best price. You will be surprised at the differences, especially if you print more than 500 brochures at a time.

The Marketing Plan

If you've made a good business plan, a separate marketing plan may not be necessary. But some smart business people prefer to keep the two plans separate. After all, the primary purpose of a business plan is to attract investors; and potential investors don't usually care about the details of marketing and promotion.

Another point: You may show your business plan to lots of people. Why give them every marketing detail? There's mot much to steal in the general plan of a business—but there can be ideas to steal in the specifics of how you plan to reach your market.

In my example, the plan starts with generalized goals and objectives. More simply put, what do you want to accomplish? Whether you are manufacturing a product or providing a service, certainly, recognition of your brand name is very important.

Everyone knows Roto Rooter drain cleaning or Frigidaire refrigerators. But that was not always the case. Most people don't need a drain cleaning service—or at least not very often. After years of television advertising, people know the Roto Rooter name. When you need a refrigerator or a washer/dryer, the Frigidaire name is likely to pop up. Again—years of television advertising.

The basic outline of a marketing plan looks like this:

1. Goals/Objectives
2. Strategy
3. Target Market
4. Marketing Mix
   a.   Promotion Strategy (pushing and pulling)
   b.   Distribution
   c.   Price
   d.   Tactics
   e.   Product
   g.   Promotion
   h.   Distribution

For the rest of this chapter, I'll consider each of these parts in turn.

Goals and Objectives

As the song goes, "...everybody wants to rule the world." If your goal is to control the entire market, think again. You won't and it ain't necessary. Moreover, for a start-up business, capturing between five to ten percent of the marketplace in the first five years is just fine. So be realistic. Set obtainable goals and do that which is required to get there. Then move on to the next goal.

Strategy

Okay, so you know what you want to do, now it is time to be the Ways & Means committee and figure out how to get there. This is especially important when you have a limited budget. And let's face it: if you had unlimited sources of money, you probably would not be engaged in starting up a new business.

The plan provides a number of strategies. However, the first thing to do is look at similar products or services. What do they do, where do they advertise, and do consumers know their name?

Part of this process is to identify your target market. Just like my college friend running regional ads in the *National Enquirer* for the breast enhancer, you can identify your market by charting the demographics. Ask yourself:

- Who *needs* your product or service? Teenagers or young adults? New parents or older folks?

- Who *wants* your product or service? Are there any significant differences between the people who need it and want it?

- Is your product affordable to most people—or only to high income earners?

- Where are the people who want or need your product? In certain regions of the country? In cities? Suburbs? Campuses?

- What other things do your target customers buy? Houses? Cars? Clothes? Candy?

- What activities do your target customers spend time on? Watching TV? Driving places? Working? Traveling? Reading?

While this may seem obvious, the challenges in providing a product or service that is unique are quite different than distinguishing your products or services from those of others.

Even the best marketers sometimes trip over the right markets. In the early 2000s, Honda Motors spent a lot of time doing market research on a boxy but versatile SUV it eventually called the *Element*. After spending millions of dollars on database research and focus groups, Honda concluded that the best market for the Element would be young males recently out of school and looking for their first new car.

When the Element reached the showrooms, it was a modest success. But an entirely different sort of person was buying it. The young guys weren't so interested; but mothers with small children liked boxy but versatile a lot.

Go figure.

Target Market

Sketching the *who* of your market equation allows you to reach other conclusions. Where do products similar to yours sell? *How* do they sell? One advantage to observing those who have come before you with a similar product or service is that you can glom on to their market research.

For example, if they are using a yellow wrapper, chances are they spent tens of thousands of dollars to determine that the yellow wrapper causes the most people to purchase the product. Did you really think the M&M's with peanuts is in that wrapper by accident?

The most successful retailers cater to specific demographics. For example, lower income families shop at Wal-Mart; higher income families shop at Macy's. But it's not always easy to know which is the best channel to market for a given product. And the best profits don't necessarily come from the highest demographics.

Consider Mossimo, a clothing line designed for the young and the hip. At the start, Mossimo made deals with high end department stores. In the *sounded-like-a-good-idea-at-the-time* category, the projected profit margin looked quite high. One problem: High end stores have a tendency to pay when they feel like it and return merchandise when only a single thread is out of place.

Eventually, the profits on paper became losses in reality. Rather than pull out of department stores altogether, Mossimo made a deal with Target stores and created lower cost items to be sold at prices affordable to middle income families. The change has proven to be a success. Businesses that cannot adapt to changing market conditions fail. At one point, Mossimo was close to bankruptcy. Today it is a success.

Even more important than the stores, the consumers love to get the "great buys." Recently, a local supermarket chain ran a promotion called "10 for 10"—a mix and match, no-limit sale where you get 10 items for 10 dollars, ranging from boxes of Kleenex and trash bags to makeup remover and navel oranges. So customers flocked there to snag this great deal, speeding through the isles grabbing 10 packages of this and 10 packages of that.

My assistant, being the frugal shopper that she is, got to the checkout counter, she loaded twenty items onto the belt and then asked the checker about the deal. He quietly informed her that she didn't have to buy ten items to get the discount. Everything was one dollar. But, the chain advertised this as "10 for 10" knowing that people would come in to buy a couple of things and then leave with ten. Good plan? I think so.

Marketing Mix

Once you identify your target market, you need to develop a promotional strategy commonly known as advertising. Radio? Television? Newspapers? Magazines? If customers need to know your telephone number then radio ads may present a problem to listeners who are driving (or maybe not). The *Wall Street Journal* contains advertising for high end luxury products such as Mercedes, Lexus and Infiniti automobiles. Alternative newspapers like the *L.A. Weekly* contain ads for liposuction, botox and Internet dating services. A strange symmetry.

Price point is another issue. As we discussed, with respect to products, your concern needs to be price point and profit margin. In retail, you can't charge substantially more than the five similar products the store already carries. Additionally, if the difference between the store's cost and the retail price is substantially less than the other products, then the store has no reason to purchase your product.

> For service providers, you can't charge substantially more than the competition. If the carpet cleaner company down the street charges $49.95, a charge of $69.95 will serve only to get you to a bankruptcy sooner. The same constraints apply at every level. On the high end of my profession, expensive New York law firms watch carefully the fees that their rivals charge—and match quickly and precisely.

Still, pricing isn't always uniform. Different regions pay different amounts for the same things. And, even within the same region, more affluent areas will usually pay more money for the same service. Investigate your competition—check local retail stores everywhere you can—examine their prices and set yours accordingly.

Chargebacks and Product Returns

And speaking of stores, we have discussed the time lag between fulfilling the order and payment. Also, be prepared for charge backs and product returns. Charge backs occur when a consumer returns your product. Returns occur when the store returns the product.

> With consumers, the returns are the likely result of a defect. If you mass produce any product, you can expect a certain number of defects on a consistent basis. With stores, the returns consist of *their notion* that a defect exists. If a retailer has too much of your inventory or your products aren't selling as fast as the store would like, it will often invent defects so that it does not have to pay for the some or all of the units.

For the past five years, a company I operate has been shipping products to a major Internet retailer. Recently, we received a box of nine units and a note stating that the enclosed units had broken packaging. In fact, only the first unit had broken packaging—probably broken once in the seller's care.

I e-mailed the company three times asking why the other units were returned before it responded by stating that it never makes mistakes and that I must not have examined carefully the returned units.

Of course when I asked for contact information on the person who rejected the units, I did not receive any response. I then returned to the retailer the remaining unbroken eight units in the next order, and viola! They accepted them.

If you manufacture and sell a product, you will learn quickly about *spillage* **and** *shrinkage*. **Originally referring to missing ounces of beverage,** *spillage* **refers to the mysterious percentage of merchandise that just doesn't make it to the warehouse or from the warehouse to the customer—mostly due (whether real or imagined) and sometimes due to theft. Also, the major department stores are notorious for returns whether the merchandise is defective or not.** *Shrinkage* **means the same thing, with a slightly heavier focus on theft.**

If you don't plan for these little inconveniences or if you count on payment simply because you shipped your products, you are in for a rude awakening. It is a wise idea to include provisions in your budget for situations such as these. Again, your marketing company or independent representatives know which retailers are more prone to spillage. Ask for their advice.

In 1983, I noticed that the "Cabbage Patch" doll was coveted by every child. Mothers everywhere stormed the beaches of Normandy just so that their child would not miss out. The maker of the doll was Coleco. Just before Thanksgiving I purchased shares of Coleco. A week later, after the mother invasion, I sold the shares. I made a profit of $6.50 per share.

Conclusion

Marketing is about observing— what people want and the lengths they will go to obtain it. Or how you can make them think they can't live without it. I'll bet that if you received a Cabbage Patch doll you have no idea where it is now. But boy how you wanted one in 1983.

Don't reinvent the wheel. Large corporations spend millions on market research. If bright colors are used for laundry detergent boxes it is because those companies know that bright colors are needed to sell the product. Don't buck the trend with light pastel colors. Watch, listen, and learn. It works!

References

Bangs, David H., Jr. *The Market Planning Guide: Creating a Plan to Successfully Market Your Business, Product, or Service* (6th edition). Dearborn Trade Publishing (October 2002).

Debelak, Don. *Marketing Magic: Action-Oriented Strategies That Will Help You: Find Customers, Promote Your Products or Services, Create Exciting Marketing Plans, Increase Your Sales.* Adams Media Corporation (March, 1997).

Klymshyn, John. *Move the Sale Forward: Position Yourself and Your Business to Make Things Happen.* Silver Lake Publishing (March, 2003)

Parker, Roger C. *Market Planning Guide: A Handbook to Help You Design, Write, and Use a Marketing Plan Tailored to Your Specific Business Needs.* Upstart Publishing Co. (December, 1989).

Ryan, J. D., et al. *Small Business: An Entrepreneur's Plan* (The Dryden Press Series in Management). International Thomson Publishing (January, 1999).

Stanton, John, and Richard George. *Success Leaves Clues: Practical Tools for Effective Sales and Marketing* (2nd edition). Silver Lake Publishing (September, 1999).

Vyakarna, Shailendra, et al. *Action Plans for the Small Business: Growth Strategies for Businesses Wondering Where to Go Next.* Drake Beam Morin (DBM) (November, 1995).

Wood, Marian Burk. *Marketing Plan: A Handbook with Marketing PlanPro* (edition with CD-Rom). Prentice Hall (April, 2002)

Chapter 9

Leases, Landlords and You

When Marx spoke of 'private property' he was not referring to 'personal property.' Private property meant the means of production of the capitalist who hires property-less individuals under conditions the latter is forced to accept.

—Erich Fromm

I remember the days of rotary dial telephones and answering machines the size of stereo receivers. Today, computers with modems and high speed data lines give a lot of flexibility to small businesses. The biggest effect of these technology advances: You can operate a fairly sophisticated business from home. Certainly, costs are reduced—especially because there is no lease of space required.

But, running a business from home can blur any sense of separation and boundaries. The expression "taking your business home with you" takes on a whole new—more literal—meaning. And, while running down to the office at 2:00 a.m. to get a brilliant idea into the computer may seem like a great idea, I guarantee you that your spouse and your children will be less enthusiastic about it.

Also, if clients are an important part of your business, you lose some privacy when you have meetings in your living room. Some people are more at ease with this proposition than others.

> Some people are better at managing distractions—the dog barking, the telephone ringing, the kids playing, the gardeners mowing—than others. Some people ably negotiate a 15,000-unit purchase order with SpongeBob Squarepants yelping in the background. Others can't concentrate like that.

At some point in the growth of any business, it's time to move into commercial space. This is a happy—and scary—rite of passage. In this chapter, we'll talk about how to make the move well.

Commercial Leases

If your main experience with leases has been renting a house or apartment, throw out all that you think you know.

Commercial leases are far more complicated, cover many more issues and require meticulous examination. The laws governing commercial leases are quite different, often far more favorable to the landlord, and have significantly different consequences in case of a breach by either the landlord or the tenant.

As we discussed previously, in purchasing an existing business, it is likely you will want to continue operating in the same location in order to preserve the going concern value.

If this scenario applies to you, A first piece of advice: Get a lawyer and a broker. Despite claims or implications made by other books, my experience has been that almost half of the litigation faced by any business relates either directly or indirectly to its lease.

Many of these disputes could have been prevented if the business had an expert review the lease at the beginning.

Transferring of an Existing Lease

Whether you buy assets or the stock of a business, the advantage of remaining in the same location is that customers already know where to find you. This reduces your advertising costs significantly.

> **As part of the purchase, you will want to review the seller's lease. If the terms and conditions meet your needs, then set up a meeting with the landlord.**

It is important to note that most commercial leases do not allow for the seller simply to transfer or assign the lease to a buyer without the landlord's permission. If you intend to stay in the same location, you should include a contingency in the escrow for the transfer of the lease. That way you can cancel the sale if the landlord rejects the assignment or refuses to provide a new lease.

The landlord will probably want to see your financial records. If your business has operated for more than two or three years, then the tax returns will be important; other relevant information will include profit and loss statements and income and expense statements. Even with this information, if your business is just getting started, the landlord will want to know your *personal* financial history—including the amount of money you have in the bank and whether you have ever filed a bankruptcy. The landlord may also want to run your credit report.

All of this seems terribly intrusive; but landlords know that, in the event of a business failure or in the event of a bankruptcy, it may be many months before the space is returned to their control...and several additional months before the property is rented again.

Negotiation of a New Lease

If you are starting a new business or if you prefer a different location for an existing business, then choosing a location and negotiating a lease will be your first step.

> Unlike residential or apartment leases, commercial leases are almost never month-to-month or for one year. Rather, landlords often require a minimum of five years often with an option for an additional five year period.

In most cities, vacancies are indicated by signs that tell you space is available and then include the name of the broker and company in charge of the lease. Call the broker and tell him or her you would like to visit the property.

Don't be afraid to ask questions. Important questions may include maintenance, security, access on weekends, plumbing, or trash disposal. Also, you will want to review the financial condition of the building owner to ensure a bankruptcy is not near. And you will want to review past charges to tenants for maintenance and upkeep.

Further, though you may like the size of the space and the location, you may not like where the walls are located. Other than "load bearing" walls, many can be torn down and rebuilt to fit your needs. Also, certain businesses must meet certain unique requirements.

> For example, doctors often have x-ray equipment on their premises. Many states require that the walls surrounding x-ray machines have lead shielding in the dry wall. Also, developing equipment requires certain plumbing needs and disposal of potentially hazardous waste. So make sure the broker (or landlord) fully understands your business' needs.

Many landlords recognize that each business is different and if you are intending to execute a long-term lease, the landlord will offer "tenant improvements." This is money spent by the landlord customizing the space for your needs. The longer the term of the lease the more money a landlord is likely to spend.

If you have partners or if you have trusted employees, you might bring them along. Since they will be working in the space too, their opinion is very important.

Tip: the landlord's broker works for the landlord. He or she traditionally gets paid by the landlord based on a percentage of the lease amount. You too can have a broker. Just like a real estate agent, a commercial broker is familiar with landlords, locations, lease terms and maybe even the specific needs of your business. However, unlike a residential real estate transaction, the commission is not always paid by the landlord.

Once you have found the space you want, the broker will hand you a monstrous document he calls a lease. You will call it *War and Peace*.

Generally, the lease comes in two parts: the standard form and the addenda—attachments that apply specifically to your situation.

The Standard Form Lease

The real estate departments of most states have created forms for residential and commercial leases. If you have ever purchased a home, then you will have seen similar documents. This form contains the terms commonly found in leases such as the name of the parties, the term of the lease, and the monthly payment and when it is due. It also contains other clauses that bear review. These include parking spaces, assignment and sublet, and HVAC—the air conditioning system. Settling all issues and discrepancies *before* you sign a lease will relieve business headaches much more quickly and much less expensively than any after-the-fact legal Excedrin.

While we've discussed the general issues facing a tenant, the specific issues within the agreement are addressed below. We won't discuss every term as many are what lawyers consider *boilerplate*, or terms generally found in all agreements.

Most of these are self-explanatory; other terms—and those that are not easily understood—we will address.

Specific Provisions of the Standard Form

Commercial leases generally run 30 to 100 pages of small type (and you thought this *book* was long). On the surface, this does not make a lot of sense; once you understand all of the contingencies, you will understand why these agreements rival *Gravity's Rainbow*.

Description

The opening paragraph contains the names of the parties and the date the agreement is effective. Thereafter, the lease contains a description of the premises. The description is extremely important, especially with respect to square feet. It is not uncommon that the advertisement for the lease contains a measurement with a disclaimer that the measurement is only an approximation. Fine. But you should always confirm the amount of square footage in the lease to the advertisement.

Term

The term of the agreement provides for the length of time the lease will bind you. In commercial leases, five years with options for additional years is quite common. If the space is going to be modified, you may try to set the commencement date for a period shortly after the completion of the modifications. After all, why should you pay for a space you cannot move into?

Rent

While this part may seem simple, it is likely the most significant section of the lease—especially if the lease will be in effect for a number of years. Some leases have specific increase amounts; others have increases based on increases in the cost-of-living index.

You may also responsible for a pro rata share of "operating costs." In this case, your share includes insurance, property taxes, parking lot maintenance, and any and all state and local taxes related to the tenancy.

At least the tenant receives an itemized list of the expenses included in the lease and has the right to object to any items. You should be sure to include a right of accounting that includes copies of the actual bills. Also, this lease specifically defines *pro rata*. But in other leases the term could refer to a percentage based on the number of tenants or based on the square footage of each tenant. Obviously, if you have a large space then the former is a better deal.

Security Deposit

Tenants are required to pay a security deposit. The amount is usually provided in the first few pages of the lease. Fair enough. However, the uses to which the landlord can put the money should be spelled out somewhere in the agreement.

As the lessee, you want to make sure that the landlord keeps your deposit in a reasonably easy-to-access place. If the lease ends sooner than expected, through no fault of yours, you don't want that money tied up somewhere it can't be obtained.

Permitted Use and Use Prohibited

These seem like a simple phrases. In fact, this part of the contract can cause serious problems. Most lessees have a pretty good idea of the type of business they intend to run. But, if the marketplace changes, so might the business. If the business simply makes minor changes—such as selling football helmets instead of baseball caps, the landlord has no basis to complain. If you change from selling helmets to selling sex toys, though, you may expect an eviction notice.

> Also note that any change in the business that results in an increase in the landlord's insurance premiums will be passed on to you. Any activity that prevents the landlord from retaining or obtaining a policy of insurance will be prohibited.

While anyone creating a new business has no expectation of abandoning the leased premises, it happens for two reasons:

1. the lessee is going out of business and simply leaves; or

2. the lessee finds a better space and moves out.

Another possibility, though less likely, is that the business goes under but no one moves out.

Condition of the Premises

The condition of the premises concerns what you are getting and whether the space is ready to go. Here, the landlord states that he is not responsible in the event the particular business you have is not proper for the zoning regulations or other similar regulations.

The condition is also an essential element of when the lease should begin. If the former tenant made a mess that has yet to be cleaned up, the landlord should provide for the janitorial services needed. However, if the landlord isn't willing to clean the space, then the *start of payment* under your lease should be delayed until the premises are ready to be inhabited.

Insurance

Insurance is always a requirement. Most landlords require that tenants maintain at least $1 million of insurance and that the landlord be named as a co-insured. This is a fundamental issue in any lease.

Several years ago, a client of mine was cleaning with linseed oil. He was not careful in checking the disposal bin where he threw away the rags with the oil. The bin was full of other flammable materials that, mixed with the linseed oil, had the ability to start a fire. They did. And his business went up in flames.

Other Common Topics

In most agreements, the tenant pays for utilities. This is easy when separate meters are installed for each unit; but that isn't always the case. Instead, these charges are divided in a *pro rata* manner between all tenants. Also, the lease makes the tenant responsible for personal property taxes. Many states have eliminated this tax. But other states have not.

As in most agreements, alterations of any significance require permission from the landlord.

Also, a number of other requirements may be added. For example, while in most agreements the tenant can employ any professional who holds proper credentials, many landlords insist on the tenant retaining professionals only after approval from the landlord. The disadvantage of this is that the landlord has full control over the work, when it is done and how it is done. Since the landlord has a vested interest in anything structural but also in saving money, corners might be cut.

On the other hand, when the landlord retains the professionals, the landlord bears responsibility for anything that goes awry.

In some lease situations, maintenance and repairs provide the toughest of issues for the tenant and the most likely paths to future litigation.

In most contracts, the maintenance and repairs section begins with a waiver by the tenant stating that, when he or she moves in, he or she accepts that the premises are in proper condition and ready for use. If your lease includes this kind of language, make sure you have a professional inspector examine the space carefully—and agree that it is, in fact, in good condition. Don't let a pressing schedule or anything else prevent this. It will matter a lot, the first time the HVAC system breaks down.

Most agreements require the tenant to pay for any and all expenses including the hiring of air conditioning service companies and other similar professionals. However, structural issues such as the condition of the roof, foundation and exterior walls are the responsibility of the landlord. This section also provides for notice by the tenant. It's vital that the tenant notify in writing the landlord of any repairs needed. And keep a copy of the letter just in case litigation ensues.

Another critical issue is *entry by the landlord.* As a general rule, the tenant enjoys an absolute right to control over the space. But, if you have requested repairs, the landlord or any repair person must have access—especially if safety issues are involved. Otherwise, most agreements require advance notice, usually 24 hours.

 Parking and the use of common areas also provide fodder for legal actions. As we've discussed, you will need a certain number of parking spaces for your employees. But don't forget your clients and patrons. Also, if your business receives deliveries on a routine basis, be sure to check out the delivery bay, if any, and service elevators. It is common for landlords to limit when heavy materials can be supplied or removed.

Several years ago, one of my clients decided to increase the size of his business after his neighbor moved out. The landlord provided permission to open the wall that separated the two offices and to build the area into one larger office. With the larger office, came more staff and more patrons. But my client failed to request any additional parking.

The issue came to a head when my client received threats of canceling the lease because patrons and staff were using too many spaces. The result was a client having to move out in less than a year after the build-out at a loss of thousands of dollars.

Common areas can vary significantly from building to building. Over the past twenty years, the larger complexes have made efforts to provide areas for lunch or for cigarette smoking. Rules for the uses of these areas are often included with the lease. If your lease does not have these rules, ask for them.

We've discussed the issue of insurance and the need for a policy. Many business policies provide for business interruption payments. So, if you burn down your unit, the insurer will pay a certain sum to make up for the loss of business. But, when your unit is damaged by your neighbor's fire, neither your insurance nor your neighbor's insurance nor the landlord's insurance may provide any coverage. Also, you may not be entitled to break the lease and move out. Often, certain types of destruction do not permit the tenant to break the lease unless the landlord does not intend to repair the premises.

Another famous contract phrase is *force majuere,* also known as an act of God. A tornado or an earthquake that destroys the premises constitutes such an act. Generally, if the landlord can make and will make speedy repairs, then the tenant is not permitted to break the lease. But there are no hard and fast rules as to how long is too long. Make sure you and your insurance agent or lawyer review carefully the terms of the lease and the parameters of the insurance with respect to interruption.

A lesser known issue is condemnation. This is *not* a diplomatic term for what a righteous man does to cheese eating surrender monkeys or for roach-infested apartments. It refers to a situation where a government agency, under a right of eminent domain, decides to take over the land where a business or residence is located in order to place something else on the land. For example, new freeway construction often requires the removal of businesses and residences. In the lease, either the landlord or the tenant can terminate the lease.

But, if the termination comes from the tenant, he receives nothing other than a bill from Manny and the moving guys.

One of my clients is in the car rental business. He's been informed by his local government that a new line of the subway system is going to run under his business and a station will be placed on his land. He has been told he has to leave the property. However, the government agencies involved must pay the fair market value for the property, for the improvements and for the relocation of the business.

Assignment and Subletting

Two of the most confusing terms in a commercial lease are *assignment* and *subletting*.

An assignment occurs when the tenant finds another party to take over the lease. A sublet occurs when the tenant permits another party to come onto the premises without a transfer to the lease.

An example of assignment: You decide your business needs more space than it can get at its present location. But your landlord won't let you out of the lease; So, you find another business that needs the kind of space you have, does something like what you do and has good credit. With the landlord's approval, the lease may be assigned to the new tenant. The landlord may not remove you from liability to the lease. So, if the new tenant goes bust or fails to pay, you may be liable for the lease payments.

In a sublease, you decide you need more space but you don't want to give up your existing lease over the space. Maybe rents have gone up so much that you can make a few extra bucks by renting the space to someone else. You invite another business to take over the premises. You still make monthly payments to your landlord; but you become landlord to the subtenant.

 Increasingly, commercial leases state that—if you sublease the space for more than you're paying—you have to split the profit with your landlord.

The other likely sublease situation arises if you have more space than you can use. So, you bring in another tenant to take some of your space and pay a *pro rata* share of the rent.

This occurs often with doctors and lawyers or with similar professionals. The tenant remains liable under the lease and the subtenant is liable to the tenant.

Most commercial leases specifically require the approval of a subtenant or assignment before the tenant can enter into any such agreement. However, many states provide statutes that prevent a landlord from rejecting a sublease of a part of the tenant's space when the sublessee is in the same or similar business.

To limit assignment and subleasing, some leases state that a tenant is in default when it abandons the location.

Finally, two obscure legal terms—*subordination* and *estoppel certificate*—have to do with the landlord's version of assignment and sublease. They refer to a situation where the landlord is attempting to refinance or even sell the building.

A subordination occurs when the landlord uses the proceeds from the lease to secure financing. In essence, the agreement acts like a deed to property. If the landlord fails to pay the mortgage, the mortgage company has the ability to obtain payment by demanding that you send the rent to it and not to the landlord. The estoppel certificate is a verification that the tenant has a lease and the amount it's paying under the deal.

The remaining clauses are standard fare. However, the work of the tenant is not finished.

Addenda

The addenda to a lease often run longer than the agreement itself. The first addendum in our template lease concerns the work or "build-out" that the landlord has agreed to perform. In addition to the writing, a schematic or floor plan should be included. That way there will be no question about the nature and scope of the work

Rules and regulations also take an appendix. These rules cover operational issues such as identifying the common areas and the behavior permitted there. They also cover signage such as that on the door and that on any larger billboard or sign at the front of the premises. And the rules might provide for logistics such as parking, trash disposal, and use of the service elevator.

On the surface, these rules and regulations may seem like minor details; but you can trip up on them if you're not careful. One of my clients moved into a building as a subtenant—taking a portion of space from the main tenant. Because my client and the tenant were friends, my client didn't bother to read the rules and regulations that had been provided to the tenant. They stated plainly that the building was not readily accessible on weekends. My client needed to see customers on Saturdays. Call in the lawyers.

Make sure that any and all terms meet with your needs before you move in.

If you've ever rented an apartment, then you know to ask whether the rent includes utilities. Commercial leases that include utilities are often referred to as "gross" leases. Unfortunately, most leases do not include such amenities.

These leases are known as "net" leases.

The most common form of net lease requires the tenant to pay for a proportionate share of utilities, operating costs such as security, cleaning service and trash disposal and so-called "common area maintenance" (CAM) charges. These might include gardening and landscaping and other expenses related to the upkeep of the building and its grounds.

While you have little chance of bargaining to eliminate these charges, it is most important that you know for what you are paying and figure that into your expenses. Here's a tip: Spend the money to retain a real estate attorney to review the agreement. The cost of having a professional review the lease and explain to you many of the clauses will save you money in not having disputes or litigation.

In my experience, landlords or their brokers sometimes "forget" to include the additional parking spaces you requested or that first month discount for having signed a five year lease. With the multitude of pages and clauses, it's easy to miss something. Paying an attorney is like purchasing an insurance policy.

And, if he gets something important wrong, just think of the fun you will have suing *him*.

One of my clients entered into a sublease for a portion of a suite occupied by the main tenant. After six months, the main tenant filed for bankruptcy, nullifying the main lease and leaving my client high and dry.

My client hadn't considered the financial situation of the tenant and didn't meet the landlord in order to form his own relationship—either legal or personal. He was left with the choice of moving out or taking over the lease of a space that was twice what he needed. Unfortunately, there wasn't much I could do for him.

Another client, Yolanda, entered into a lease with a receiver during a bankruptcy proceeding. She realized that this could be trouble; but she thought it was going to be a good deal.

Yolanda had heard horrible things about the landlord owner; she entered into a five-year lease anyway because she figured that the owner was unlikely to get the building back and the receiver was offering a good rental rates.

The receiver is an official appointed by the court to manage assets during a bankruptcy proceeding. In real estate bankruptcies, the receiver acts like a substitute landlord. But many businesses don't like renting from receivers, because no one's ever sure how bankruptcies will turn out. (This is especially true of *real estate bankruptcies*, where judges often encourage landlords and their creditors to work out deals that allow the landlords to keep their properties...but manage them differently.) As a result, receivers often have to offer discounted rents to attract tenants.

As luck would have it, nine months after Yolanda moved in, the nasty owner took back control of the building.

Had Yolanda consulted with me before she signed the lease, we might have added a clause that allowed for her to terminate the lease and vacate the premises in the event the bankrupt owner took back the building. (That's a clause I always suggest if you're considering renting from a receiver.) Instead, the landlord lived up to his bad reputation and Yolanda was stuck for another four years.

When the Landlord Fails to...

Obviously, the lease contains all sorts of requirements for the tenant. But it also provides for the landlord's responsibility. This responsibility mostly consists of actions that render the property or space usable for the purposes specified by the tenant at the time the lease was executed. These actions might range from fixing leaky faucets to maintaining smoke detectors or security systems.

For example, tenants generally are not permitted to make structural repairs. So what happens when the rain leaks into the rented space and the landlord fails to uphold his or her end of the bargain?

The answer depends on the size of the problem and the cost of resolving it. Similar to residential leases, in most states a tenant has the right to make repairs and deduct the repair costs from the next monthly payment. Before the tenant does this, I always insist that my clients contact the landlord in writing when a problem is discovered and that the client follow up all telephone calls with letters confirming the problem, the solution provided and the response of the landlord or representative.

 If several telephone calls and letters yield no results, I advise my clients to inform the landlord in writing that—if the necessary repairs are not performed within 48 hours—the client will hire a professional to perform the repairs and then deduct the cost from the rent payment. If the repairs aren't made, I advise my clients to proceed.

For many repairs, repairing and deducting from the rent resolves the problem. But what if the costs of repairs far exceed the rent payment?

There are few good solutions in this scenario. Most agreements contain "warranties" made by the landlord that the premises are fit for the purposes of that which the tenant intends to do and that the premises are habitable. Even where no warranties are specifically stated, most states have statutes that provide for fitness and habitability.

> **A statute is a law passed by the state legislature and signed into law by the governor. Often you will hear these referred to as "codes."**

In residential leases, tenants have a right to "quiet enjoyment." This means they have the right to be free of any disturbances that make living difficult. Noisy neighbors, leaky roofs and toilet overflows violate this right. A failure of the landlord to resolve a significant or expensive problem is grounds to terminate the lease.

In commercial leases, a similar principal applies. If the problem is too expensive to repair and deduct and the landlord refuses to make the necessary repairs you have the option of terminating the lease and moving out.

However, under no circumstances are you permitted to remain on the premises and refuse to pay the rent.

One of my clients was renting a little office space in a ten story building. The building owner filed for bankruptcy and another party purchased the building.

> Unlike residential leases, commercial leases can usually be terminated upon the purchase of the property by a new party.

The new owner first stated that all of the tenants could stay. Two weeks later, the owner told the tenants to leave—because it wanted to renovate the building. So, my client made plans to move out. Then, the new owner informed the tenants that *some* of them *might* be able to stay; but they would have make a formal request and get a specific confirmation. My client sent several letters requesting to stay. No one responded. So, three weeks later, he moved.

Imagine his surprise when he was served with a lawsuit from the new owner for breach of lease.

It only took a few days to get the lawsuit tossed out of court; but this example illustrates the level of confusion that occurs when ownership changes. Fortunately, my client had put everything in writing and could back up his claims that he made every effort to advise the new owner of his predicament.

Sometimes, even diligent efforts can't prevent major landlord trouble—because the landlord or its representatives are just scheming weasels. I was involved in a residential rental case that stands out in this regard. Even it wasn't about a commercial lease, it's still a memorable example.

My client and his wife found a house to rent. On the day they viewed the house, it still had paper over the carpeting that had been cleaned the day before. When they inspected the garage, they found that it smelled of cat urine. Not a big problem—or so they thought.

Within two weeks of moving in, the entire house reeked of urine. Of course, the broker and the owner denied any knowledge of the problem.

My clients were beside themselves over the smell. I suggested they do some detective work about the carpet-cleaning job that just taken place when they inspected the house. They did, asking around until they found the carpet cleaner who'd done the job.

That guy told my clients that he'd been hired specifically to mask the urine smell left by the previous tenant. And, at that time, he'd told the landlord's broker that removing the smell could cost up to $3,000. One firm letter (with a copy to the landlord), telling the broker that he seemed to have knowingly misled my clients, resulted in the clean-up job that should have happened in the first place.

Ask About the Landlord

As I wrote earlier in this chapter, you will want to review the financial condition of the landlord. Reputable brokers often will know the details of which landlord is easygoing, which is difficult, and who may be going out of business soon. But often times the larger players will hide their financial distress for fear of tenants leaving and new ones looking elsewhere.

In most states, a residential tenant is not automatically displaced by a bankruptcy or a purchase of the building or house from the trustee of the bankruptcy court—at least not until the lease expires. But the rules for commercial properties are different.

In the event of a bankruptcy and a sale of the premises, a new landlord may not be required to honor the leases. While you will receive notice, moving a business unexpectedly in 30 to 60 days can result in chaos and a loss of income during the time of the relocation and office set up.

In some of these situations, you can file suit for breach of contract and collect damages including the costs of moving and any business lost due to the problem and/or the move from the premises. But you will need a lawyer, money and time to press these claims. And, even though most

The Elements of Small Business

lease agreements provide for the attorneys fees and costs to the prevailing party, the time and expense of litigation is rarely worth your while.

 A point on attorney's fees in lease or contract disputes: Judges rarely award businesses all of their attorney's fees—even when the business wins the suit. So, anything you can do to resolve the situation short of litigation *is* worth your while.

Several years ago, I was retained to file a suit against tenants who had leased a client's car wash with an option to purchase it after a certain amount of time. When one of the three partner lessees could not come up with the rent, the other two partners refused to help. For several months the rent remained unpaid.

I filed a suit to force out the tenants and to recover damages in the amount of the rent and other damages caused by the tenants.

> A suit to remove a tenant is called an "unlawful detainer" action. Unlike typical civil matters, unlawful detainer proceedings are "expedited" proceedings. For example, unlike the typical thirty days to file an answer to a complaint, in unlawful detainer the defendant has only five days to file an answer.

After two hours of trial, the judge entered a verdict in favor of my clients. Then came the motion for an award of attorney's fees. The judge gave my clients one-half of the fees they had requested.

The judge's reasoning: The case had been heard in a rural area of California and she figured that the average local attorney fee was $150 an hour—half of what I was charging my clients. None of the attorneys involved in the case was local and my clients' request was quite reasonable under the circumstances. But the judge wouldn't change her mind.

The judge's ruling on an award of attorney's fees doesn't have any impact on the fees. It only applies to how much the *losing side* has to pay. If she says they have to pay half, you still have to pay the other half. So, don't base your decision to sue or be sued on the clause that provides for attorney's fees.

When *You* Get Sued...

In another weasel landlord case, my client rented a space that had a heating unit in the floor of an old building. Little did she know that the landlord had failed to clean or maintain the furnace. During the first cold day in October, the furnace turned on automatically and debris in the heater caught fire.

Luckily, my client was there when this happened and put out the fire with minimal damage. But the trouble was just starting. She didn't receive a call from the landlord to thank her for saving his building from certain destruction; in fact, he decided not to fix the heater and claimed my client was at fault for "waste."

Then, the landlord filed for unlawful detainer.

We responded by threatening suit for habitability and fitness and got the furnace fixed. But, a few weeks later, my client got a bill charging a ridiculous sum for "maintenance and repair" which was promptly taken out of her security deposit at the end of the lease.

Bad landlord! Bad! We had to sue to put an end to the nonsense.

 If you have requested necessary repairs to no avail and you have had to deduct their cost from your rent, you can bet the landlord will make all possible efforts to make your life a living hell. And one recourse is to file a suit for unlawful detainer.

In many states, the prelude to filing an unlawful detainer action is a notice to pay the rent your landlord claims you owe. The notice sets forth the amount of rent due and provides a timetable as to when payment must be made in order to avoid a suit. When you have not paid and the time specified in the notice has expired, the unlawful detainer action will be filed and served on you. [Form 9-1]

As we discussed earlier, unlike typical civil suits, an answer to an unlawful detainer complaint is required much faster. If you fail to heed the deadline, a default will be taken against you.

A default is not a judgment. But is does prevent you from participating any further in the judicial proceedings. Ultimately, the landlord will apply for a "prove-up" hearing where he will put on evidence of how much he is owed under the lease. The landlord does have a duty to mitigate—to make every effort to re-rent the premises. But, of course, this has not happened in circumstances where you have failed or refused to vacate the premises.

So you should answer the complaint and appear at the trial. While jury trials are available in most jurisdictions, unlawful detainer suits are rarely tried before a jury. You should hire an attorney to represent you from the first moment you receive the notice to pay or vacate. But if that is not an option, bring with you all of your documentation with copies for the judge and the other party.

 Keep in mind that the judge has heard it all and seen it all before. Judges are quite capable of determining whether you are just another deadbeat or whether you had a legitimate problem that the landlord failed to solve. Make sure to have your documents in writing and even bring witnesses whenever possible. Also, dress the part. An organized and prepared party neatly attired always impresses the judges. If you look like a deadbeat, the court will see you that way and it will taint your case, regardless of its merits.

If the issue is not payment or deduction of the rent for repairs, your landlord might give you notice based on waste. This occurs when you cause serious damage to the leased space. Just like a failure to pay the rent, the destruction of the premises also is a ground to terminate the lease and have you removed.

Conclusion

As we discussed in the introduction, owning your own business can be quite satisfying. But that does not alleviate the need to retain professionals to protect your rights. If you are a manufacturer or a retailer, you will have enough legal issues arise. If you provide a service, you will have plenty of issues with clients. You do not need trouble with the landlord.

Read your lease and then provide it to a qualified attorney for review. Believe me, it is money well spent.

References

Mayer, David G. *Business Leasing For Dummies*. John Wiley & Sons, Inc. (September, 2001).

Mitchell, Thomas G., et al. *The Commercial Lease Guidebook: Learn How to Win the Leasing Game!* MacOre, Intl. (January, 1994).

Portman, Janet and Fred S. Steingold. *Leasing Space for Your Small Business*. Nolo Press (February, 2001)

Willerton. Dale R. *Negotiate Your Commercial Lease* (2nd edition). Self Counsel Press (January, 2003).

Zankel, Martin I. *Negotiating Commercial Real Estate Leases*. Mesa House Publishing (February, 2001).

Chapter 10

Insurance

If all our misfortunes were laid in a common heap whence everyone must take an equal portion, most people would be contented to take their own and depart.

—Socrates

In Woody Allen's movie *Take the Money and Run*, Allen plays a failed criminal. After he disobeys the warden, he is ordered to spend a night in the box—with an insurance salesman dressed in the appropriate seersucker suit. Now that's torture!

About the only people disliked more than attorneys are insurance salesman. But the fact is you cannot run a business without insurance. There are two types: Protection from things that go wrong (liability and workers' compensation); and continuity of the business (disability protection and key man policies).

A good general insurance agent is essential to any business. Having insurance often provides for legal representation with the fees paid by the insurer. Since most litigation can cost in the tens of thousands of dollars, making your insurer pay is well worth the expense of the premiums.

It is also worth noting that, while corporations or limited liability companies often provide insulation from liability for individual partners or shareholders, sole proprietorships or simple partnerships have no such protection. As a result, getting the best policies with the highest coverage limits protects not just you but also your family from an economic calamity related to your business.

Types of Damages

Small business is subject to two types of legal entanglements. These are called *tort damages* and *contract damages*. They will either arise from breach of an agreement or arise from injuries incurred by consumers of your products or services.

A tort damage consists of two elements:

1. Unquantifiable damages, such as pain and suffering and referred to by lawyers as *general damages*.

2. Actual or quantifiable damages, such as a broken leg with resulting medical bills—often called *special damages* by lawyers.

A contract damage takes on of one of three forms and depends on the circumstances of the breach:

1. Reliance damages. If I order widgets for $1,000 and you promise delivery in two weeks and you don't get it to me for eight weeks—causing me to lose profits from the sale of the widgets—then my reliance damage would be any increase in costs (e.g. a "rush" production to meet the deadline) and lost profit from sales.

2. Restitution damages. If I pay you $1,000 for an order of 6-inch widgets and you give me 4-inch widgets, I can return the nonconforming goods. If you refuse to refund my money, I can sue for the $1,000 plus any costs in having to obtain the right widgets somewhere else.

3. Expectation damages. This measure is similar to restitution damages but focuses almost exclusively on lost profits, because let's face it: you don't care about widgets; you care about the profit that would have been used to by the Porsche 911.

Because calculating expectation damages can get very complicated, many business contracts already include provisions should any damages be incurred during the term of the contract.

Clauses that fix the loss are called *liquidated damages provisions*. Many standard real estate purchase forms provide a liquidated damage in the event the buyer or seller backs out of a real estate transaction.

Standard business insurance policies are designed to protect you against claims for both tort and contract damages. The coverage for tort damages is relatively broad; the coverage for contract damages is defined more narrowly.

Start With Property Coverage

The term business insurance includes a number of different kinds of coverage. The most basic coverage is a Commercial Property Policy (CPP). This insurance protects your premises—offices, warehouse, factory, shop, etc.—your inventory and your equipment against damage, loss or court judgments.

A CPP is roughly analogous to a homeowners policy. It protects structure as well as possessions; and it offers a basic level of liability protection. However, it's usually defined more specifically to the type and needs of your business.

The Elements of Small Business

A CPP is the "insurance" that your landlord will require if you lease commercial space…or your lender will require if you buy it.

For smaller businesses, some insurance companies offer a package of coverages called a Businessowners Plan (BOP). These policies usually offer lower coverage amounts, a broader range of things and actions covered and are cheaper, generally.

BOPs make the most sense for small businesses that are at the stage of moving out of a home-based environment and into a more formal commercial one. Some landlords will accept BOP coverage as sufficient to support a commercial lease, other will not. The landlord's position will usually reflect how much—and what kind of—space you're leasing.

Workers' Compensation

After property coverage, the risk that most businesses dread is injuries to their employees.

In the early 1900s, many states were concerned that the uncertainty of damage awards from lawsuits and judgments obtained by employees could result in the bankruptcy of many businesses. To fix this problem, workers' compensation insurance was created. The advantage of having workers' comp coverage is the fixed amount you pay each month. If you have three accidents within a one-month period you won't have to bankrupt your business in order to pay for the injuries.

Worker's comp also pays injured employees replacement wages while they recover from a work-related illness or injury.

If your employee drops his pen at work and bends underneath the desk to pick it up and bumps his head on the way up, suffering a concussion that prevents him from being able to work for a week, he gets as much as 75 percent of his wages for that week through worker's comp.

> Through this type of insurance, employees receive a range of benefits for both minor injuries to death or serious disfigurement in industrial accidents. The injury doesn't have to take place on the factory floor; it can happen anywhere, as long as it occurs in the course of work. And workers' comp also covers illnesses or conditions—like lung problems, carpal tunnel syndrome or even psychological problems—that might emerge over a long period.

Workers' compensation is a *no-fault system*. Businesses pay premiums to insurance companies. In exchange, a worker injured while on the job receives medical benefits and lost wages; but, unlike in personal injury lawsuits, the worker does not receive general or pain and suffering damages. If the injury prohibits return to the same type of job, monies are provided for retraining in a different job.

Each state regulates workers' comp coverage in its own way. In California, worker's comp insurance is calculated using the employees' salary and the number of hours worked per week. California's premiums are among the highest in the U.S. In Texas, on the other hand, rates are relatively cheap and the state doesn't even require very small companies to carry the coverage. Contact your state's Department of Insurance for the details that apply to you.

In most states, every company that has even one employee must have some form of workers' comp coverage. Many states fine (or otherwise penalize) businesses that don't have the coverage; and most provide the coverage to businesses—usually smaller ones—that can't get the coverage from a private-sector insurance company.

Liability

Commercial property and workers' comp policies can protect your business from most of the liabilities you're likely to face. But, as your business grows, you may need to arrange separate business liability coverage.

Also, depending on your business, your landlord may require separate or additional liability coverage. This is especially true if you run a high-traffic retail business.

In insurance jargon, this separate coverage is provided by a Commercial General Liability (CGL) policy.

A standard commercial lease often requires that you obtain liability insurance, usually consisting of $1 million in protection so that if an injury or death occurs on the leased property you and the landlord are protected. While costs vary from state to state, you can expect to pay about $2,000.00 for such a policy if the business is relatively safe and a whole lot more if you have vats of hydrochloric acid on the premises. There are software programs available with the American Association of Insurance Services (www.aais.org) to calculate costs for all commercial liability policies.

For a number of years, I have been retained by a client that produces laser light shows. The company has been in business for almost 35 years. Recently, a venue negotiated with the company to put the show in one of its theatres. Negotiations lasted a few weeks, a contract was drawn and executed and equipment delivered. Then came the problem—the venue required a $1 million liability policy.

In 35 years, my client had never been sued and it was not aware of any injuries. Moreover, the type of laser used would not be likely to cause injury. Nonetheless, to comply with the venue's requirement, it sought the liability insurance. The price quotes for one year ranged from $35,000 to $50,000. But the projected net annual profits of the show would be substantially less than the cost of the insurance. My client called agent after agent to no avail.

When my client informed me of the problem, I investigated its plight. A standard liability policy would in fact cost between $35,000 and $50,000. Time for *Plan B*. And I found one—an insurer that would charge the client a certain amount for each ticket sold based on an immediate annual estimate of ticket sales and adjustments made quarterly. That reduced the price of the insurance to $11,000. And that premium could be financed. Problem solved.

Negligence and Liability

A customer comes into your store and slips on a banana peel that some other customer left on the floor. She breaks her leg and sues you for *negligence*. The damages totals $10,000. Aren't you lucky that you bought that liability policy? The issues in determining whether you are liable for negligence are:

A. Did you have a duty to make the premises safe?

B. Did you breach that duty by committing an act or failing to commit an act that resulted in the premises being unsafe?

C. Did your act or omission proximately cause the patron to break her leg and could you have reasonably foreseen that your act or omission would result in an injury to the patron?

D. Was there a resulting measurable damage?

If you open the business to the public, you have a duty to make the premises safe. Simple enough. Obviously, the woman would not have been injured had she not been in your store. However, whether you breached your duty may depend on the color of the banana peel. That's right. The "Banana Peel Rule" has been plaguing law students since the days of early days of America.

If the banana peel were yellow, a jury might conclude that the peel had recently fallen to the floor and no reasonable manner of diligence on your part, other than luck, would have led you to find the peel and remove it. On the other hand, if the banana peel were brown, the jury might conclude that the peel had been on the floor for quite some time, and your failure to spot it and remove it constituted a breach of your duty.

This is why lawyers like me get paid the big bucks... and why every small business needs a good one.

Product Liability

If you intend to sell any product, whether directly or through retail outlets, you will need a policy of products liability insurance. In fact, it's likely that no retail store will sell your product unless you have the policy. These policies commonly provide $2 million in coverage and name the retailer(s) as an insured.

One of the factors that make this protection so valuable is the strict liability that attaches to products.

> **"Strict liability"** doctrines provide that, as long as the buyer uses the product in a manner foreseeable to the manufacturer or to the seller, those parties and any other parties that assisted in placing the product into the "stream of commerce" can be held liable for damages resulting from the product's use.

You decide to sell gel candles. Some you sell yourself and some you sell through a retail store. A man buys a candle from such a store. When he lights it the whole things blows up and burns his hand off.

In traditional negligence cases, the injured party has to prove that the defendant breached its *duty of reasonable care*. But that is not the case regarding the purchase of products. Simply put, duty and breach of duty are not in issue. If you sold it, you are responsible for it even if you did not make it.

Because the man was using the gel candle in the manner with which it was intended, he is entitled to compensation. If you manufactured it, the store will look to you and to your insurance carrier for the retaining of competent attorneys and coverage for any loss.

Prices of product liability insurance vary depending on the product being sold. Items that are dangerous or potentially dangerous, such as chemical cleaners or ladders, require policies with premiums in the thousands of dollars. However, most benign products require policies costing in the upper hundreds or a little over $1,000.

Social Host Liability

Insurance companies also sell various kinds of speciality policies that cover particular kinds of liability that can come up the course of business.

If you start a business where alcohol will be served, you may consider getting social host liability or tavern-keeper liability insurance. This specialty coverage isn't usually required by law—but, if you're renting the space, the landlord may require it.

Someone comes into your bar, has a few drinks and drives away drunk. A few blocks away, he causes an accident, killing someone in another car. Whoever served the drunk driver alcohol can be held at fault. Although this seems ridiculous, the repercussions from this occurring even once can be severe.

You need to run a bar to need social host liability coverage. If you have an art galley where you serve beer and wine at openings…or, if your business involves a lot of boozy client dinners…you might consider it.

Social host liability isn't cheap. But, like most speciality coverages, it's usually priced very specifically to your business circumstances.

Key Man Insurance

A partner's death can mean the end of the business, and when partners have an agreement providing for a surviving partner to purchase the interest or shares of the deceased partner, insurance can save the day. But "key man" insurance is not exactly the typical personal life insurance you may be considering to protect your family.

> The "key man" is logically defined as the key person or persons in the business without whom the business might fail. It could be the owner, the founder, or a couple of senior employees.

Should a key man die unexpectedly, the insurance policy will pay for the business either to shut down properly (pay off debts, distribute monies to investors, and pay employee severance) or to pay the estate or heirs of the key man in exchange for his ownership in the company. With continuity being a critical issue in any business, shareholder or partnership agreements should provide for contingencies including the death of a partner.

In the absence of such an agreement, the heirs can seek an evaluation of the business and then demand that the surviving partners cough up the dead person's share. To avoid valuation issues, the partners often agree to a set value of each other's interest and then purchase a policy covering that amount. Depending on how much you can afford and the relative value of the business, your insurance agent can obtain competitive quotes for policies ranging anywhere from $100,000 to $1 million and beyond.

Most life insurance agents will be able to sell you key man insurance. But be aware that life insurance agents often over-sell their products. Buy a policy within your budget that will accommodate your financial needs in the wake of tragedy. Just don't forget that the business is likely to grow. So, try to get a policy that covers expected growth or that can be modified to cover increases in value.

A $100,000 key man policy might seem like plenty right now. But it won't in 10 years, when the business is worth millions and you try to pawn off a hundred grand on your partner's widow.

Can you say "Litigation?"

Directors and Officers Liability

For those in charge of larger corporations, errors and omissions insurance—sometimes also called directors and officers liability insurance—is often a good idea. These coverages protect individuals from financial liability for the *reasonable* decisions they make or actions they take in the course of running the business.

This insurance is especially valuable in two cases:

1) where other shareholders or joint venture investors might sue if revenue or profit falls far short of projections on any given deal; and

2) where you want to attract well-known people to the Board of Directors. Chances are they will not want to serve if they could be liable for any decisions of the Board that they ratify.

Note that you might consider putting well-known people on your board of directors especially if you intend to raise money. I don't mean celebrities (the troubles faced by Planet Hollywood proved they're not worth so much on a board); but, rather, people known in your particular industry for their expertise. Investors tend to trust companies directed by people who have good reputations.

Sexual Harassment

Many states have adopted specific statutes with respect to sexual harassment. These statutes have limited the liability of companies for failing to prevent continuing harassment or ignoring the complaints of workers claiming they are being harassed.

> For example, if the harassed employee fails to report the incidents or fails to follow guidelines contained in the employee manual, damages to the business may be limited.

But, if the employee reported the incidents and the owners or managers were asleep at the wheel, the business could be in big trouble. That is also true if the harasser has a known history of harassing—and the harasser doesn't have to be another employee. It can be a client or other business contact.

Standard Commercial General Liability policies specifically exclude coverage for sexual harassment. The specialty insurance that does cover things like sexual harassment (and racial or gender discrimination) is called Employment Practices Liability (EPL) coverage.

EPL coverage is expensive—and gets sharply more so if your company has had harassment problems in the past. If you don't have or can't afford a policy to cover sexual harassment, at the very least create a clearly-stated procedure by which complaints shall be investigating and make sure that the employees are aware of that mechanism.

Health Plans

The mechanics of health coverage in the U.S. are complex and constantly changing. There's not enough room in this book to discuss them in detail. But a quick review of the basics should be useful.

First and most important: While most Americans get their health insurance from plans offered at their work, businesses are not required to provide health insurance for their employees. Companies that do offer health coverage usually have made the decision that the benefit attracts better employees. If you're at the point that attracting and keeping good workers is important, offering health coverage is—next to paying more—the best way to do this. But be aware that some states are toying with the idea of requiring businesses with a certain number of employees to provide health coverage. Beware of these changes.

While large corporations provide employee benefits from disability and life insurance to health and dental insurance, small business rarely have the purchasing power to provide these benefits.

Nonetheless, for small businesses the number of options has grown over the years. While including dental and vision care and disability and life insurance may be too much, medical insurance premiums are not as prohibitive as you might think. Also, if the city where you operate your business has more jobs than employees to fill them, your company will be competing with other companies for those workers—so, offering coverage can help.

Meet with a qualified and experienced insurance agent and map out an affordable strategy. If you can be competitive, you will get the better employees and retain them. In the long run, it beats turnover and training and turnover and training...

Conclusion

While only certain types of insurances are required by law, the longevity of your business depends on your ability to prevent litigation from bankrupting the company. Liability protection and continuity protection are essential elements and part of the cost of doing business successfully.

References

Florence, Mari. *Sex at Work: Attraction, Orientation, Harassment, Flirtation and Discrimination*. Silver Lake Publishing (September, 2001).

Harrington, Scott E., and Gregory R. Niehous. *Risk Management and Insurance*. The McGraw-Hill Companies (July, 2003).

Hungelman, Jack. Insurance for Dummies (Dummies Trade Series). John Wiley & Sons, Inc. (January, 2001).

Newkirk, R. & R. *Business Insurance*. Dearborn Financial Publishing, Inc. (September, 2000).

Russell, David T. *Insuring the Bottom Line: How to Protect Your Company from Liabilities, Catastrophes and Other Business Risks*. Silver Lake Publishing, (June, 1996).

Silver Lake Editors. *The Insurance Buying Guide*. Silver Lake Publishing (November, 1999).

Silver Lake Editors. *The Insurance Dictionary*. Silver Lake Publishing (March, 2002).

Skipper, Harold D. *Life and Health Insurance*. Pearson Education (September, 1999).

Walsh, James. *Workers' Comp for Employers* (2nd edition). Silver Lake Publishing (April, 1995).

Chapter 11

Business Equipment

It is questionable if all the mechanical inventions yet made have lightened the day's toil of any human being.

—John Stuart Mill

It might seem obvious that, to have a successful business, you need to have equipment. If you are in the service industry, then computers, printers, fax machines, copiers and possibly vehicles will be required.

If you are manufacturing a product or two, then you will need lots of equipment and possibly equipment especially made for your needs. If you are selling wares to the public, then you may need a little of both.

In obtaining equipment, you have many options. You can lease, you can buy, or you can lease to own. Often, some form of leasing option sounds quite appealing since most equipment leases provide that you own the equipment at the end of the payment term and you do not tie up precious capital in the meantime. But beware. Not all leases are the same.

The equipment most common to any business is the computer system, telephones, faxes, printers and copiers. Unless you are hiring many employees at once and installing a computer network with a server, computers should always be purchased, not leased unless the lease provides for system upgrades along with maintenance and repairs. Printers, fax machines and other peripherals are often provided with the computer system. As such, the decision to lease or purchase these devices generally falls into the same analysis as we use for computers.

Copiers are an entirely different matter. Most major manufacturers of business equipment provide a line of moderately sophisticated equipment at reasonable lease prices. For example, if you make less than fifty copies each day, a sophisticated copying system with double side copying that collates, staples, hole punches and generally throws out the garbage once a week is unnecessary for very small businesses.

Tip: Though your copy count may be less than fifty today, you should consider what your needs will be next year or the following year. Whether you purchase or lease, be sure that expansion will not result in a financial disaster. Ask whether the supplier has a plan for trade-ins or replacement.

Another Tip: We are inundated with copy centers. From Kinko's to Office Depot to Staples, these stores provide copying services at a reasonable cost. They have the machines and they pay for the maintenance. So why should you? Before you commit yourself to anything, check out the copy centers in your neighborhood. If you can charge clients for the costs of copies, then you only give up a small convenience by owning or leasing your own machine.

For those who need sophisticated copiers, the experience of choosing the machine and executing a lease is quite unsettling. First, most manufacturers do not sell or lease their products directly to the consumer. Rather, the lease comes from an unaffiliated finance company that could care less whether the leased product works. Second, just like cellular phone dealers, copiers are provided by independent companies. And third, also just like cellular phones, knowing which brand is the best will require a little research. Or maybe a lot.

If you have friends or relatives in similar businesses, ask them about their systems and repair contracts. Also check with magazines like Consumer Reports that research products and rate them. It is easy to allow some salesperson to convince you that his copier is the best. Maybe it is. But maybe it is not. While name brands abound, not all make great copiers. And each has its own unique design and features that render it easy or difficult to repair.

What Is "Lease to Own"?

When you finance that multifunction machine you will notice that the paperwork will likely refer to the financing as a "lease" and not a purchase even though you will own that machine when all forty-seven payments are made. The reason is hyper-technical at best. Leasing permits the finance company to charge you in ways that it cannot if the transaction is defined as a purchase.

The most significant difference is the manner in which the interest is charged. While each state has its own rules with regard to financed purchases, most require that a certain portion of each monthly payment must be applied to principal.

For example, if the copier you have been eyeing is priced at $5,000 and you finance it over five years at an interest rate of ten percent, each monthly payment must have a certain percentage applied to the reduction of the $5,000 price.

This just ain't so in a "lease." And the consequences can be devastating if you have any intention of replacing the copier prior to the end of the lease.

A client of mine in marketing and sales decided to enter the wacky world of product videos— five minute presentation on the inner workings of "Crete Clean." No, not a method by which one scrubs Mediterranean islands; it was a method for cleaning your driveway.

Since my client had no familiarity with video equipment or production, a "partner" had to be located. He was. And my client provided an unlimited budget to "purchase" the equipment necessary.

The purchase was really a lease-to-own arrangement. When the partnership ended—and it did, rather abruptly—my client decided to sell the equipment and pay off the finance company. He was shocked to learn that, after two years of payments, the principal had not been reduced.

How is this possible? In a lease-to-own transaction, finance companies take the total sum owed over the term of the lease including the totality of the interest. When you make a payment, you reduce the total. Depending on the interest rate and the term, the total may be almost double the original sum.

Two years of payments brought my client back to even. Meanwhile, the equipment had deteriorated and depreciated by almost two-thirds of its original value. The result? My client still owed the original purchase price on equipment with equipment worth less than half its original value.

Interest-only financial packages might make sense in real estate. They make no sense in equipment leasing.

The "Security" Interest

The other important factor in a lease or purchase to own is that the finance company has a "security" interest in the leased or financed product. In the event you fail to make the payments, the equipment can be repossessed.

Chapter 11: Business Equipment

 Warning: The company that supplies the copiers or faxes or computers or printers, etc., often is not the same company that finances them. This poses a problem: If you have difficulties with the equipment or if the sales company provided you with lemons when you ordered limes, you still have to pay the leasing company. Moreover, check the contract you signed. Chances are it places jurisdiction for any legal action in some state you never visited and is not geographically desirable.

While a lawyer may not be required to review the agreement, make sure *you* read it carefully. The young kid who hands you the agreement is interested only in his commission. He knows nothing about the lease/purchase agreement and does not care. So don't expect to get answers (or at least not good answers) from him.

Again, check the venue for any legal disputes arising out of an equipment; many lease agreements make it a different state than the one where you are. Unless you enjoy meaningless and expensive travel, try to negotiate for the venue to be your state and county. If that doesn't work, cross out the venue clause and initial it before signing the agreement.

Several years ago, a client retained me to reengineer his business. "Reengineering" is a fancy term for restructuring a business—usually a bigger or older one—to remove antiquated systems or equipment and replace them with updates to make the whole operation more efficient.

On the first day, the client informed me he had a problem with the two copy machines he had leased. Now this client was one of those who spent more of his productive day negotiating for the better deal on anything rather than making money. When confronted with a copier salesman, he had badgered the guy into a "great deal." Rather than 3.5 cents per page, the client received a deal of 3.0 cents per page.

As we have discussed, the sales and leasing company is not the financing company. And therein came the problem...

Two months later, when the machines broke down, the sales company could not be located. Apparently, it had folded. But that did not stop the lessor financing company from sending a monthly bill. Two lawsuits, countless telephone calls and lawyer letters later, the finance company agreed to pick up the machines and drop the lawsuit.

The half-cent-per-page savings ultimately cost far more than anything that could have been saved from cheap copies.

Technology Updates

Those of you who have cellular telephones know that your carrier's rate plans change all the time. For the most part, the plans become cheaper. But your carrier usually chooses to share this information with you or any other information that might result in lowering your costs only when you ask for it. So it pays to look at the carrier's Web site and visit its official store if one is near you.

 All technologies, including those for fax machines, telephone systems and copiers advance very rapidly. If you don't block out some time every few months to review pricing changes you could be wasting money.

Since the mid-1970s, a family member held a 50-percent interest in a travel agency. The agency was run by the other partner until his death in 1997. It had only one full-time employee, who had worked in the agency for more than fifteen years. He was given authority to manage the joint. He did any adequate job…but the agency seemed stuck.

Shortly thereafter, I wandered in. The business had two problems. First, it was located in a low rise office building on the second floor where no one could see it; second, it had a computer system more than 10 years old. The system barely ran—and had a slow dial-up modem.

Worse yet, the computer had no Internet access and, therefore, in order to book fights, cars, trains, hotels, etc., it used a direct dial system to the appropriate approved booking company.

Because the system was a relic, the cost for the direct dial system was $400 per month. The cost of logging into the site by Internet was $50 per month. Now here's a no-brainer: Spend $1,000 on a viable upgraded computer and spend $35 per month on a cable modem. We did—and have saved thousands of dollars per year on better and faster technology.

Conclusion

You need equipment—and have to deal with equipment costs. Whether you are buying or leasing or leasing to buy, read the contract very carefully, ask questions and always comparison shop.

Tip: Some companies offer great deals on financing equipment. Often the contract provides that if you are late with even one payment, the interest rate on the financing jumps from three percent to thirteen percent or higher. Some states allow for interest rates on financing or leasing up to twenty-five percent. Now that hurts. And finally, always ask the dealer/agent what the consequences would be if the dealer/agent went out of business. You don't want to get stuck with broken equipment on a financing contract where you are still required to make monthly payments.

The old saying applies: If the deal looks too good to be true, it probably is. Make sure you understand the financing options and any interest on the remaining balance.

Also, read the lease—no matter how impatient the salesperson is. Read the purchase contract. And read the financing disclosures. If you don't understand, ask someone who does. Also, check the reputation of the company providing the product and don't be penny wise and pound foolish.

References

Contino, Richard M. *Complete Equipment-Leasing Handbook: A Deal Maker's Guide with Forms, Checklists and Worksheets.* AMACOM (July, 2002).

Mayer, David G. *Business Leasing For Dummies.* IDG Books/ John Wiley & Sons, Inc. (2002)

Nevitt, Peter K. and Frank J. Fabozzi. *Equipment Leasing.* John Wiley & Sons, Inc. (August, 2000).

Mitchell, Thomas G., et al. *The Commercial Lease Guidebook: Learn How to Win the Leasing Game!* MacOre, Intl. (January, 1994).

Willerton, Dale R. *Negotiate Your Commercial Lease* (2nd edition). Self Counsel Press (January, 2003).

Chapter 12

Accounting and Taxes

In business, the earning of a profit is something more than an incident of success. It is an essential condition of success. It is an essential condition of success because the continued absence of profit itself spells failure.

—Justice Louis D. Brandeis

If you have never owned a business, then balancing a checkbook is the closest thing you likely have ever done by way of accounting. And I'll bet you never found that $13.95 deficit from three years ago....

Accounting skills, or a lack thereof, often become the downfall of many businesses. Sure, you enjoy operating that restaurant or coffee house or golf store or foundry. So who has time for bookkeeping?

You.

First, you need to pay taxes—payroll taxes, income taxes, sales taxes, city taxes and possibly property taxes. A failure to pay these taxes or even to pay them on time can result in penalties and interest in addition to the principal sum that should have been paid.

Second, some states charge additional penalties. For example, the California Labor Board charges $1,000.00 per each employee who is not currently covered by Worker's Compensation insurance. While the states and the Federal government seem forgiving and are willing to provide payment plans, why would you want to tie up your operating capital in back tax payments with exorbitant penalties and interest rates?

Third, you need to evaluate your expenses regularly to determine whether monies are being wasted or whether expenses are too high in any particular area.

Several years ago I was retained to restructure a mortgage loan business. The mortgage brokers spent most of their time in the field with clients or potential clients while processors in the office input the data and information into the computers. All of the brokers had cellular phones and all with separate companies and separate rate plans. The total bill per month ran as high as $6,000. No one actually knew because no one ever reviewed an expense statement.

When I began my work, my first step was to gather all expenses and review the various costs to see where monies could be saved. Simply by putting all of the brokers under the same cellular phone company and under one plan, the monthly costs decreased from $6,000 per month to $1,200 per month. That amounted to a savings of more than $50,000 per year.

Fiscal Year or Calendar Year? (Huh?)

It is well understood that on April 15, tax returns and tax payments for individuals are due for the previous year. That is, the previous calendar year. Sole proprietorships, limited liability companies or partnerships and corporations filing under Subchapter S must file their returns on a calendar year basis.

Corporations not filing under Subchapter S have the option of filing their taxes on a calendar year basis or on a fiscal year basis. By fiscal year, we mean a 12-month period that begins on the first day of a month other than January 1. The exception is corporations that perform personal services. For example, if you and your corporation perform consulting services, the IRS requires that your corporation file its taxes on a calendar year basis.

What is the advantage of filing on a fiscal year basis? Who knows? In this day and age, the calendar year and fiscal year probably make little difference to the small business.

> For larger corporations, fiscal year filing allows the corporation to prepare its financial statements and returns during the period where business is slower or where the previous quarter's profits were so high that they mask the lousy quarters that came earlier in the "year."

For small business, the advantage of fiscal year filing is that you can deal with your corporation's finances at a time where it does not interfere with your personal return and beating that April 15 deadline.

If you have more than one business, spreading out the taxes may be quite helpful.

Also note that corporations, regardless of type or type of business, do not file taxes on April 15. Calendar year corporations file on March 15— two months plus fifteen days. If the corporation's fiscal year runs from July 1 to June 30, then the return would be due on September 15.

Businesses are expected to make tax payments quarterly based on an estimate of their income. If the business is a corporation, then estimated payments are due on the fifteenth day after the end of the quarter.

If the business is a sole proprietorship, then estimated payments are due on April 15, June 15, September 15 and January 15. Leave it to the IRS to come up with oddball dates.

If you fail to make estimated tax payments quarterly and instead wait until the annual tax return is prepared, you will pay interest on the monies you *should* have paid.

Cash or Accrual Method (Huh...Huh?)

The next issue, which applies to all forms of business entities, is whether to account on an accrual or cash method. This is simpler than it sounds, but there are specific reasons for doing either one.

The Cash Method

The cash method is the most common. Under this method, revenue is counted when it is received. You receive payment of $100.00. You then book that amount of revenue. Simple, eh? If you don't get paid, you have no income.

The Accrual Method

The accrual accounting method consists of booking the revenue at the time the services are rendered or the time that goods are provided regardless of whether payment is received.

For most small businesses, the cash method is the best way to account for revenue. Firs, it is simple. You receive payment; you record having received it. Second, at the end of your tax year, you know what the business made.

For larger businesses, the accrual method has two advantages. First, if you sell products to clients who pay on thirty or sixty or ninety day schedules or whenever they feel like it, the accrual method will show an even cash flow. Second, if you intend to sell the business, the accrual method might indicate a higher income—thus improving the books.

Federal Income Taxes

It is said that the only certainties are death and taxes. While medical science or cryogenic labs may prevent death, taxes appear to be omnipotent. You owe them and you must pay them. In fact, whether you are a sole proprietor or you choose to operate under a corporation, as we discussed above state and federal income taxes are paid quarterly based on your projection of income during the course of your fiscal or calendar year. That's right—Uncle Sam has no desire to wait a year to see its share of the take.

 Don't spend too much time buying those books or listening to those who tell you that you are not required to pay taxes and that the collection of taxes is illegal. Taxes are not illegal. You owe them. And if you don't pay them intentionally, you will surely find yourself in a room at the federal country club penitentiary with Big Bubba and his tennis racket.

State Income Taxes

Most states require payment of income taxes on businesses. Payment is also made on a quarterly basis and is due at the time the Federal quarterly taxes are paid.

A few states don't have an income tax. But be wary that the lost revenue is not replaced through other assessed taxes.

Local Business Tax

Many businesses do not know that they owe local taxes until the tax assessor sends that nasty letter informing them that in addition to owing the monies, they owe interest and penalties as well. Cities love to charge businesses simply for the privilege of being located in their area. Some cities charge a flat rate, some charge based on a percentage of estimated revenue, and some charge based on the number of employees.

As you can imagine, these taxes are not very popular. As a result, many businesses simply "forget" about them. Local governments have responded to this by making arrangements with the state taxing authorities to review the business returns of those who list their city as the principal place of business. When the listing is made on the state return but no local filing has been made, the business is up a creek without a paddle. You will get a nasty letter and an even nastier bill.

Payroll Tax

In addition to income taxes, any business with employees must pay certain taxes to cover a portion of the employees' social security along with unemployment compensation, and disability. Additionally, employers withhold income taxes owed by their employees.

 If you use a payroll service, the payroll taxes will be automatically debited from your payroll account on or near the same day that the service delivers your checks. If you do your payroll yourself—or your accountant does it—you'll usually make two checks with your payroll checks. These other checks are usually made payable to your bank and include a coupon with your tax identification information for the Federal government and state government. Your bank then forwards that money to the appropriate agencies.

Payroll taxes can be paid monthly—or even quarterly—instead of every two weeks, with payroll. However, if you pay the taxes on these other schedules, make sure that all of your paperwork and the payments are sent in on time. If you don't make payroll tax payments on a timely basis, the IRS and state agencies take collection actions quickly.

Sales Tax

If you are selling a product directly to consumers, you will be required to charge a tax on all of those sales. That tax consists of a state imposed tax and a local (city or county) imposed tax. The highest total rate currently in the United States is approximately 8.6 percent. The lowest rate is approximately 4.0 percent.

> You collect the sales tax and then you pay it to the state and local governments. Many states require payment of sales taxes on a monthly basis. Payment is made with a form you or your accountant fill out and you or another partner or officer signs. The form requires information on gross sales and gross taxable sales, as not all sales are taxable to the buyer.

So what sales are taxable? That question is not always as easy as it seems. Most states have some authority of appointed bureaucrats that decide these things. Merchants then have to decipher the convoluted rules and regulations. Food sales are the most confusing because ready-to-eat snacks are treated differently than a bag of potato chips. However, most sales are going to be taxable events. The only exception is interstate sales and Internet sales, and even these sales can be tricky.

Interstate sales occur when someone is Akron, Ohio purchases a product from a business in Tucson, Arizona. In theory, the buyer is supposed to pay the sales tax to his or her state. Some do.

Internet sales are a bit trickier. When "e-commerce" first became a hit, Congress decided that taxes would not be charged on sales. Since then, many states have complained that they are losing revenue that otherwise would be theirs. As a result, intrastate purchases are often taxed and some Internet companies are now voluntarily collecting taxes. If your business will include Internet sales, check with your accountant for current requirements and any future changes in the tax laws.

Recently, a client purchased a bar. The owner had placed it for sale and my client decided he just had to buy it. As an attorney, I keep a template for the purchase of stock or assets of any business. These templates require the seller to warrant (guarantee) that all of the taxes owed have been paid including payroll taxes, sales taxes, and income taxes. The templates also require the seller to warrant that he has the right to sell the business.

In the case of the bar deal, no one bothered to ask for my help and no such agreements were prepared or executed. Guess what? The purchase price didn't even cover all of the taxes owed. Since my client had chosen a stock purchase and was about to assume all of the liabilities along with the assets, he would have been responsible for more than $250,000 in unpaid taxes, penalties and interest.

> Sure, he could have sued the seller—if my client could find him and, having won the case, collected such a large judgment. Two big *ifs*. In the meantime, all of the capital needed to run the business would have been paid to tax authorities and to lawyers.

Luckily—for my client—he did ask me to review the purchase agreement before he signed. I saw it didn't say anything about taxes owed and was able to raise the right questions before my client signed anything.

Resale License

For those of you who are buying or are intending to purchase goods for resale to the public, you will need to obtain a resale license.

> Under this license, the business does not pay sales taxes on goods it purchases and does not have to collect taxes on goods sold to other licensees who intend to sell to the public. However, the business does have to pay sales taxes collected from sales made to the general public.

Financial Statements

Of course, there's more to running a business than paying taxes—even though it's easy to forget that sometimes. And the reporting aspect of accounting can be an important management tool.

The ability to "see" your income on a quarterly basis can provide other benefits. While some businesses are truly seasonal (such as the beach resort that makes more income in the Summer than in the Winter), other businesses are not so obvious. The ability to determine when your business receives its greatest revenue helps you to establish a budget and the number of employees you will need to meet demand.

On the expense side, as we discussed earlier, it is hard to know where or what to change if you do not know how the money is being spent. If you are ordering supplies, either as a component of manufacturing or for sale or for the continuing operations of your business, the time you buy and the quantity of materials you buy can save you thousands of dollars.

> For example, the cost of those paperclips may be significantly cheaper if you make one bulk purchase of paperclips at the beginning of the year rather than purchasing throughout the year. Your expense reports can help you see how you spend paperclip money over the course of a year—and make any adjustments that you might need.

Reviewing expenses also assists in tax planning. For example, most businesses are required to pay taxes to the Internal Revenue Service on a quarterly basis. If you know that in the first quarter your income will be significantly less than your fourth quarter income, then you might consider paying one-fourth of the total projected taxes at each interval so as to fix your expenses. Or you may opt to utilize the additional operating capital to develop new products. At least you know where you stand.

The Balance Sheet

The balance sheet is probably the most common financial document. While it does not contain itemized income or expenses or itemized profits or losses, it does measure the health of the company. [Form 12-1]

While a balance sheet can be created for any business, it is a tool normally reserved for corporations or limited liability companies or partnerships. In a nutshell, here is everything you need to know (but were afraid to ask).

The left side of the balance sheet consists of the assets. This may include cash on hand, receivables (monies due and owing), tangible property, real property, and possibly intellectual property such as patent or trademark. In short, the left side of the balance sheet consists of all things that give the business a value.

The right side of the sheet provides for the liabilities and comes in two parts. The first is actual liabilities— those debts or costs that reduce the value of the company such as accounts payable, loans due, tax liabilities etc. The bottom portion (referred to in corporations as "shareholder equity") is the difference between the assets and the actual liabilities.

So if the assets amount to $1 million and the liabilities amount to $500,000, the value of the company to its shareholders can be assessed at $500,000.

In a publicly traded company, one can realize the "book value" by multiplying the number of shares outstanding to the price at which those shares are selling on the exchange. When the price of the shares on the market falls below the shareholder equity as reported by the corporation in its annual report, you might be looking at a good investment opportunity.

Ultimately, the balance sheet of a small business or of a large business may be of little value since it does not take into account the external financial conditions such as a recession or such as competition and because it does not provide a sense of whether the product or service m̥ become obsolete in the near future.

Also, as we will discuss below, certain expenses such as capital expenditures do not have to be included. But it adds to the picture and it acts as just one more method by which you can measure the relative success or failure of your business or a business you want to purchase.

Income and Expense Statements

As we discussed earlier in this chapter, knowing the sources of your income and expenses can make a significant difference to the profitability of your business. [Form 12-2] Depending on the size and revenue of the business, these statements should be prepared either quarterly or semiannually.

Your accountant can prepare these statements. Also, most of the accounting software you are likely to use will be able to create an income and expense table or even a pie chart and in living color.

Once you know where the biggest cuts of the budget are being paid, you can work on reducing those costs.

Profit and Loss Statements

For small businesses, profit and loss statements may not be necessary as the income and expense statement since for a small business the information on them will be the same. But there are a few subtle differences. For example, fringe benefit monies spent on employees for coffee or bottled water or paper or printer cartridges or telephone service or insurance are "expenses" and are applied against earnings to determine the business' taxes. But they are not losses. [Form 12-3]

Then we have the "capital expenditure." Purchased items designed to increase profits, either in the short term or long term, are not treated as an ordinary "expenses." That is because these are "investments." If the office computer system runs on a P2 Intel processor at 250 megahertz, and that is resulting in long delays in file processing, then you may wish to buy the newest system: a P4 processor at 2.5 gigahertz.

For purposes of taxes, this purchase is still an expense to be applied against income. But it may not require you to characterize it as an "expense" on your balance sheet. In fact, it could be an "asset" because the cost (the amount you paid) can be depreciated.

Simply put, because you bought something that helped the business operate and make money, you can take certain tax deductions for the related expense. That deduction reduces your taxable income and thus reduces your taxes. As a result, expenses that can be classified as capital expenditures are positive.

Capital expenditures remain one of the most abused areas of corporate finance. In the past few years a number of well-known publicly traded companies have been investigated for listing items of ordinary expense as capital expenditures and then depreciating the purchase price. That is a big no-no and could land you in the hoosegow.

Tip: Over the years I have seen accountants play all sorts of games with their client's returns— often because they don't think the IRS will catch the questionable activity and sometimes because they don't think the client will catch it. Sometimes overzealous accountants will try to "help" you and your business by restating expenses and other taxable items in order to reduce your taxes. While the tax forms can be terribly complex, make sure you go over the forms with your accountant and be sure to ask questions about anything you don't understand. If the accountant is unwilling to explain the issue to your satisfaction, fire him. Just like lawyers, there are a lot of good accountants—and a lot of bad ones.

Cash Flow Statements

The most valuable information may reside within the cash flow statement. Cash flow statements show the ebb and flow of dollars. It helps small businesses understand from where their income is derived and where their expenses get paid.

More significantly, it provides a business with "seasonality." For example, a golf store in Montana will make most of its income from April through August. After all, who needs a new set of irons when the snow is four feet high? Or consider accountants who spend January through April preparing tax returns often working fourteen hour days but may have less than eight hours of work per day in all other months. [Form 12-4]

If your business has certain seasons when sales are higher, you will want to consider the timing of any significant purchases and whether you will need to borrow money or draw down from a line of credit during the off-season in order to replenish inventory.

Many accounting software programs provide for the creation of cash flow statements based on the income and expenses you provide.

Popular Software Programs

The most popular software programs (such as *Quicken/QuickBooks* or Microsoft *Money*) can help you create financial statements including balance sheets, income and expense, profit and loss, and cash flow.

Just remember the adage: *Garbage in, garbage out.* If you get lazy and fail to input the information, your statements will not be accurate. So, if you choose to utilize the software, it can help you immensely—but it's imperative that you make time to do the work.

The more you know, the more likely you will make the right decisions for your business. While small businesses don't require all of the bells and whistles of a Fortune 500 company, the various financial statements still provide a wealth of information. Between you, your accountant and the software you choose, these statements are easily created and easy to read. So don't be afraid just because math was a foreign language to you when you were in school.

Conclusion

For some, accounting is not rocket science. For me and for most of us, it is. And when God realized that Adam could not keep track of the apples in the garden, he created the Certified Public Accountant.

Find one with a solid reputation and experience and never make a move without his or her advice and consent. You will be amazed at the monies saved in the long run.

Yes, Virginia, it is worth the price.

References

Brelsford, Harry. *Teach Yourself Microsoft Small Business Server 4.5 in 21 Days* (book and CD-ROM edition). SAMS Publishing (June, 1999).

Burton, E. James and Steven M. Bragg. *Accounting and Finance for Your Small Business* (2nd edition). John Wiley & Sons, Inc. (December, 2000)

Daily, Frederick W. *Tax Savvy for Small Business: Year-Round Tax Strategies to Save You Money* (7th edition). Nolo Press (September, 2003).

Fishman, Stephen. *Working for Yourself: Law and Taxes for Independent Contractors, Freelancers and Consultants* (4th edition). Nolo Press (August, 2002).

Fox, Jack. *Accounting and Recordkeeping Made Easy for the Self-Employed*. John Wiley & Sons, Inc. (October, 1994)

Kamorof, Bernard B. *422 Tax Deductions for Businesses & Self-Employed Individuals* (4th edition). Bell Springs Publishing (December, 2002).

Langer, Maria. *Quicken 2002 Deluxe for Macintosh: The Official Guide*. McGraw-Hill/Osborne Media (October, 2001).

Negrino, Tom. *Quicken 2003 for Macintosh: Visual QuickStart Guide*. Peachpit Press (September, 2002).

Nelson, Stephen L. *Quickbooks 2003 For Dummies*. For Dummies/John Wiley & Sons, Inc. (January, 2003)

The Elements of Small Business

Nelson, Stephen L. *Quicken 2003 For Dummies*. For Dummies/John Wiley & Sons, Inc. (September, 2002).

Pinson, Linda. *Keeping the Books: Basic Recordkeeping and Accounting for the Successful Small Business* (5th edition). Dearborn Trade Publishing (January, 2001).

Savage, Michael. *Don't Let the IRS Destroy Your Small Business: Seventy-Six Mistakes to Avoid*. Perseus Publishing (January, 1998).

Weltman, Barbara. *J.K. Lasser's New Rules for Small Business and Tax* (5th edition). John Wiley & Sons, Inc. (December, 2001).

Weverka, Peter. *Microsoft Money 2003 for Dummies*. For Dummies/John Wiley & Sons, Inc. (October, 2002).

Chapter 13

Computers and E-Commerce

In a few minutes a computer can make a mistake so great that it would take many men months to equal it.

—Merle L. Meacham

So the only thing you know about your computer is where to turn it on. And a floppy disc is that condition requiring back surgery. That's okay. For many Americans, a computer and the Internet can be extremely intimidating. My mother fears that, if she hits the wrong key, the computer will explode and planets will collide. They won't. And it doesn't have to be that way.

In this chapter, we will discuss the *hardware* and *software* available to assist you in operating your business. For those of you who think software is a cashmere sweater and hardware is a set of tools for the holidays, welcome to the 21st century. In this section we will explore the basics of your computer and how it can make you money.

This is not intended to be a crash course in computers. Rather, it is an overview of the systems, the software and related technology. Most community colleges and private learning companies offer computer classes for all levels. And there are a plethora of books that take you step by step through the programs. Whether you are creating a Web site strictly to provide information to potential customers and the public at large or whether you are considering a virtual store where customers can purchase items over the Internet, there is a class and a book right for you.

Common Hardware Issues

Want a computer? Start with some plastic and add a motherboard, a processor, a few slots for cards, a few ports (serial, parallel and USB), maybe a CD or DVD player/burner, a 40 gigabyte hard drive, a floppy disk drive—and voila! Mass confusion.

Actually, all of this stuff is quite simple. The hard drive is the storage area of your computer. It is where your programs sit until you are ready to use them. When you create a file—whether it's a program for making 3-D holograms or a letter to your mother—the hard drive is where the file is stored.

The motherboard is simply the large rectangular thing that contains all the soldered electronic connections. (Sure, that helped.) In this time of "solid state" electronics, every stereo, television or transistor radio has a motherboard. It is the group of electronic processors to which and from which all roads lead.

> The processor is the device that makes the system work—a little like gasoline hitting the spark plugs. It is the conduit through which the data travels, whether to you because you have requested certain information or to the hard drive to be stored. In most computers made in the 2000s, the main processor is about the size of a quarter. But it's the computer's main brain; it determines how quickly and how reliably the machine works.

Today, most processors for new computers are ten times faster than they were ten years earlier. And storage space has quintupled. So, the likelihood is you will never run out of room.

Each motherboard has slots for certain *cards*. Cards are translators between the hard drive and processor, on the one hand, and some unique function. For example, to hear sounds—whether from a CD you decide to play or from the nice AOL guy who says "You've got mail!"—the sound card translates information or data into sound.

Likewise, the video card translates data into video images. For example, if you want to see that report from *National Geographic* on lemur migration patterns, the data is translated by the video card into an image just like the picture you would see on the television.

Ports are the places where other devices are connected to the computer. For example, the printer is a separate device. A cable connects the printer to the computer so that when you print a document, the computer can send the information to the printer. The most common types of ports are serial, parallel and USB.

> **The serial port usually connects the monitor (screen); the parallel port usually connects the printer. The USB ports are the wild cards of connectivity. There are usually at least four in most new computers; they connect other devices, such as digital cameras, wireless keyboards, specialty printers, CD players not built in, etc.**

Also, many newer computers have ports for "fire wire" connections. These ports are often used to load large volumes of data into your computer such as the video from little Jimmy's third birthday party.

What Kind of Computer Should You Buy?

For most small businesses, two types of computers are most common: The *PC*, which stands for personal computer and is based on the combination of processors made by companies like Intel and software made by Microsoft; and the *Mac*, which stands for Macintosh and operates on its own, proprietary software.

The Elements of Small Business

Many companies manufacture PCs, including Sony, IBM, Compaq, Dell, Gateway, and Hewlett-Packard. Macs are built by Apple Computer and no one else.

For the most part, anything a PC can do a Mac can do—and vice-versa. Those who swear by their Macs claim that it has the most stable operating system so it freezes up the least. Many users also claim that the Mac is the simplest system to use.

 The stability issue is debatable. What's more certain is that, for years, Mac has been the standard computer system in graphic design field. As a result, most of the best-known design software programs were built for Mac machines...and then modified to work on PCs.

If you intend on performing desktop publishing or designing brochures or creating graphic arts or editing music or video, then most experts agree that a Mac is the better buy.

But Macs are usually more expensive and have fewer software titles available to them.

Also, as we will discuss in more detail later, businesses and their clients often share files or send information between themselves through files attached to e-mail. If the sender is using a PC system and the receiver is using a Mac system, the receiver may not be able to read the attached file.

PCs use Microsoft's *Windows* operating software. And most of what we call *computers*—that is, not industry-specific workstations or high-end supercomputers—fit in this category. More than 85 percent of the general-use computers use some version of *Windows*.

That phrase "some version" covers a lot of ground. Most new PCs come with the *XP* version of *Windows*. Previous versions include *Windows 95*, *Windows 98*, *Windows 2000*, *Windows ME* and *Windows NT*. Most of these versions are just updates of earlier versions, adding some quicker features and fewer reasons for system failures. However, some of the versions are intended for specific uses. *NT* was meant for computers that serve as the central hub of a computer network—anchoring systems in which each of many users can access the same databases, programs and files. *ME* was meant for nonbusiness home use.

The current favorite, *XP*, is more user-friendly for people who like to use multimedia software, such as programs that edit music or videotape you shot at the family Christmas party.

Most computer experts (those not employed by Microsoft) say that the most stable version for business uses is *Windows 2000*. It provides the best overall performance with the fewest errors or problems.

Common Software Issues

Most current business software (financial accounting programs, sales and marketing database programs and legal or business forms packages) will run on any version of *Windows 98* and newer. On the other hand, some older software does not enjoy the *XP* experience. So, look for software that states on the box that it is compatible with your system.

Installing computer software is a lot easier today than it was a decade ago. Most programs come on a CD; you just turn on the computer and place the CD in the CD ROM drive. Most programs automatically open and guide you through the installation process on screen. If not, they come with simple instructions for installation.

Sometimes, your computer will reject the installation of new software. This can happen if particular programs (often called *drivers*) related to the new software conflict with drivers related to other software already on the computer.

Drivers are like bridges that connect software to the operating system (*Windows* or other) and the hardware of your computer. This bridging—computer geeks call it *interfacing*—involves lots of variables. For example, if you have a Compaq computer with an Epson printer, the people at Compaq and Epson have loaded their various machines with programs that control how the keyboard types and how the printer prints. When you install Intuit *QuickBooks* accounting software onto this computer, it needs to load drivers that will interface with the Compaq and Epson programs.

On my system, I have an Epson printer and a Hewlett-Packard printer. The first is an inkjet that prints in color; the second is a laser jet that prints in black. Both are connected by way of USB cables. When they were installed, I put the H-P into the first USB slot and the Epson into the second USB slot. I tried to print. Nothing happened. So, I switched them. They worked.

Why did this happen? Probably because the Epson drivers were trying to read the H-P code even when I had sent the document to print on the H-P printer. That caused the drivers to collide and nothing got past the traffic accident.

Another solution is to turn off the computer, turn it on and try again. And, when you do, make sure that other programs are not running, as they may interfere with the process of transferring the software from the diskette, Web site or CD to the computer's hard drive.

If simple solutions do not work for you, call a computer technician. Whether you are running one computer or a small network of computers, you'll probably need to have a local tech available to maintain your system and to make any needed repairs. A good tech doesn't have to be Bill Gates to help you. All he or she needs to have is a lot of experience with smoothing out the kinks and conflicts in small business and small network systems.

Some software comes in bundles, meaning that several programs that integrate with each other are available as a unit. The most widely-used software bundle is *Office*. Another Microsoft product, *Office* contains *Word*, a word processing program, *Excel*, a spreadsheet for accounting or other organizational documents, *Powerpoint*, a presentational program, *Access*, a database for information such as customer names and address, and *Outlook*, a program for sending and receiving e-mail.

The value of this—or any—bundle is in its integration. For example, if you enter the name and address along with an e-mail address of a client in *Access*, you can send an e-mail to that person from *Outlook* just by importing the information from the first program to the second.

Or, if you are writing a letter that requires the inclusion of financial information and you want to place the information in the body of your letter, you can create the financial document in *Excel* and import that information to a letter you write in *Word*.

You don't *have* to buy bundled software. Software manufactured by companies other than Microsoft is usually designed to integrate with Microsoft programs or programs created for the PC by other companies. But it's always a good idea to do some checking before you buy any software program. Ask your friends who use their computers for business. If they have been using computers for awhile, they will be a terrific source of information on what works and what does not. Just try to ask more than one—people are sometimes eccentric about which programs they like.

One last general note on software. In the 2000s, a growing number of computer experts have started using Linux as an alternative to *Windows* and other Microsoft programs.

Linux is an operating system, like *Windows*; but it's more than that, too. It's the basis for a number of specific applications that compete with programs like *Word*, *Excel*, *Outlook*, etc.

> The main distinction about Linux is that it's free. Its developers, a group of European programmers working on their own time, believed that if they built a computer operating system that was *open*—available to everyone at no cost—then people would develop a wider range of applications that would ultimately be better than anything made by corporate giants.

In order to run Linux, you have to download the Linux operating system "kernel" from the Internet and remove *Windows* from your system. This is more than most businesspeople feel comfortable doing; so, Linux has been limited somewhat to computer geeks with time and hardware to spare.

Still, some larger companies have switched at least parts of their computer systems to Linux. And more are likely to do so in the coming years. Even if Linux itself doesn't catch on with business users, some form of open programming may. Eventually.

Software Specifics

In the meantime, the most popular word processing program—for both PC and Mac systems—is *Word*. This Microsoft program provides everything you will need to write business letters. It comes with templates or pre-designed formats for letters, labels and other documents. It also can offer tips on how to improve your writing (though some people find these tips annoying and disable that function).

The second most popular program is *Word Perfect*. Prior to *Windows*, the operating system most widely used was *DOS*; and *Word Perfect* was the top word processing program in that era. Today, *Word Perfect* comes in a Windows version and can perform essentially all of the same functions as *Word*.

The most popular spreadsheet program is another Microsoft product—*Excel*. A spreadsheet is simply a fancy name for a place where lists of data can be placed. When opened, you see rows and columns where the information can be placed. When the information is numbers, columns or rows can be added with the click of a button.

Excel also can perform other, more complex functions. Each box can be tied to a formula or a component part of a formula. For example, during your business career, a common issue we have already discussed is whether to lease equipment or purchase it. Using Excel, a series of questions can be created with either "yes" or "no" responses and/or with numeric responses. Since each box is set to a component of the desired formula, the responses can provide a conclusion of yes or no to the lease.

Access is another type of database. Say you have clients all over the country or even all over the world. You will want to manage those contacts—by *manage*, I mean place that information in some usable application or program. That information may consist of the name, address, telephone number and type of merchandise purchased. With *Access*, you can sort the data by name, location or product.

If your business is managing a rock band and the band intends to perform in Tulsa, being able to send an e-mail to fans in that area is quite valuable. Or if you are in the clothing business and you are preparing to order more merchandise, the database can provide information on how many of each item was sold. If 1,000 t-shirts were sold but only 100 sweatshirts were sold, you might want to modify that order for 550 of each.

The combination of Microsoft's email program *Outlook* and *Access* may be one of the best business tools available. *Outlook* is used primarily to receive e-mail—but it also contains a calendar of events and contact information. And the information you placed into the *Access* database, including e-mail addresses, can be moved into *Outlook* with the click of a few buttons. This permits the business to send the e-mail to all fans in the Tulsa area.

> If you still don't see the value, take a look at your mail. I bet that on any given day you receive between five and 10 pieces of junk mail. Each piece costs money, even at bulk rates. But e-mail is free—that's right, it's free! (Well, it doesn't cost anything more than buying a computer, loading it with software and setting up a Web site or on-line email account.)

Powerpoint is used for presentations. Most recently built computers can be connected to screens or televisions. If you want to make a presentation but putting pen to paper just is not glamorous enough, then this program is for you. It comes with templates and examples so that you can simply input the information or create your own look. And the presentation has moving parts. *Powerpoint* can be bought already installed or you can buy it as a separate software program.

For example, if you want to show how four elements of your business come together, *Powerpoint* takes your information and displays it as any of several prefabricated graphics. For your presentation, you choose a group of jigsaw puzzle pieces. The pieces spin around and dance around before coming together—and all before the eyes of those whom you are trying to impress. In *Powerpoint*, a particular display page is called a *slide*. In addition to jigsaw puzzle pieces, other templates are available for creating slides.

It is hard to believe that just ten years ago most small businesses did not operate with the assistance of a computer and did not have available to them the plethora of software programs available for less than $100. You can purchase programs for accounting, for check writing, for general business agreements, and for corporate operations.

My rule of thumb about software is, if I have to read the manual to figure out how the program works, then I ain't buying it. So, with that in mind, let's consider the programs available to the business owner that resolve common issues and are not so complex that you will need to hire an information technology specialist in order to run them.

Printing Checks and Other Documents

Until recently most businesses and individuals could not print their own checks because those wacky looking numbers on the bottom were printed with magnetic ink.

Now, the systems use optical scanners so the composition of the ink makes little difference. Companies such as Versacheck provide the software and the blank checks for printing.

This program is simple to use. It requests your name and address, the name and address of the bank and the numbers printed on the bottom of the check. Then it asks for a file name so that the information is saved as a file. This comes in handy when you or your business uses multiple accounts. And then you print the information onto pre-designed blank templates. Also, Versacheck is compatible with *Quicken* and with Microsoft's *Money*, the two most widely used personal finance programs.

Accounting

The best selling accounting software is the *Quicken* series released by Intuit. *Quicken* makes programs from the simple check register to the complex business proposals and bid estimating for potential jobs. If you are not operating a business that requires forecasting and estimating, then the middle-end program, *Quicken Home & Business* probably is your best buy.

Home & Business provides a check register where you enter deposits and withdrawals or transfers just as you would in a checkbook register. It allows you to write checks by filling out a template that looks like a check and then by printing that information on the Versacheck templates. Voila! Instant checks suitable for bill paying.

QuickBooks, from the makers of *Quicken*, is a more complex accounting program. Many community colleges offer courses to learn how to use *QuickBooks* and other widely used business software programs. It is probably also the bestselling program for a more complicated and involved businesses.

Some love *QuickBooks*—and others hate it—for its ease of manipulation. The advantages of Quickbooks are its ability to forecast, to create proposals and estimates, and to change data previously entered. Adjustments on the ledger, for example, are easy to make, so unlike other programs, your profit and loss statements can be changed around, much to your accountant's dismay!

The boxes containing the *Quicken* programs provide a comparison of the differences between each. *Quicken* is like a Chevrolet, whereas *Quickbooks* is a Cadillac—same basic platform but with a number of additions and variations. There is no point in purchasing the Porsche just to drive to the supermarket; likewise, you don't need to buy more software than you need.

But don't forget to consider growth. If cost estimation or competitive bidding is in your future, get the program that will meet those needs.

Computer-based Legal Forms

Intuit, the company that makes *Quicken*, also makes a program called *Family Lawyer*. The program contains forms routinely used by individuals and families. These forms include simple wills, dispute letters and some basic agreements. If *Family Lawyer* doesn't fulfill your latent Perry Mason tendencies, then *Business Lawyer* will. It contains employment agreements, articles of incorporation, powers of attorney, bills of sale and other documents routinely used by business.

 Both *Family Lawyer* and *Business Lawyer* are full of disclaimers about not giving legal advice. And they don't. They're just collections of standard legal forms. If you're at all uncertain about how to use a form...or any language in it...call your real lawyer for a few minutes and discuss the matter.

After the Intuit products, the most well-known legal forms packages come from Nolo Press. Nolo was started and is run by lawyers, so its material tends to be more technically precise and—in some cases—a little less easy to use. But its forms are usually thorough and well-explained.

Nolo Press also has a particularly good Web site (www.nolo.com). If you're interested in legal forms for your computer, that site is often a good place to start.

E-Commerce

There is an old adage: *Your output is dependent on your input.* Or *garbage in, garbage out.* Or, *if you lie down with dogs, you get up with fleas.* But enough of the platitudes. So far, few companies are making a profit selling their wares via the Internet. And those that do fill a niche or an area where a traditional marketplace does not exist.

For example, the most successful Internet company is E-Bay. Unless you have no knowledge of the computers or the Internet and believe World War II is not yet over, you know that E-Bay provides a platform for owners of almost everything—including, literally, the Pet Rock—to sell their items to others, auction style. The company makes money by charging a fee for the use of its service.

The Elements of Small Business

With hundreds of thousands of items listed for sale, E-Bay collects a lot of fees.

If you want to win a bet with friends, just bet them that you can find used socks up for auction on E-Bay. I won $10 doing this. There were more than eighty pairs listed. And most had bids of more than one dollar.

 Some small companies decide it's faster, easier and cheaper to list their products for sale on E-Bay than develop their own Web sites. Others market on E-Bay in addition to setting up their own sites. Generally, selling on E-Bay works well if you have one-of-a-kind items to sell. If you mass-produce things, it's not as effective a channel.

Another well-known on-line commerce company is amazon.com. This company began as a seller of books and then quickly moved to compact discs, DVDs and other entertainment products. It now sells an assortment of consumer items in many categories.

Despite its popularity and high revenue, amazon.com has lacked profitability. Simply put, it receives less money than it pays out every year; and some on-line business experts say that amazon.com's most profitable activity is charging publishers and record companies for preferred placement on its site.

If your business model consists of Internet sales as a primary or sole source of the company's revenues, you may want to rethink your model. But that does not mean that the Internet has little value even if your business plans do not include sales of goods. The Internet can take the place of expensive brochures by informing customers about your products or services. And it can be used to create a database or list of customers.

When you are conducting a sale, you can send an e-mail to those customers. Imagine being able to reach hundreds or even thousands of potential buyers without the cost of U.S Mail.

Building Your Own Web Site

After years of unofficial sites carrying the load, a well-known rock band launched an official Web site. The site included a forum for its fans and a store for merchandise. In order to use the forum, a user had to sign up. Great idea. That way, the band and its management would have a database of core fans. That would come in handy when offering discounts on merchandise or holiday specials or even on publicity of upcoming concert events. When a new CD was released, one fan told management that it should let the fans know about any radio stations receiving the new CD so that the fans could e-mail or call the station to request that songs from the CD be played.

One problem: Neither the band nor its management understood the Internet or how to use it. There were no discount sales on merchandise; there were no holiday gift ideas; there were no discounted tickets. In fact, the fans who signed up received absolutely nothing for their troubles. So, the band lost out on tens of thousands of dollars, maybe more than $100,000. Sometimes you can't teach an old dog new tricks.

Still, if you're in business, you probably need a Web site. If nothing else, it's an inexpensive brochure and a place for employees to received email; and, in some markets, you will seem out of touch if you *don't* have a site.

The first thing you will need is a *domain name*. Internet sites are designated by an address known as a universal record locator or URL. This address is actually a series of numbers. But who can remember those? So, you can link your URL to a catchy name—called, less formally, an Internet address. For example, Cable News Network has the address www.cnn.com. When the address is entered on an Internet browser, your computer searches for code numbers connected to the address. And voila! Up pops a list of Larry King's guests for that night.

Because of the sheer number of businesses with Web sites, your first choice in names may not be available. You can check name availability and actually obtain a URL at Network Solutions, the best-known of several firms that specialize in issuing domain names.

In fact, (as if this were a surprise) the easiest way to secure the name of your choice is to log onto www.NetworkSolutions.com and follow the instructions.

You may have heard of or seen Internet addresses ending in ".com" or ".net" or ".org" or ".edu" or others. Originally, these designations were created to inform the Internet user about the type of business with which he or she was viewing. The ".com" designation indicated a commercial for profit business or information site. The ".net" designation generally referred to a business directly involved in the Internet. For example, several portals (Internet service providers)—such as Earthlink—use this extension.

The ".org" designation usually was and is held by nonprofit groups (ORGanizations). Finally, the "edu" designation is used by schools or universities (EDUcation).

Since these designations were created, many countries have created and reserved their own extensions. The most popular is ".tv" since television stations can use it instead of ".com."

Hosts and Servers

Once you have picked an address and designed a few pages that explain your business, you need to load everything onto a server. A *server* is a computer that provides for a direct connection to the web. As we've discussed, the name of the site you type in the box is really a number sequence. When you attempt to view a Web site, your computer is searching for a match of code numbers. This also works in reverse. When you have a Web site, customers need to find it when they type in the name of the business. This occurs through a computer linked directly to the Internet—the server.

The *host* refers to the company that owns the server. While anyone can have their own server, this can be expensive to build and maintain. *Fortune* 500 companies usually have their own servers. Small businesses usually pay a monthly fee to let some other entity do this for them.

The cost of renting the host's space varies and mostly depends on the amount of computer space you need. If your site consists of a few pages of information or even a method by which customers can order product, then the costs likely will not run more than $30 to $50 a month.

Costs can vary between hosts companies. And so can the quality of service. This is yet another opportunity to ask friends and your web designer for referrals. You will want to know if the server has ever "crashed" or "gone down." Simply, has the server been broken before and how long did it take for the company to fix. Also, you will want to know whether a technician is available twenty-four hours each day to resolve any problem. Can you call the technician? Can you call anyone in the event of a problem?

While describing all of the qualifications to look for in a host company is easy, finding a good designer and webmaster can be far more challenging. Unfortunately, the yellow pages are not the most helpful for finding a good webmaster. Once again, if you have friends with sites, ask them for recommendations.

If that does not help, search the web for companies similar to your business. Often, the webmaster will have his or her contact information on the bottom of the "homepage" or the first page that comes up when you enter the site address. If they are good for your competitors, they are good for you.

Conclusion

Computers are an integral part of business. E-commerce and technological dependence provide for more and more businesses basing computers around their everyday operation. Computers provide better organization of the office and daily business activities to networking throughout the world and marketing products and services. Familiarize yourself with the types of computer systems and software packages available to you in the marketplace. Your business in return will most likely become more efficient and productive in today's competitive market.

References

Fulton, Jennifer, et al. *Learning Office 2000*. DDC Publishing (July, 1999).

Ketchum, Bradford W. (editor). *Tips and Tactics for Using the Internet to Run Your Business*. Business Resources (February, 2001).

Nelson, Stephen L. *Quicken 2002: Using Quicken in Business*. Redmond Technology Press (January, 2002).

Reynolds, Janice, and Roya Mofazali. *The Complete E-Commerce Book: Design, Build, and Maintain a Successful Web-Based Business*. CMP Books (October, 2000).

Xiradis-Aberle, Lori, and Carig L. Aberle. *How to Computerize Your Business* (revised edition). John Wiley & Sons, Inc. (June, 1995).

The Elements of Small Business

Chapter 14

Employees and Contractors

I think that maybe in every company today there is always at least one person who is going crazy slowly.

—Joseph Heller

You have the corporation and the location and the computer system with software and the copier. Now you need someone to operate all of it.

The toughest thing you may ever do is go through the process of hiring (and firing) employees. That is because there are many rules and regulations, questions you can ask and can't ask, acceptable conduct and unacceptable conduct, and responsibilities for the conduct of the employees toward each other. So let's get started.

The Hiring Process

Most businesses require employees. Obviously, everyone wants to hire workers qualified to do the job. While placing a *Help Wanted* sign in the window may attract attention and maybe even a few applicants, it is not likely a sign will bring in all of the qualified personnel necessary especially if your business requires certain special skills.

Finding qualified people can be time consuming. But you will soon discover that the costs of firing an employee, searching for a replacement, interviewing potential candidates and hiring a new person with the right training are significant—and draining of time and money.

The Search

In addition to advertising in the window of your business (unless you are located on the twelfth floor) and in the newspaper, you might consider occupational colleges. For example, if you are an attorney and you need a secretary who knows something about law, you could post an ad with a vocational college that provides paralegal or legal secretary training. Or you can post an ad in relevant trade magazines. If you need a welder, try a magazine or periodical about construction.

In the 2000s, the Internet has emerged as a location from which employers and potential employees can hook up. There are a number of sites where those searching for jobs can post their resumes and where employers can review them.

On the corporate end, there are popular Web sites like www.monster.com and www.careerbuilder.com; on the creative end, www.craigslist.com is among the most popular.

There's a fee for posting a job on these sites (usually under $100); but that's cheap, when you consider that the services of an executive recruiter often cost one to three months of the employee's starting salary.

If the position is a skilled position, resumes should be requested in advance of any scheduled interviews. Generally, most job applicants will have a resume that provides you with their education and experience. You should review the resumes and choose to interview personally those individuals who meet your needs. During the interview, you will want to question the candidates about their past experiences and their relationship with other employees and bosses. You have a right to call previous employers and inquire as to the candidates' past job performance.

> If a job candidate previously worked for a large business, the response likely will be nondescript and relegated simply to "yes we employed Mr. Smith" and "these were the dates of his employment...."

The terse responses are a result of former employees filing defamation lawsuits after the statements of former employers resulted in a rejection from a potential employer. On the other hand, a ringing endorsement should be taken as a positive sign.

When I graduated from law school, traditional law-firm jobs were hard to find. One classmate found a temporary job with a local firm. After a few months, my classmate discovered that some of the activities of the partners were not up to ordinary ethical standards. Without too much fuss, he found a way to exit gracefully. Then he applied for new jobs with several firms.

Of course, those firms wanted to contact his previous employer. While my classmate did not know whether the potential employers were calling his former bosses, he did realize that no one was hiring him. So he asked me to call the old bosses and pretend to be a potential employer. I called. The old bosses were saying bad things about this former employee. There was a sickened silence on the other end of the phone when I described the lawsuit their firm was about to receive.

Each state has established guidelines as to what potential employers are entitled to know and what cannot be asked. Often, these rules are convoluted and difficult to enforce. But, in the abstract, the rules are quite simple and are designed to avoid any invasion of privacy or any collection of private information that might be used to disqualify wrongfully a potential employee.

The Elements of Small Business

> For example, as a prospective employer, you can ask whether there are any circumstances under which a candidate might not be able to work a full 40-hour week. But you cannot ask whether the candidate has children that have to be picked up occasionally before 5:00 p.m.

An employer cannot ask about sexual orientation and cannot ask about religious affiliation unless there is a direct relationship to the job. For example, if the position requires the candidate to work on Saturdays, asking whether his or her religion might prevent him or her from working on Saturdays might be appropriate. However, the better question would be, "Is there anything that would prevent you from working here on Saturdays?"

Also, employers can order a drug test and can test employees before or after they have been hired. Even lie detectors can be used regarding any statements made the candidate during the interview process or placed on the resume. Of course, this might scare away potential employees, not because they take drugs or lie, but simply because the perceived restrictive work environment may not be viewed as a pleasant place to be. And it probably isn't.

One of my clients applied for a job as a receptionist at a plumbing conglomerate. The company required a urine specimen and a lie detector test. Another client applied for a position as a computer software programmer. He had to provide hair samples for drug testing. Since the potential employer informed my client of the test several days in advance, my client spent a lot of hours combing the Internet for hair treatment products that would remove any trace of drugs. Whatever he found must have worked because he got the job.

Asking questions of job applicants is a little like selecting a jury. You have very little time to assess the pros and cons, strengths and weaknesses. A little known trick—er, I mean *question*—we lawyers ask potential jurors is to state the magazines and newspapers they read regularly. If they get *Newsweek*, then it's likely they are slightly liberal and a "progressive" thinker. With *U.S. News and World Report* or *The Wall Street Journal*, then they probably have a college degree and lean toward traditional family values. If they read *InStyle* and *Us*, then…well, then the job had better involve clerical work.

You get the picture. There is no law that prohibits asking about magazines and periodicals. On the other hand, certain questions may yield little data. A few years ago, Jay Leno stood on the grass just below one end of the podium as college graduates received their degrees. As the first walked by, he stopped her and asked, "How many moons does the Earth have?"

"I don't know, I didn't take Astronomy," was the shocking reply.

Then her friend, also a new graduate, walked over. Again, "How many moons does the Earth have?"

Without missing a beat: "Three," she insisted.

So much for the college degree.

 An attorney friend usually asks a series of questions during the interview. But only one question is pivotal. If the applicant fails this one question, he or she does not get the job: "What is seven times eight?" Ninety percent of the applicants either answer incorrectly or do nothing other than explain that they have lousy math skills——apparently regarding concepts known to most second graders.

Even if the job candidate seems to pass the interview, make sure they fill out an application form that requests information about past jobs, education and experience. [From 14-1]

While you may not need to refer to this document during the interview, it can be of great advantage if the employee is ever terminated and considers suing you or your company. That is because there is a growing trend throughout the states that, if the employee lied on the application, they lose all rights to sue except for discrimination-related issues.

Employee Leasing

Chances are that to date the only thing you have ever leased is your car and maybe—if you'd never read my Chapter 11—a copy machine or two. Well, you can lease employees too.

Small businesses often have difficulties attracting employees because they cannot offer the same benefits that larger companies can offer—benefits such as health care, dental care, vision care, life insurance, disability, retirement plans, etc. Also, in certain states, such as California, workers' compensation insurance for a small business with five or six employees might charge more money than an employer can afford.

One solution to these problem is employee leasing. In this scenario, workers that you would hire are actually hired by another company that does nothing other than hire employees who work for other businesses. This is not a "temp agency"—but it's similar in some critical ways.

> Leased workers work for you full-time and permanently, under a contract between your company and the leasing agency. But, because they're actually employed leasing agency, the agency's purchasing power for benefits and insurance reduces your costs and gives you access to the benefits necessary to attract a qualified workforce.

The leasing experience also solves the issue of complying with federal and state laws. For example:

- For companies with 15 or more employees, the Civil Rights Act prohibits employment discrimination based on race, color, religion, sex, or national origin and the Americans with Disabilities Act prohibits employment discrimination against qualified individuals with disabilities.

- For companies with 20 or more employees, the Age Discrimination Act prevents job termination of workers who are 40 years of age or older.

- For companies with 50 or more employees, the Family and Medical Leave Act requires the employer to provide job security and unpaid leave for those who have family health emergencies.

- For companies with 100 or more employees, the Worker Adjustment and Retraining Notification Act requires you to provide notice to employees 60 days in advance of covered plant closings and layoffs.

Some states have even more stringent requirements. With the lease, these issues cease to be your problem.

Now, this doesn't mean you can sexually harass an employee. You can't. And if you do, suit will be filed and a judgment likely. But you do not have to concern yourself with compliance of so many rules and regulations. Rather, the leasing agency does that for you.

> **The U.S. Department of Labor projects that by the year 2020, more than half the employees in the United States will be working through some form of leasing agency.**

Advantages of Employee Leasing

1. It saves money. You can probably get a better rate on workers' compensation through a leasing agency because the policies they offer and their know-how about the policies are not available to you. Leasing agencies tend to handle claims efficiently and know how to root out fraudulent claims that can end up costing big bucks. Savings gained through risk management alone can offset the fees paid to the leasing agency.

2. Business focus. As a business owner, you want to focus your time and energy on the "business of your business" and not the "business of employment." Using a leasing agency allows you to concentrate on your business.

3. Human Resources expertise. Most business owners don't have the necessary human resource training, payroll and accounting skills, knowledge of regulatory compliance, or background in risk management, insurance and employee benefit programs to meet the demands of being a good employer. That is one of the greatest resources you gain when you use a leasing agency.

4. Legal advice. A leasing agency can help with guidance concerning terminations, as well as any obligations to comply with employment and workplace laws and regulations that seem to change every year.

5. Paperwork. Background checks and other hiring services are usually done through the leasing agency, which saves time, expense, and trouble.

6. Better benefits. You can secure all your employee benefits at the same time, from general health insurance to dental coverage and retirement plans. You can save a great deal when purchasing these for you employees, or you can make them available to your employees without you paying for them.

7. Taxes. Once you have signed on with a leasing company, there's no longer any need to collect, process, and forward your workers' FICA, SUTA or FUTA payments. The agency is responsible for all of these.

8. Hiring decisions. When you want to hire a new employee, you can rely on the advice of the agency about your hiring decision. Because the agency will be the employer of the record, it would make certain you are hiring the right employee.

I have several clients who swear by this method of employment. The Internet is a good tool to learn more about these companies; also, it is likely your accountant will have clients using these agencies. So before you hire, check with your accountant to determine if employee leasing has benefits for your business.

Executive Search Firms

If you are hiring a waitress or a busboy, you risk less by doing it yourself. If your business needs management-level employees, you might consider the services of an executive search firm.

These businesses represent skilled personnel looking for new employment or a change of employment from their current job. The advantage is that a reputable firm will have screened the potential employee and will provide only those who meet the qualifications you set.

 The disadvantage is the cost. You usually have to pay the search firm a fee equal to a percentage—often a third—of the employee's first year salary.

Posting the Rules

Once you've hired your employees, the real fun begins.

Most states require that employment rules and regulations, such as minimum wage, withholding, workers' compensation rules and disability benefits be posted in plain sight of employees. If you have a break room or dressing room, those are good spots to post the legal disclosures.

In addition to government rules, you need to articulate your own rules for employment. The best way to do this is to assemble your company's workplace policies in a employment handbook that is given to every new employee on his or her first day.

A good employment handbook should state, as clearly as possible:

• normal business hours and the hours employees are expected to work;

• dress and grooming codes for various positions;

• standard break and meal periods;

- expected late and sick notices, if an employee is either;

- vacation and sick day allowances and rules for use;

- standard review cycles and periods;

- the company's definition of and any requirements related to professionalism and professional behavior;

- the company's policy toward alcohol or drug use on the premises and in the course of employment off-premises;

- the company's policy—zero-tolerance is best—toward illegal racial, gender, age, disability or other discrimination (including harassment);

- reporting and/or complaint policies which employees can follow if they witness or experience any illegal discrimination;

- the company's policy on receiving tips, gratuities or gifts from clients or customers.

This is by no means a complete list of what your employment manual should include. But it will give you an idea of the sorts of things that you need to establish with employees from the start.

The actual form of the handbook can be anything from a leather-bound folio to three sheets of paper stapled together. The key point is that it's written in clear language and everyone reads it.

The value of the handbook does not rest in the ability to send an employee home for wearing Bermuda shorts. Rather, it provides cover for the employer.

For example, many states do not permit recovery for sexual harassment claims from the employer if the employer did not know about the allegations. If the company offered a procedure for reporting a problem and an employee fails to do so, it will reflect poorly on any complaint the employee makes later.

In fact, for certain causes of action to be viable, the employee either has to report the situation to a superior or the superior had to have known the situation was occurring.

A number of resources are available for the creation of a handbook. Check out software at your local office supply store. Also, your attorney may have a template for the handbook and can make simple changes or additions to meet your specific needs.

It's a good idea to include with the employment manual a page which states that the employee has read and understands the contents of the manual. Have every employee sign and date this page within a few days of accepting the job. Keep the signed statement in his or her employment file.

If you have a employment manual, make sure that every new hire—without exception—reads it and signs the statement that he or she has. When it comes to employment matters, consistency is essential.

Employment Contracts

Should you offer an employment contract? If so, on what conditions? For how long?

There is seldom a right or wrong answer to any of these questions. If your type of business has a high rate of employee turnover, especially employees moving laterally (same job, different company), then locking a good hire in with a contract may be a good idea.

However, if you are operating an ice cream parlor where skilled labor consists of washing the scooper before re-use, then contracts would be a waste of time.

> Most employees in the United States do not work under a written contract. When no contract is involved, the employee is considered terminable *at will*—which means he or she can be fired for no particular reason (unless the firing occurs as a result of discrimination or similar violation of some public policy). When possible, this at will status is a good thing for an employer to keep.

On the other hand, a contract locks in the employee for the term specified in the document. It specifies the duties of the employee and the compensation to be paid by the employer. It also provides a basis for termination with cause (good reason) or without cause, including whether severance pay will be provided. [Form 14-2]

A well known company hired one of my clients as a middle-level manager. The company gave her a five-year contract. She could be fired either for cause (such as failing to show up at work or committing illegal activities) or without cause. If she were fired for cause, then she would be owed nothing. If she were terminated without cause, she would continue to receive her salary and benefits for the remainder of the contract term.

Fair enough.

About two years into the five-year term, the company chose to downsize. My client's employment was terminated. Since the termination was without cause, the company had to keep paying her salary.

This was a strange decision. Rather than reassigning my client or finding special projects for her to tackle, the company terminated her with the requirement of paying her for three years...of nothing. The company's stock price had been depressed for several years (part of the reason for the layoffs). Any wonder?

Employee Retention

How do you keep the good employees from leaving? And what makes them want to leave? Employers, executive search firms, psychologists and sociologists disagree. While intuitive logic suggests that everything is about money and that periodic raises equal higher retention, the statistics prove otherwise.

Recently, a major recruiting firm—Mercer Human Resource Consulting—conducted a survey on employee retention. Mercer reviewed data from large corporations over a 10-year period. The survey concluded that employees moved on when they felt that their supervisors were not listening to them or when they felt that their supervisors were not treating them fairly or were not appreciated for their efforts.

Providing raises made little difference.

The survey also found that the higher a company's retention rate, the higher its productivity. In other words, the more turnover, the less profits. So, whatever it takes to keep employees at your company, do it.

Spying on Your Employees

The fact is few rules exist about when, where and how you can run surveillance on your employees.

Most states do not prohibit video surveillance in the office. However, many states do not permit audio surveillance. The states do not prohibit reviewing e-mail or e-mail accounts of employees.

Don't assume that years of watching police dramas on television have taught you anything about spying on your employees. The constitutional limits that apply to police searches don't apply to private employers. But hold on, Big Brother: Federal and local privacy statutes sometimes do.

The United States Supreme Court and most state courts have held that, where a reasonable expectation of privacy exists, employers or business owners cannot spy. Obviously this leaves a lot of gray areas. Before you engage in undercover action or allow others to do it for you, check with your attorney for the status of current laws in your state.

Payroll and Payment for Services

If you have employees, you have payroll taxes.

So, you've been operating your business for awhile and you realize that those payroll taxes are taking a big bite out of your profits. You decide to make everyone an independent contractor to lessen your tax burden. Bad idea.

If you incorrectly categorize those working for you, the Internal Revenue Service and your state taxing authorities will be happy to explain the rules as they charge you for the unpaid payroll taxes plus interest and penalties. Also, your "independent contractors" may sue you for the benefits such as unemployment compensation or disability that they should have received and would have received had they been classified properly.

The Internal Revenue Service and many state taxing authorities have created rules with respect to classifying those providing services to you or your company. Note that these rules are not always in sync. For example, while a worker may qualify as an independent contractor under the IRS guidelines, the worker may not qualify for such status under the state law.

To make things even more confusing, the IRS has a "safe harbor" statute that provides for the classification of a worker as an independent contractor even when the requirements are not met if the type of business you own commonly and traditionally classifies the workers as independent contractors. But states are not required to follow the rules of the IRS and often do not do so.

Also: Just because the IRS classifies a worker as an independent contractor or allows for an exception, the state in which you reside does not *have* to recognize the exemption. In California, real estate sales people do not qualify as independent contractors under the IRS test or the California State Franchise Tax Board rules. However, an exception has been created by the state and is recognized by the IRS. So, real estate sales people—who receive commission for each property they sell—are considered independent contractors. But this exception is an exception to the rule.

The Test

The following IRS guidelines provide the test for employment status:

a. Does the worker only work for one company?

b. Does the worker have the autonomy to come and go as he or she pleases?

c. Is the worker able to complete the task in any manner he or she sees fit or are the guidelines set by the company?

d. Is the worker paid by the hour or by the task?

e. Can the worker do some or all of the work at a location of the worker's choosing?

f. Is the job one that traditionally has been considered that of an independent contractor?

> As with the real estate agents in California, some states recognize independent contractor status where the guidelines would otherwise not support it. But this is an exception, not a rule. So don't count on an exception to save you. More importantly, it makes no difference if the employee wants to be classified as an independent contractor.

In the infamous case of *Borello & Sons*, the California Supreme Court was asked to examine the following situation: Borello was a produce grower in California's Central Valley. One of its fields was used to grow cucumbers for a pickle company. The contract with the pickle company permitted the pickle company to purchase or not purchase the cucumbers as it saw fit. As a result, one year Borello chose not to grow cucumbers or anything else on the land.

The soon-to-be-out-of-work employees visited Borello's upper management. They had a proposition: They would be given full control of the field for the purposes of growing cucumbers. They would plant, water, grow and harvest the cucumbers. They would use their own tools. If the pickle company purchased the cucumbers, then the profits would be split; if not, then Borello would not have lost a dime. Borello agreed.

The Worker's Compensation Board audited Borello and discovered this special arrangement. To the chagrin of the workers and the company, the Board claimed that the situation should have been classified as employee-employer and not independent contractor. Ultimately, the California Supreme Court agreed with the Board.

Changing the status of workers from employees to independent contractors is never a good idea.

A more recent example: One of my clients owned a gentleman's club. The bartenders, disc jockeys, security personnel and management were paid as employees. The dancers were not. They were contractors, paid a percentage on each private dance and all tips when they danced on stage.

Because they're in a cash business, most of the dancers never filed a tax return. However, the average dancer in my client's club was making more than $50,000 per year, an amount well above minimum wage. One testified that she routinely pocketed more than $17,500 per month. (Don't reach for your calculator: That's $210,000 year…more than most lawyers, doctors or publishers make.)

All this money didn't stop the dancers from filing a class action lawsuit against more than 10 clubs—including my client's—to recover the minimum wage they supposedly did not receive.

A few points of interest here.

1) Several years before the suit, the dancers had been paid wages by my client with all appropriate taxes withheld. But, when other clubs changed to paying a percentage of private dances (and, thus, eliminating *any* taxable income), the dancers told my client that if he didn't follow the practice they'd go to other clubs.

2) "Employees" cannot chose their designation and any agreement between the worker and the company that the worker is an independent contractor does not stop a reclassification from the IRS or from your state's taxing authority.

3) The penalties in most states are not just the taxes. They can include fines and penalties for failing to pay proper payroll taxes and for failing to have workers' compensation insurance.

By the way, my client settled the case just before declaring bankruptcy and avoiding *payment* of the settlement.

Keeping the Record Clean

If a worker is an employee, at the start of the employment you will provide the worker with a W-4 form. [Form 14-3] This short form requires the worker's legal name, address, and social security number. It also requires the worker to include the number of "dependents" or those people the worker supports financially such as a spouse or children. The higher the number, the lower the taxes removed from each paycheck since the worker will have more deductions from his or her taxes.

Every paycheck to an employee will contain a check for the net sum being paid along with a stub containing itemized information about each deduction taken by the employer. Often, the stub will also contain the total amount taken year to date for each category. On or before January 31 of the following year, you will be required to provide to your employees a W-2 statement. [Form 14-4] This statement contains the gross total of monies paid and the gross totals of the monies removed for taxes.

For independent contractors, a simple check will suffice as no monies are deducted. You will need to obtain their tax identification number, either a Social Security number or another identification number obtained from the IRS, if you intend to deduct from your gross receipts the amount you paid the independent contractor. [Form 14-5]

On or before last day of February—unless your accountant files electronically, in which case you have until the end of March—IRS form 1099s for all contractors from the previous year must be filed and a copy sent to the contractor. [Form 14-6] That statement provides the total sum paid to the contractor. The contractor is then responsible for his or her own taxes. If the contractor is an individual, he or she will place the gross sum and any relevant deductions on a Schedule C attached to the 1040 form.

Remember, monies paid to employees or independent contractors are tax deductible to the employer. When you file the tax return on behalf of the business, the sums paid including the taxes are subtracted from the total income generated by the business.

Employee Grievances

At some point in the life of your business, you can expect grievances. Sometimes complaints are minor, such as a request to change an uncomfortable chair; but the complaint may be very serious, such as an employee complaining that his or her immediate supervisor is sexually harassing (don't snicker at that *his*—sexual harassment complaints by men are a booming business for labor lawyers) or that the supervisor of the widget manufacturing unit is allowing defective widgets to be shipped.

If the complaint is serious, you need to take it seriously. The easiest way to ensure an employee lawsuit is to dismiss a complaint or act in such a nonchalant manner that the employee believes you don't care about the problem and you have no intention of investigating or resolving the matter.

As I mentioned earlier, a good employment handbook goes a long way to providing a procedure both for the employee and for the employer to investigate and adjudicate the dispute. In smaller companies, you might consider retaining the services of an outside ombudsman who arbitrates or mediates the dispute.

One problem arises when one employee accuses another of wrong-doing—especially sexual harassment—but has no witnesses to support the claim. In that event, it would be difficult to fire the accused but also difficult to reject the concerns of the accuser. The best anyone can hope for is that the parties can be separated so that their contact is limited.

Tip: Bad people do not all of sudden act in a bad manner. Harassers harass. For example, if a female employee complains that she is being harassed by a male counterpart, you will want to question other female employees who work with the male employee. If their experiences are markedly different than those of the accuser, there is a chance that either the accuser is exaggerating the behavior (either intentionally or unintentionally) or she has an axe to grind with the accused. On the other hand, if other have had the same experience as the accuser, time to call the lawyer.

Termination

There is nothing easy about terminating an employee. First, if the termination is for cause, make sure that you have documented in writing the incident(s) that provide the grounds for the termination. Second, if possible, the employee should be given the opportunity to correct his or her behavior before termination. Third, when terminating an employee, have at least one other person in the office during the conversation. In the event a wrongful termination lawsuit is filed, at least you will have a witness to the issues raised and discussed in the fateful meeting.

In the absence of a contract, employees are terminable at will. If you have reason to believe an employee will be a problem, provide some severance pay in exchange for a waiver of any rights to sue the company.

The Elements of Small Business

And by the way, put all that in writing with the help of a lawyer. You will save tens of thousands in lawsuit prevention. Also, while most employees will not sue, the few dollars needed to provide a severance in exchange for a waiver of any rights to sue the company can be quite cheap.

> Many states have reduced the risk of wrongful termination by placing it under the rubric of contract law and not under personal injury (tort) law. The result: Pain and suffering or "general" damages are not available. Instead, the former employee can be awarded lost wages less any monies that he or she would have made had they mitigated their damages by finding another job. This is a good thing for businesses.
> However, if the termination was conducted in violation of "public policy," such as illegal discrimination or a refusal of the employee to engage in an unlawful activity, additional damages and potentially punitive damages can apply. That is why making a record of the employee's performance and placing any warnings in writing is so important.

If you plan to fire an employee or if you are interviewing an employee as a result of a grievance, it is a good idea to have a witness present or to audiotape the interview. Note: if you audiotape or videotape an employee, make sure that they state clearly their permission for you to do so as some states have prohibitions against taping without permission.

Tip: Termination does not come solely from firing an employee. Most states recognize "constructive termination" as a situation where the workplace becomes so intolerable that any reasonable person could not and would not continue to subject him or herself to the nefarious condition. In that sense it is similar to a constructive termination of a lease agreement where the landlord creates an environment where the business can no longer operate— such as failing to repair the air conditioner during summertime.

Several years ago a friend called me. He had been terminated from his job working in a bank and wanted to know if...there was anything I could do. When I asked him what the reason was for the termination, he explained that he had been late for work on a few occasions. I asked whether he had received written or verbal warnings. The bank had provided warnings orally and had him sign the written confirmation. That confirmation was placed in my friend's employment file.

It turned out that my friend had been late more than 50 percent of the time and had received three warnings over twelve months before the bank finally let him go. No wrongful termination suit there.

Tip: Many state courts have held that a former employee who sues for wrongful termination can have the suit dismissed if the employer/defendant discovers that any part of the employee's resume was false or that the employee lied or mislead the employer at the time of the interview. This rule applies even if the lie had nothing to do with the termination. So take copious notes at the time of the interview and save the employee's resume.

Conclusion

It only takes one rotten employee to kill a small business; so, don't take the hiring process lightly. Make your interview questions count and do your homework. And, above all, interview more than one person for the job.

There is no magic formula for hiring the best employee or asking the right questions that get you there. Asking about previous employment and verifying that the employee's resume is accurate are a good start. Referrals also help. If the potential employee worked for a company you know and respect then that may increase the chances for success.

References

Adams, Bob, and Peter Veruki. *Streetwise Hiring Top Performers: 600 Ready-To-Ask Interview Questions and Everything Else You Need to Hire Right*. Adams Media (March, 1997).

Fein, Richard. *101 Hiring Mistakes Employers Make...and How to Avoid Them*. Impact Publications (February, 2000).

Fishman, Stephen. *Consultant & Independent Contractor Agreements* (3rd edition). Nolo Press (December, 2002).

Fishman, Stephen. *Hiring Independent Contractors: The Employers' Legal Guide* (4th edition). Nolo Press (June, 2003).

Inland Management Services. *Successful Hiring: A Practical Guide to Interviewing & Selecting Employees*. Inland Management Services (June, 1997).

Klinvex, Kevin, et al. *Hiring Great People*. McGraw-Hill Trade (October, 1998).

Quinn, Carol. *Don't Hire Anyone Without Me!: A Revolutionary Approach to Interviewing & Hiring the Best*. Career Press (December, 2001).

Walsh, James. *Rightful Termination* (2nd edition). Silver Lake Publishing (August, 1998).

Chapter 15

Lawsuits and Lawyers

If you think that you can think about a thing, inextricably attached to something else, without thinking of the thing it is attached to, then you have a legal mind.

—Thomas Reed Powell

Speaking of soap operas, George Carlin points out—that regardless of that title—doctors and hospitals always show up. The soap doesn't have to be about doctors. But just wait; they'll appear.

In business, lawyers will appear. Whether you are entering into a contract or suing for failure to pay an invoice, you will have a lawyer, they will have a lawyer and even the lawyers likely will have lawyers.

The statistical data suggests that your business has a one in three chance of being sued at any given time. In reality, despite the claims of Dan Quayle, the United States has only 13 percent of the world's lawyers. However, 90 percent of the lawsuits involve business disputes, not fender benders or other personal injuries. Simply, it is a fact of life that parties breach contracts—sometimes with reason and often without.

In this chapter, we'll explore those heinous possibilities along with ways to protect yourself.

The first point: Don't count on courts for *justice*. It's estimated that, in the Los Angeles County civil court system, each judge has approximately 10,000 cases assigned to him or her at any one time. That means the judge knows little about you, little about your opponent and little about your dispute. Judges don't have time to care.

So, an ounce of prevention is essential.

Causes of Action

At the formation of this country's legal system, two types of courts heard civil disputes: Courts of law and courts of equity. Courts of law concerned themselves with disputes under common law—issues that had grown out of cases and situations. Such issues included breaches of contract, fraud and negligence.

> Courts of equity were concerned with fairness and therefore were less structured. Also, courts of equity solved problems where actions in law were not available. Typical equity actions include promissory estoppel (a/k/a *detrimental reliance*), *quantum meruit* (the value of services provided) and unjust enrichment (the resulting value of the services conferred on the receiving party who hasn't bothered to pay for the services).

For example, if two parties enter into a written agreement, then chances are that, when one party fails to perform, the other will sue in a court of law for breach of contract.

But what if there were no written contract when you painted your neighbor's house? Your neighbor said he would pay you $100 if you did. You never said "yes." He leaves for a week-long vacation and while he's gone you paint and paint and paint. He returns to a freshly painted house. You go to collect your money only to hear, "Hey I was just kidding and you never said yes to the offer."

Since no contract existed between the parties, no remedy would have been available in a court of law. In a court of equity, the judge would recognize that a benefit had been bestowed on your neighbor. If you showed that your reliance on your neighbor's words was reasonable, the judge might enter judgment for the value of the services or the benefit bestowed.

It is worth noting that courts of equity did not have juries. During the later half of the 19th Century, the two courts merged so that remedies in law and equity were heard before the same court. However, even to this day, causes of action in equity are not decided by juries, only judges.

Retainer Agreements

In every state, lawyers are required to provide a written agreement to clients regarding the scope and terms of any legal representation. Though each state has its own requirements, the agreement should set forth the names of the client and attorney and the matter in which the attorney will be representing you. Then it should provide for the "retainer"—the initial payment and then the hourly rate.

If other attorneys or paralegals will be involved, it should provide for their hourly fees. And it should describe other charges, such as photocopies, faxes and postage. Finally, it should provide for remedies such as lawsuit or arbitration in the event of a dispute between you and your lawyer. Some states require attorneys to state whether they have malpractice insurance and, if so, whether the policy meets certain minimum limits.

Read the agreement (sometimes called a *letter of engagement*) carefully. If it is silent as to malpractice insurance, ask the attorney if he carries insurance and make him add that information to the agreement.

 If the agreement states that the attorney will represent you through trial only, then be sure to ask what happens if an appeal is required. If the attorney says that he or she does not "do" appeals, you may have to find other representation. Since the new attorney will have to familiarize himself with your case, the switch could cost additional thousands.

Issues in Law

Most disputes between businesses consist of failures to pay bills or failure to manufacture some item in the manner specified in the contract. Most disputes between businesses and customers consist of harm from a product sold to the customer or the failure of the purchased item to perform as advertised.

Below are the most common issues from which lawsuits arise. In addition to arming you with information, understanding the potential liabilities may prevent you from acting in such a manner that could result in being sued. Note that not all states recognize the causes of action listed here. And some states may recognize causes of action not mentioned. Your attorney will know these things and will act accordingly.

Between businesses, causes of action include:

- breach of contract,
- fraud,
- interference with contract,
- interference with prospective economic advantage,
- breaches of warranty under the UCC,
- bad faith denial of contract, and
- slander or libel.

Breach of Contract

A breach of contract occurs when one party fails to perform per the terms required while the other party performs all of the terms required of it. Generally, the term must be material; put more plainly, delivering the widgets in a gray tub instead of a black tub is not likely to be a good case. But delivering four inch widgets when the contract requires six inch widgets is the kind of situation that makes lawyers salivate.

Fraud

Fraud results when one party makes misstatements to the other party that the first party knows are false but are made with the intent of getting the second party to rely on the representations and thereafter perform some action that results in damages to the second party.

When the second party relies on the misstatements and injured as a result, the fraud has been completed. In addition to the compensatory damages, acts of intentional wrongdoing can result in punitive damages, especially if the defrauding party acts maliciously or in conscious disregard of the other party's rights.

Interference with Contract

Most states recognize interference of contracts between businesses or businesses and their customers as being a viable cause of action. Interference is not the same as competition. Businesses have the right to compete against each other. Offering a better deal is not interference. Instead, the interference comes when a person or party intentionally tries to disrupt the business operations of another, usually for no other reason than simply to harm that business.

> **For example:** A landlord decides he does not like a tenant and asks the tenant to vacate voluntarily the premises. The tenant refuses. So the landlord or his representatives begin a campaign to disrupt the tenant's business—by failing to keep the premises open on weekends, by making surprise inspections of the premises during business hours and in the presence of clients, by strictly enforcing rules never enforced before or by filing meritless legal actions.

I was involved in a case once where a former employee sued for wrongful termination. She knew that her former employer had an insurance claim outstanding after a water leak at a storage facility damaged various goods. The former employee believed the claim had been inflated—but she had no proof. In order to force a settlement of her suit, she contacted the insurer and informed it that the claim had been "padded." The insurer investigated her charge…but concluded *it* was the bogus story.

Still, the processing of the claim was delayed by several months thus preventing the business from restocking its inventory and selling new goods. That's an interference with contract.

Interference with Economic Advantage

If a contract does not yet exist, then the actions of the employee might constitute an interference with potential monies earned from a future contract.

For example, if the business in last case had been searching for an insurer and the employee had told the potential insurer that the business had inflated a previous claim, that would be interference with economic advantage.

More commonly, this kind of suit arises when an action is taken to disrupt the business' ability to make sales or gain new ventures.

A virus strategically placed in a computer that disrupts the business' systems would qualify as interference. So would the making of false statements to potential clients and customers.

And that takes us to trade slander/libel.

Trade Slander/Libel

Slander is a false oral statement of fact made against another. Libel is a false statement of fact made in writing against another. In business, making false statements that a particular product does not perform as advertised when the speaker knows that it does is slander/libel.

> Some readers may remember "rumors" about a certain imported beer that used less than pure water in its brewing. If that rumor had been started by a competitor who knew the statement to be false, then "trade" slander/libel may be present.

As in personal matters, statements of opinion are not actionable. If you think the beer tastes bad, you can say so. Competition between businesses is highly respected; competitors making similar products often use comparisons in their commercials. If the statements are false then a suit might follow. But a lawsuit is more likely if the statements of one company are intended to harm the revenue of the other.

Within the pharmaceutical industry, many manufacturers make similar medications. For example, for heartburn and stomach upset, you have Prilosec, Prevacid and Pepcid. It's one thing for the manufacturer to represent that *its* product works the "fastest" or the "longest" by some standard or according to some study. But, if the manufacturer claims that the *other* product is no better than a placebo, you can expect the lawyers to be working overtime.

Bad Faith Denial of Contract

This cause of action is fairly new and not recognized in all states. In fact, I am aware of only one case on the subject. However, I have seen situations arise in recent years that lend themselves to this kind of lawsuit.

In a day and age where individuals seem more willing to lie, even under oath, business professionals have been known to lie as to whether a contract was ever formed between them and other businesses in the first place.

The gravamen of this action occurs generally when parties have a series of agreements. When one party contends that a breach has occurred in a contract and the other contends that a contract never existed between the parties, the first party can assert a bad faith denial of contract—especially if the second party has used the claim of breach to stop performing on the other agreements or on other aspects within the same agreement.

Violations of the Uniform Commercial Code

In all states (except Louisiana), the Uniform Commercial Code (UCC) has been adopted in whole or in part. So who cares? Well, you do if you are involved in the sale of goods.

While parties may contract in any manner they desire, in the absence of contract terms covering certain issues, the Uniform Commercial Code governs.

Section Two of the UCC covers the sale of goods. And it states that the sale of any product comes with a warranty that the product is fit for the intended purpose.

So, if an auto parts store sells you a distributor for a 1976 Datsun B-210, it is likely you will not have to execute a contract. So there are no terms to that sale other than you gave up your hard earned money and received a distributor. Well, it turns out that the distributor is for a 1978 Toyota Corolla. You go back to the store and tell the store manager.

Certainly, there was an express or implied contract that acknowledged your purchase as being specifically related to a part that would function in the B-210. But you don't have to go that far. In the absence of a separate and distinct contract term regarding this issue, the customer is protected by the UCC and the store must replace the part with the correct one.

Section Two of the UCC covers almost all issues likely to arise regarding the sale of goods. If you are starting or acquiring a business where the sale of goods plays a significant role, you should review the code's provisions and make sure that any contracts cover those issues where you do not like the applicable code's provisions.

You might also take some interest in the first section of the Uniform Commercial Code. Under *that* section, you can retain a security interest in the product you have provided to the buyer or in some other property owned by the buyer.

For example: I represented a client that sold or leased meat packing and meat smoking equipment to restaurants. Since most restaurants cannot afford to purchase equipment outright, they request and enter into payment plans or lease payment plans.

Under a lease, the owner of the title is the lessor, so the lessee can't run off with the goods or otherwise try to pawn them. But, when the situation is a purchase and the purchaser will be paying over time, it would nice to have the ability to retrieve that model 6661 Ticonderoga Meat Smoker in the event of default.

There is another advantage to having a UCC security interest: In the event the lessee files for bankruptcy, you won't get paid but you will get your smoker back.

Issues in Equity

One of the most common questions I hear from my clients is: "Well, we really never finalized the deal so there is no written contract. But I did what they asked and now they say they don't need the widgets I built to their specifications. Can you help me?"

Despite the error in judgment in failing to hire the attorney in the first place, the law has provided equitable solutions to the current problem. These include:

    a. Promissory estoppel
        b.   Quantum Meruit
        c.   Unjust Enrichment
    d. Specific Performance

As we discussed earlier, promissory estoppel arises when one party relies on the representation of another and the reliance was reasonable in light of the circumstances.

For example: A party promises a $40,000 contract to an individual if he helps find investors for the project. He uses his contacts and finds the investors, just like he was asked. In the interim, he was paid a couple thousand dollars. When the investors signed on to the project, the party promptly fired the individual and revoked its contract offer.

Because no contract was signed, the hiring party isn't obligated to pay him the $40K; however, the individual can collect the money on the grounds of promissory estoppel.

Quantum Meruit/Unjust Enrichment

Quantum meruit provides the party performing the services a sum equal to the value of the services performed. Unjust enrichment provides to the performing party the value received by the other party.

These actions often occur together.

For example: An individual and a company negotiate for a long term contract. During the negotiations, the company asks the individual to perform services using the promise of a longer contract as an incentive. The individual performs certain services that will likely add significant value to the company, but before a contract is executed, the company terminates the services of the individual.

> Since no contract was ever signed, a breach of oral contract action might be available, but may prove difficult to prosecute. But the company utilized the services resulting in a significant profit. Quantum meruit will provide the value of the services provided and unjust enrichment is available to provide the individual with compensation for the value the company received.

Specific Performance

This cause of action is most often associated with real estate. In general business, it often arises when a property lease contains an option to purchase the land.

For example: Your business leases the land where a factory is built and the lease contract provides for the right to purchase the property upon notice. You give the notice—but the landlord refuses to execute the sales documents. Specific performance would be available in the form of an order from the court requiring the landlord to complete the sale.

One other issue that comes up from time to time is declaratory relief. This comes in the form of a request to the court that it declare…something. Often that *something* is a clause in a contract. For example: You suffer a loss for which you file an insurance claim. The insurer refuses to cover the loss on the grounds that the loss is not covered by the policy. Among other causes of action, you might ask the court to declare whether the policy does cover the loss.

The Elements of Small Business

Of course, the best advice is to take all necessary precautions to prevent litigation. Do business with reputable individuals and companies who sign agreements and abide by them. Interestingly, reputations abound. Ask others about their experiences with a potential supplier or manufacturer or client.

But if you can't stop all litigation, and the statistics show that you can't, then there are steps you can take to minimize costs. As we have already discussed, insurance may be available if certain events occur such as a product liability lawsuit or a sexual harassment suit. Moreover, you can place certain terms in your contracts that may reduce legal costs and judgment or provide for costs to the prevailing party.

The Litigation Process

If you are sued or you have no alternative other than to sue, the first step will be to retain a reputable attorney. If you have friends in business, especially similar businesses, it is likely they will know of an attorney or will have retained an attorney in the past.

Over the years, I have had a number of clients whom I have never met—either because their matter was resolved quickly or because the legal action I filed on their behalf did not require their participation. Sounds strange. But certain kinds of lawsuits require little or no participation of the plaintiff.

However, unless you've had the same attorney for years, take the time to visit him or her before signing a retainer agreement. Be sure to ask questions about the attorney's background and whether he or she has represented clients in similar matters. While attorney-client privilege may apply in certain situations, you can always ask for references.

If you don't feel comfortable with the attorney, don't retain him or her. You will be working closely together—and you will probably have to trust this person with intimate personal and business details—so, make sure you and the attorney have no personality clashes.

Tip: Don't have Aunt Sadie's third cousin who mostly handles workers' compensation claims represent you in complex contract litigation. I know that $50 per hour sounds like a good deal. It isn't. I make the majority of my income as an attorney cleaning up the messes made by predecessors. If you want to make people like me rich, hire that third cousin.

Once you have selected the attorney, you will be asked to execute a "retainer agreement." All states require attorneys to place the terms and conditions of their representation in writing. Other requirements vary from state to state.

> In California, a retainer agreement is required for any services where the fee is likely to exceed $1,000. In the event there is no such agreement and the client refuses to pay the bill, the attorney cannot sue for breach of contract. Instead, he or she must take his or her chances with a judge on quantum meruit.

Also, some states require that the retainer agreement must declare whether the attorney carries a policy of malpractice insurance and whether that policy meets or exceeds the minimum value set by the state. The minimum value is usually $100,000. If your matter is worth more than that, you might ask the attorney for the name of the insurer and the value of the policy.

Tell the lawyer everything. Let me repeat that: *Tell the lawyer everything*. During my years in practice, rarely have I heard the full story in the first meeting. Everything you say is confidential and can never be disclosed to any other party. Attorneys have heard it all. And while you may feel a little uncomfortable or embarrassed because you did something dumb, get over it quickly.

A failure to do this will only slow down your case, especially if you are the party being sued.

 But don't go the other way. Your confidentiality *only* extends to the attorney and his staff. It does not extend to anyone else. So don't tell your troubles to everyone. Friends and business acquaintances can be required to testify and, if any of them do not like you at the time their number is called, you won't fair well.

A little-considered issue is what court and in what location can the suit be filed. There are federal courts and state courts. Federal courts have jurisdiction over two types of matters. The first is known as "federal question." This type of jurisdiction occurs where an issue touches and concerns the Constitution or a federal regulation. It also occurs when you drink too much at the Yellowstone Park Lodge and then get pulled over by a park ranger.

The other type of federal jurisdiction is "diversity." This occurs when the parties come from different states. For example, you drive from your state to Las Vegas where you get into a car accident with someone who drove to Las Vegas from another state. Diversity jurisdiction currently requires damages over $50,000.

If the damages are below $50,000, you have to file the suit in the state court where the other party resides. If you are suing a business or individual residing in your state, then the suit will be filed in the state court. Generally, the proper venue within the state is within the county where the defendant resides.

The next step will be filing the complaint or responding to the complaint. There are a number of different ways to respond to a complaint. However, they are too complex to tackle in this book.

Shortly thereafter, discovery will commence. Discovery is exactly that which the name implies. It is the search for information to support your claims or defeat those of your opponents. It includes interrogatories (written questions), requests for production of documents, requests for admission (such as "Admit that the widgets you constructed are greater than six inches in diameter), and depositions where a party or a witness answers questions under oath posed by the opposing attorney and sometimes by the witness' own attorney.

After all of this fun, finally you get to spend a week or two in a courtroom. While lawyers can never accurately gauge the total cost of litigation, you can expect fees and costs to rise above $100,000 if you proceed through a jury trial.

Warning: Beware of cocktail party attorneys. Fairly often, I get a call on Monday from a client. He or she was at a cocktail party on Saturday night and met an attorney. The attorney chose to comment on my lawyering skills having reviewed nothing or investigated anything. It always ends up with what I am doing wrong and how he can do it better. With so many attorneys in our country, this loose talk is inevitable. It rarely turns out to be worth anything.

Usually, I ask the client whether he or she relayed certain facts, usually the embarrassing facts, to the attorney. Often that terminates the conversation, at least on that issue. With other clients, I simply ask: "What time do you intend to come by and pick up your file?" They respond: "You mean you don't want to represent me anymore?" Or they get the implication and just break into an apology.

If you file a suit, you can expect the other side will conduct reasonably extensive discovery. You sued, so you must answer the questions. Your attorney will object to anything improper. But you are now a participant and you have forced others to participate involuntarily. There are requirements, there are deadlines and you must meet them.

In certain matters, I have been forced to *fire the client* for failure to work with me to prepare his case. The worst instance occurred when a client sued his doctor for malpractice. The doctor's attorney sent out interrogatories and scheduled my client's deposition. My client continually asked me to get extension after extension on both.

After the fifth occurrence, I gave up. I explained to the client that he could not sue someone and then claim a busy schedule as the excuse for noncompliance with the rules. He then commented on my abilities as a lawyer or lack thereof and then suggested that I do something anatomically impossible. I was happy to mail him his file the same day.

On another occasion, I filed suit for a client against his former law firm. The firm had filed a complaint which it amended the following day. Bad sign. The firm then filed a motion for a preliminary injunction, which it lost. The opposing firm filed a motion to dismiss the lawsuit. It won and the action was thrown out. Then my client got the bill.

Before I disclose the amount, you should note that the firm did not have to research anything because the client's *other* former attorneys already had done so and had included all of the research in the materials provided to second firm.

Why did my client change attorneys? He thought that a major firm with a name and reputation was better suited to handle his case. It wasn't. And he didn't feel that way anymore, after his suit was dismissed and the bill for $95,000 came in the mail.

In addition to insurance, there are other ways to reduce litigation costs. For the rest of this chapter, we explore a few of them.

Arbitration

If you have been to a doctor lately or if you belong to an HMO, then you might have seen the arbitration clause in that fine print. Arbitration is an adjudication of a dispute without court intervention. An arbitration is commenced by one party filing a "claim" with the arbitration service named in the agreement or some other reputable service. The two largest organizations are the American Arbitration Association and the Judicial Arbitration and Mediation Services

Tip: Though many agreements contain arbitration clauses, they often fail to specify which service is to be used. The failure to specify a particular service can lead that service to require a stipulation from the parties that they agree to use AAA or JAMS. If the situation is contentious, when you suggest AAA, the other side will demand JAMS. Just another few thousand dollars to the attorneys who will have to go to court to sort out this mess.

Once the claim has been filed, the other party is served usually by mail, not "personal" service. That party typically files a response and may file a cross-claim. Shortly thereafter, the parties receive a list of possible arbitrators. The choices include retired judges or attorneys who specialize in the area of law appropriate to the case. Once the parties have agreed on an arbitrator, or in some cases a panel of three arbitrators, a discovery schedule will be created.

Ultimately a hearing is held where witnesses will be questioned and evidence presented. The hearing officer or officers will take the matter under submission—they will contemplate after you have left the building and then they will send a written decision.

If you do not like part or all of the decision, you can request reconsideration of a particular issue or issues. If the arbitrator says not, then you are done. Most arbitration judgments are not appealable unless the hearing office clearly violated a legal tenet in reaching the decision.

Sample Arbitration Clause

Some variation on the following clause is usually included in contracts and agreements.

> In the event that any dispute arises from the alleged breach of any term in this agreement, the matter shall be submitted to binding arbitration before the American Arbitration Association exclusively in Las Vegas, Nevada under the rules for commercial arbitration. Further, Nevada law exclusively shall govern the decision of the arbitrator or arbitration panel. The prevailing party shall be entitled to reasonable attorneys fees and costs and said fees and costs may be awarded by the arbitrator or arbitration panel. Any award may be reduced to a judgment by a court of competent jurisdiction.

But arbitration isn't the cure-all that some people make it out to be.

So, you have an arbitration judgment in your favor in your hand. Of course the other party will pay, right? Maybe. When the other party does not pay, and often it or they will not, you can take the award and file a petition with your local court requesting entry of the award as a judgment. Assuming the arbitration was conducted by a reputable agency, you should have little difficulty obtaining the judgment as the losing party has little or no grounds for an objection.

Then the real fun begins: *Collections*.

Getting the Money After You've Won

A week rarely passes without a client calling me to inquire as to why the opposing party has not paid the small claims court judgment he or she received last week. I say: "Because they don't have to." And then comes the long pregnant pause before they ask: "What do you mean?"

There is no debtor's prison in the United States (unless you fail to pay on a child or spousal support order and get held in contempt). That means the failure to pay on a civil court judgment does not result in any criminal proceeding. Nonetheless, you have options for collecting the money, all of which can make life a living hell for the judgment debtor.

- **Wage Garnishment.** If your debtor has a job, then you can obtain an order for the garnishment of wages and then serve it on the employer. It requires the employer to divert a percentage of the debtor's wages to you. Most states limit the amount of the garnishment to twenty-five percent of income. Further, your debtor can seek assistance to the court to lower the amount of the garnishment due to hardship or other related circumstances.

- **Writs of Execution**. The court can execute an order prepared by you that allows the local law enforcement to obtain funds from a bank account. Of course, you'll need to know where the debtor banks. But once you have that information, the rest is easy. The sheriff grabs the money and then holds it for a period of time during which the debtor can seek a partial or full exemption for hardship or other related problem.

- **Abstract of Judgment.** Most states permit the recording of the judgment with the office of the county recorder. That is the place where real estate ownership is recorded. The Abstract must be settled at the time the property is sold. If not, the buyer of the property will not be able to obtain a policy of title insurance thus rendering the property unmarketable. Most of the time, you will not receive your money until the property is about to be sold—but at least someday you can collect.

- **The Judgment Debtor Examination**. Similar to a deposition during the course of litigation, a judgment debtor examination can be conducted by the creditor under supervision of the court. Simply, you get to ask the questions such as where do you bank and where do you work? Most questions regarding finances and asset ownership are fair game. And many courts have created a form that debtors are required to fill out. The questions on the form are designed to elicit information regarding finances and assets. With this information, you can pursue the debtor in the manners outlined above.

- **Foreclosure**. If you have a security interest in real or personal property, you can obtain that property and sell it. For example, if you fail to pay your mortgage, the bank sells your home. If you fail to make a car payment, the vehicle gets repossessed. If you loan money to a business or individual, try to obtain some security in support of the loan.

- **Collection Agencies.** Another method available is the collection agency. Debts, whether realized in a judgment or from the simple failure to pay a bill, can be collected by an agency that is designed to accomplish exactly that—collect money.

Agencies can be successful, especially if the fear of a negative credit rating runs in deep in the heart of the debtor. But the price can be quite steep. Many agencies charge on a percentage of the amount they collect—and that can be as much as 50 percent.

You may have heard the expression that only the lawyers win in litigation. *I* thank God every day that the adage is true. However, if you start with investigating those from whom you will be purchasing goods or to whom you will be selling them, it can save a lot of heartache.

Conclusion

And now for a little dose of reality. The best news of all is that most of your clients and patrons will pay and pay on time. The economy could not survive if it were otherwise.

Businesses that don't hire attorneys and don't play by the rules are prone to lawsuits. But, as I said in the introduction, proper understanding of the pitfalls helps you to prevent them.

Proper retention of an attorney at the start of your business or when deals are going to be made is a cheap insurance policy from the costs of terminating a problem after it has commenced.

References

American Bar Association. *American Bar Association Legal Guide for Small Business: Everything a Small-Business Person Must Know, from Start-up to Employment Laws to Financing and Selling a Business*. Random House Information Group (October, 2000)

Arron, Deborah, and Deboral Guyol. *The Complete Guide to Contract Lawyering* (2nd edition). Niche PR (February, 1999).

Clarkson, Kenneth W., et al. *West's Business Law*. South-Western Publishing (February, 2003).

Menendez, Kenneth. *Taming the Lawyers* (2nd edition). Silver Lake Publishing (December, 1999).

Roberson, Cliff. *The Complete Book of Business Forms and Agreements* (book and diskette edition). McGraw-Hill Trade (October, 1993).

Tepper, Pamela R. *The Law of Contracts and the Uniform Commercial Code*. Delmar Learning (February, 1995)

Chapter 16

Miscellaneous Issues

It is a very sad thing that nowadays there is so little useless information.

—Oscar Wilde

There are other issues that deserve a mention. Some of these may apply to you and some may not. I discuss them only in passing. If some or all of them apply to you, then you may wish to discuss them with your attorney before proceeding.

Confidentiality Agreements

Whether your employees are under contract or not, you still may have trade secrets that if divulged could damage your business. A trade secret could be anything from a formula to a way of conducting business to interpersonal activities. For example, McDonalds has its "secret sauce," Coca-Cola has its formula, and KFC has it's the special herbs and spices. Many famous actors require their employees to sign agreements not to provide any information to the media, especially the tabloids.

To protect your secrets, you can have your employees sign a nondisclosure agreement that requires them not to make public anything they learn about you or your business. [Form 16-1] But what if a company wants to purchase your business? It will need to review financial information, operational information and intellectual property. An agreement will be required to ensure that the information provided and obtained is not disseminated to the public.

Non-Competition Agreements

A close kin to the nondisclosure agreement is the non-competition agreement. This measure is used to prevent an employee from learning all there is to know about your business and then starting his or her own business. [Form 16-2] Many states prohibit agreements that prevent an employee from finding another job or even starting a new business.

For example, California forbids such agreements except under certain circumstances. Once such circumstance occurs when separate consideration (i.e. money) is paid to the potential competing party.

> Also, if you purchase a business, via asset or stock, the law permits a covenant not to compete. Otherwise, if the former owner can open a competing business down the street, all of the customers may follow and thus the value of your investment may be diminished.

UPC Codes

Often referred to as a "bar" code, the Uniform Product Code is nothing more than a series of numbers represented by bars. As you know from visits to the supermarket, scanners read the code and then list the item and price on your receipt. Any product sold in the retail marketplace must have a bar code. In addition to the manner in which the cost of the item is displayed and placed on your receipt, businesses, especially retailers, use the code to determine the amount of any particular item in their inventory.

When the products arrive, their codes are scanned. The total number of items is stored in a database. At each purchase, the database is informed. When the number of any product falls below a certain benchmark, more units are ordered. The number of products reordered is determined by a calculation as to how many products sold in what period of time.

Anyone can obtain a code—for a little over $500. The Uniform Code Council is located in Dayton, Ohio. Upon receipt of your application, a six digit number is selected and sent to you with instructions. Each type of product uses a certain prefix code.

For example, a compact disc is different from a can of soup. So depending on the type of product, the first few digits/bars will describe the category of product. Then comes your six digits. Then comes your chosen numbers for that particular product. And then comes a "calculated" number. Any graphic artist or printer with the program necessary to print the UPC code on your labels will have the software program for inserting the numbers you provide. The program has a feature that takes the inputted numbers and formulates a final number.

For more information, visit the UCC Web site at www.uc-council.org.

Intellectual Property Rights

If you did not go to college (or if you attended school in California), not to worry. Intellectual property has nothing to do with intelligence. Rather, it is any idea or thought, that has a value. Typical examples include songs, drawings, writings, or the design of your latest invention.

Copyrights

Obviously, the type of intellectual property determines the method of protecting it. For creative writings, fiction or nonfiction, you can apply for copyright protection. The United States Patent & Copyright Office has forms. Its Web site is www.uspto.gov. You fill out the forms, pay a small fee and then send in the requested number of copies of the property. That's all.

Before we get too excited, let's make sure we understand what we have done. By registering the work first in time, you have provided proof, if necessary in the future, to show when you first created the work. That does not stop someone from claiming that he or she created the work first. The claimant would have to prove it. If he or she does, then your copyright is worthless. In other words, the failure to apply for a copyright does not result in a loss of rights to the creator of the work; it just makes ownership a little harder to prove.

You might have heard of the "Poor Man's Copyright." In order to prove when something was created, the creator places the writing into an envelope, seals it with wax or similar substance and then mails it to an attorney or other trusted person. That person keeps the envelope safe, secure and unopened. The postmark shows the date of the mailing.

Does this method work? Most attorneys advise against it. But in reality, it can be effective to prove when the property was created. And, for creations less likely to need protection, it only costs the amount of the postage and envelope.

Patents

Remember the better mousetrap? Maybe the new design could be patented. By that we mean that something unique about the design might be of value and thereafter unusable to others without your permission.

Patents fall into two categories: design and utility. Generally, a utility patent protects the way an article is used and works; a design patent protects the way an article looks. Both types may apply to a single invention and can be obtained for that invention if the invention resides both in its utility and ornamental appearance.

There is one other type of invention for you horticulturists out there. Since I could not figure out a way to describe this, I will let the government do it for you:

> *A plant patent is granted...to an inventor who has invented or discovered and asexually reproduced a distinct and new variety of plant, other than a tuber propagated plant or a plant found in an uncultivated state. The grant, which lasts for 20 years from the date of filing the application, protects the inventor's right to exclude others from asexually reproducing, selling, or using the plant so reproduced.*

If you think you have developed a better mousetrap or Venus Flytrap or a whole new device then you should find a reputable patent attorney. To file for a patent, an attorney must be registered with the U.S. Patent & Trademark office. And you will need a qualified attorney. Many patent attorneys majored in engineering and are capable of creating or interpreting schematics or blue prints.

A qualified patent attorney isn't cheap. You can expect the cost of patent legal fees alone to start at $5,000.

Not every new idea or improvement is worthy of patenting. Before you spend the money, you should determine whether your creation can be duplicated easily or whether others will want to duplicate your invention and could do so without copying from your design. How many cellular telephone manufacturers are in business today?

Trademarks

The trademark might just be the least understood aspect of intellectual property. Simply, a trademark is a word, phrase or drawing that has taken on such a unique look or meaning that it is associated with your product. Think of those that you see every day: Coke, Pepsi, Kleenex, Jell-O, and Band-Aid. These terms are not English words. Rather, they are names created by various companies to identify a particular product.

> In most circumstances, a trademark cannot be descriptive term or a term that simply restates the actual name of the product. For example, Kleenex is fine; "tissue" is not. Coke is fine; "soda" is not. Jell-O is fine; "gelatin" is not.

Symbols or unique methods of displaying the business' name also can be trademarked. For example, most people are familiar with Universal Studios. At the beginning of any movie it makes, you see a three dimensional Earth rotating with the words "Universal Studios" as a banner across the globe.

Some states permit the registration of a trademark. But it's usually better to register your mark with the federal government so that it applies throughout the country. To do so, you must follow certain requirements. As usual, there is a form to fill out and monies to pay. Expect this to set you back a few hundred dollars. You must choose a category covering the product or thing where the mark will be adorned.

Also, you must provide the material where the product will be displayed. If the mark is on a label, then you will provide the requested number of labels. Further, since you are applying for a trademark presumably used throughout the country, you will need to declare that the goods have been sold to a consumer in another state.

This is where Aunt Bessie in North Dakota comes in. Sell her one of the units and then declare on the application that the goods have been sold in interstate commerce.

From filing to response, you could be waiting for months. When the response comes, if it is not favorable you can contact the bureaucrat and appeal. Sometimes the issue is minor and can be resolved in a matter of minutes. Otherwise, the appeal could take more months.

Work for Hire Agreements

So you won the lottery and have chosen to cut a record. You know nothing about music but that did not stop your under-appreciated songwriting talents. So you hire a few musicians. They create a sound. The rhythm section creates a good beat and the brass creates a strong background. Guess what? Each musician owns the rights to his or her performance. Unless....

Unless you have them execute work for hire agreements or contracts with a clause that provides that anything created by the employee or independent contractor shall remain the property of the company.

 If your employees or consultants or anyone you are paying are working on anything that might have an intellectual property value, the work is owned by them, not you unless they execute a "work for hire" agreement. This agreement clearly states that the ownership of the property rests with you—a work for hire. If in doubt, have them sign one.

The following is a good example of a "Work for Hire" clause.

> **WORK PRODUCT OWNERSHIP.** This agreement constitutes a "work for hire" situation. Any copyrightable works, ideas, discoveries, inventions, patents, products, or other information (collectively, the "Work Product") developed in whole or in part by Smith in connection with the Services contemplated under this agreement shall be the exclusive property of Jones. Any royalties in any form received in connection with the Work Product shall be paid to Jones. All royalties received as a result of the publishing of the songs shall be paid to Morales or his designee. If necessary, Smith shall sign all documents necessary to confirm or perfect the exclusive ownership of Jones to the Work Product.

Power of Attorney

The most common types of powers of attorney are "Durable" powers of attorney or "Healthcare" powers of attorney. The latter provides powers to a friend or relative to make healthcare decisions for you in the event you are not competent to make them for yourself. For example, the document might contain a "DNR" or do not resuscitate order or it might describe conditions where life support would be shut off. A healthcare power of attorney is an essential part of estate planning but has little direct connection to business.

On the other hand, a durable power of attorney covers anything you specify. For example, if your house is for sale at a time when you will be out of the country, you might provide to your spouse a power of attorney that permits him or her to sign your name to counteroffers or acceptance agreements. It might also permit him or her to execute other documents to complete the sale. This works far better than sending documents to Zimbabwe by overnight express.

In a business partnership, if you will be away from the office, a power of attorney providing certain powers to your partner might be necessary. Or if you have no partners, a power of attorney to your attorney or spouse or trusted friend might be helpful. Again, the power of attorney can provide as much or as little power as you decide.

Note that powers of attorney must be signed and notarized to be valid and are void upon the death of the person who executed it. In my practice I have come across situations where the power of attorney was used instead of the probate process to transfer assets. Since the bank and brokerage did not know of their client's death, the holder of the document was able to transfer or withdraw funds. Not a good idea, especially if the beneficiaries discover that you deprived them of monies and other assets belonging to them.

References

Bouchoux, Deborah E. *Protecting Your Company's Intellectual Property: A Practical Guide to Trademarks, Copyrights, Patents and Trade Secrets.* AMACOM (April, 2001).

Elias, Stephen, and Richard Stim. *Patent, Copyright and Trademark: An Intellectual Property Desk Reference.* Nolo Press (September, 2002).

Hamam, Edward A. *Power of Attorney Handbook.* Sourcebooks, Inc. (December, 1997)

Miller, Arthur Raphael, et al. *Intellectual Property: Patents, Trademarks and Copyright In a Nutshell.* West Publishing (October, 2000)

Roberson, Cliff. *The Complete Book of Business Forms and Agreements* (book and diskette edition). The McGraw-Hill Companies (October, 1993).

Silver Lake Editors. *The Value of a Good Idea: Protecting Intellectual Property in an Information Economy.* Silver Lake Publishing (September, 2002).

Chapter 17

Retirement Planning

From the errors of others a wise man corrects his own.

—Publilius Syrus

Every morning, millions of people read their horoscope to discover what will happen to them in the future. Many people go to psychics for "readings" on their future. Apparently not enough horoscopes or psychics mention retirement planning—the simple concept that you need lots of money if you don't work.

If you're running a small business, you may think you're too busy to think about retirement...or that, when the business takes off, *it* will be your retirement plan. But don't think like this. When it comes to retirement matters, treat yourself like an employee.

There is no specific formula that can determine the amount of savings you will need to maintain your life-style in retirement. Some experts estimate that, if you plan to retire at age 65, you won't want to draw down more than four percent of your principal each year. So, if you have $1 million, you shouldn't use more than $40,000 per year.

While living on $40,000 (especially after kids are grown) may not sound so bad, getting a liquid million is tough for just about anyone.

Despite the warnings that it will take well over $1 million in savings to retain the life-style of the average middle-class American in his or her retirement, most Americans fail to take advantage of retirement plans available through their employers or available to them as sole proprietors or available to them as members of the human race. Many of these programs provide significant tax breaks and are simple to use or create.

 If you are hiring employees, any retirement benefits you can provide may make all the difference between qualified individuals choosing to work for you or choosing another place of employment. Simply put, it ain't just the salary that attracts employees or that keeps them from leaving.

I have one client that operates a business in Las Vegas, Nevada. Everyone knows that Las Vegas operates twenty-four hours a day. While that is great for tourists, especially those with insomnia, it hurts small businesses because the job market belongs to the employees. Operating around the clock requires a lot of qualified employees. As an incentive, most of the large business and the casino/hotels provide significant benefits including medical and dental coverage, disability and retirement plans.

Small businesses have a much more difficult time obtaining these benefits at an affordable cost.

The good news is that employers have more choices than ever before and can leverage their buying power through organizations designed to assist small business.

The main reason that most owners of small businesses join professional associations, industry trade groups or civic organizations is that these groups offer benefits programs—often health and retirement plans—to their member companies. This doesn't make the plans free; but it does make them much cheaper. Working through one of these groups, a business with six employees has the buying power of one with thousands.

And remember: If you are employed by your own corporation, you too are entitled to the same retirement benefits as your employees. So, if you intend to operate a small business with employees, here are a few things you might consider for yourself and for them.

The 401(k)

The 401(k) is the most common plan used by employers. Companies hire an administrator to organize and control a pool of money invested by the employees, often with contributions from the employer. The employees have the money deducted from their paychecks pre-tax and then invested.

Normally, the employee has some choice as to how the money is invested. For example, a portion might be placed in mutual funds, a portion might be placed in the company's stock, and a portion might be placed in a money market account. The administrator usually provides a booklet explaining the investment options and how to invest based on how many years you are from retirement.

The pre-tax feature of the plan is quite significant. The percentage you designate is subtracted before taxes are applied. As a result, your income taxes are based on lower earnings figure while you make the choices as to how your money is invested.

Usually, you can make changes in the allocation at any time. So, if stocks are taking a tumble, money can be reallocated to a money market fund or a bond fund.

Another advantage of this plan is that the employer can match a percentage of each worker's contribution to his or her fund. And that matching contribution—usually between 50 percent and 100 percent of whatever the worker puts in—is tax-deductible for the employer.

While there is no apparent disadvantage to the 401(k), it does come with a few rules. For example, the government has set a maximum limit as to how much money can be contributed pre-tax. Currently, that amount is $11,000 per year but is set to rise over the next few years to $15,000.

The choices made available to you by the plan administrator can sometimes become an issue, as well. While most plan administrators and companies provide many investment options, they cannot offer everything. Also, investments that might have provided solid growth five years ago may not be the best bet now. So for better or worse, you are stuck with the choices they provide.

Though subject to change, another current annoyance is the rule that if you or your spouse has a 401(k) plan available, generally you are not eligible to receive the before tax contribution benefits normally associated with a traditional Individual Retirement Account (IRA)—even if you don't make use of the 401(k).

Recent legislation has changed some of this by making available to small businesses a plan known as a Simple 401(k). So, a self-employed individual or even a corporation of one or two shareholders could create their own 401(k) plan and choose the investment options.

Other than the 401(k) investment limit, there is no income limit for these plans. So, if your spouse is contributing before tax dollars to her 401(k) and you contribute before tax dollars to your Simple 401(k), you can double the pre-tax retirement savings.

The Traditional IRA

Individual Retirement Accounts provide for the ability to deposit certain sums into an investment account without tax on the money. An account can be opened at a bank or any brokerage. Once established, the money contributed can be placed in almost any legitimate investment—including stocks, bonds, mutual funds and real estate.

Currently, at the federal level an individual can contribute up to $3,000 and a couple up to $6,000 per year. These sums are deductible from income in the same manner as the 401(k). The money can be withdrawn beginning at age 55; a certain percentage *must* be withdrawn by age 71.

> Once withdrawn, the monies taken are taxed at your tax bracket at that time. The advantage here is that your tax bracket in retirement tends to be less than that while you are working. On the other hand, the penalties for early withdrawal are harsh. Certain exceptions have been carved out recently so that monies can be deducted for major healthcare expenses or other catastrophes.

The Roth IRA

A new feature of retirement planning is the so-called "Roth IRA." Most of the rules for traditional IRAs apply to the Roth IRAs—with one significant difference. Roth monies are deposited *after tax*. So instead of the tax break you receive from a deposit into the traditional IRA, you receive no tax break with the Roth.

But when you withdraw the Roth monies, you pay no taxes on either the money or the gain on the money from your investment choices.

Life Insurance

Most people think of life insurance as money to be received in the event of the death of a specific person. Term life insurance is exactly that: You pay a premium and, upon death, the insurer pays the beneficiary. The policy has no cash value.

Whole life and universal life insurance policies are different.

A whole life policy is really an investment. While you pay a premium with benefits paid at death, the policy gains in value and ultimately reaches or exceeds the amount of the face value of the policy.

For instance, a $100,000 policy will be worth $100,000 to you at some point in the future depending on the premiums you pay. And those premiums are quite a bit higher than the premiums paid for term life. For example, a $100,000 policy might require annual payments of $1,000 per year for 20 years; whereas, a term life policy for the same value would likely cost only $200 per year.

Universal life is similar to whole life except that you control the investment vehicle. In whole life, the investment is controlled by the insurer. Thus, the insurer makes you pay a flat premium over the years that a premium is required. For a $100,000 policy, you don't pay premiums totaling that amount—because the return on the investment of your premiums covers the difference. So depending on age, a $100,000 might require annual premiums of $1,000 for 20 years.

With a universal life policy, you decide on the investment scheme. The insurer requires that same premium and increase in value from the investment. If you invest wisely, the gain will meet with the percentage increase required to hold the value of the policy. You might even reduce you premium. If you guess wrong, then in addition to the premium, you have to pay the difference (loss) in order to maintain the policy's value.

> Many financial advisors point out that paying for the term life policy and then investing the remaining balance in mutual funds or other traditional investments makes more sense. But this is highly dependent on the conditions of the market. The advice is correct, for example, when stocks are doing well or when other traditional investment are producing significant gains in value. But, when most traditional investment are flat, the whole life or universal life insurance policies provide modest increases in value.

Quick Plan Descriptions

- **401(k).** Sponsored by the employer, allows employee to investment pre-tax dollars up to a certain limit. Employers often provide matching contribution from 50 to 100 percent. Monies can be placed in almost any legitimate investment.

- **Simple 401(k).** Same rules as a traditional 401(k), but designed for small business owners, including corporations, LLCs or LLPs and sole proprietors. All can create this plan and contribute pre-tax dollars.

- **Traditional IRA.** Similar to the Simple 401(k). Individuals and couples can contribute tax free dollars into most legitimate investments. Withdrawal rules and penalties also apply. But the amount of the contribution is limited to approximately one-third of the sum that can be contributed into the 401(k) or Simple 401(k).

- **Roth IRA.** Same rules as a traditional IRA. But the contributions are not tax deductible. Good for those whose wages are subject to the lower tax brackets.

- **Life Insurance (Whole Life).** Premiums paid over a long period of time result in cash value usually up to the amount of the policy. Policy holder has little latitude in selecting investments. Premiums may be tax deductible on certain circumstances.

- **Life Insurance (Universal Life).** Similar to whole life with flexibility on the choices where investments may be placed. But possibility of having to make up difference in any losses.

Conclusion

Whatever you do about retirement, doing nothing is not an option. Consider that Social Security payments probably won't exceed one thousand dollars per month. What are your current expenses? At what age did you intend to hit the links?

Get the point?

References

Bogosian, Wayne G., et al. *The Complete Idiot's Guide to 401(k) Plans* (2nd edition). IDG/John Wiley & Sons, Inc. (October, 2003).

Dearborn Financial Publishing. *Retirement Plans for Small Businesses*. John Wiley & Sons, Inc. (October, 2003).

Gnabasik, Matthew. *Smart Choices: Selecting and Administering a Safe 401(K) Plan*. Blue Prairie Group (October, 2002).

Malaspina. Margaret A. *Cracking Your Retirement Nest Egg (Without Scrambling Your Finances): 25 Things You Must Know Before You Tap Your 401(k), IRA, or Other Retirement Savings Plan*. Bloomberg Press (January 2003).

McCarthy, Cornelius. *The Under 40 Financial Planning Guide* (2nd edition). Silver Lake Publishing (October, 2000).

Miller, Alan J. *Standard & Poor's 401(k) Planning Guide*. McGraw-Hill Trade (March, 1995).

Salisbury, Dallas, and Marc Robinson. *Essential Finance: IRA and 401(k) Investing*. DK Publishing (May, 2001).

Siflett, Jean D. *Beyond 401(k)s for Small Business Owners : A Practical Guide to Incentive, Deferred Compensation, and Retirement Plans*. John Wiley & Sons, Inc. (October, 2003).

Slesnick, Twila, et al. *IRAs, 401(k)s & Other Retirement Plans: Taking Your Money Out* (5th edition). Nolo Press (January, 2003).

Chapter 18

Marriage and Divorce

Marriage is a three-ring circus—first the engagement ring, then the wedding ring and then the suffering.

—Lou Costello

Marriage and divorce have a bigger impact on small business than academics report and economists realize. As someone who works with lots of small businesses, I've seen firsthand how many companies come undone—closed, sold or gone bankrupt—because of the end of an owner's marriage. It's a major business issue.

Like some marriages, this chapter is short but vitally important to anyone operating or intending to operate a small business. If you're like Joanne Woodward and Paul Newman, happily married for more than 40 years, you can skip this chapter; if you're like everyone else who's ever worked in Hollywood, pay attention.

Reno, Nevada, is the home of Judge's College. You'd be amazed how many great legal minds flunk the course on how to put on a black robe. (Rim shot, please.)

Actually, Judge's College is helpful to men and women who've been appointed or elected to the bench for the first time. Not all judges go; but those who do say the short courses are full of practical advice.

The Elements of Small Business

One of the most memorable lessons: Don't worry too much about criminal defendants turning violent during their proceedings. Murderers, rapists, thieves and gangsters usually want to avoid any more trouble.

Instead, the new judges are warned to be wary of the father who hears that he can only see his children every other weekend. *That's* the person most likely to pull out a weapon and lunge at his ex...or the judge.

Over the years, my experience bears out that lesson. Most acts of violence occur in the Family Law courts. While many couples have seen the light and worked out a settlement before seeing (and paying) the attorneys, other couples—often, those with the highest financial stakes—still choose to litigate. It truly is ugly out there.

My father has been an active member of the California Bar for more than 45 years. He has been a leading Family Law attorney for more than 30 years. From time to time he attends weddings.

He hates weddings but does especially enjoy the aisle seat. As the happy couple marches toward wedded bliss, in a voice only a few can hear, he says, "There goes inventory." He's not kidding. By now, most Americans know that divorces occur in a little over half of all marriages.

When I was in college, my father was involved in a high profile case that made the news almost every night. One of my professors was in the process of his own tough divorce at the same time; he watched the nightly news and saw my father. Eventually, the professor figured out who I was and would occasionally vent to me about some of his experiences. Before class one day, we were talking about the costs of a divorce when another student overhead the conversation.

"How much is it costing you?"

"About $25,000," replied the professor.

The student was incredulous. She just could not comprehend such a high price for a breakup, even the breakup of a marriage. However, the professor told the student that such a price tag was cheap, especially when juxtaposed with the emotional trauma of a lengthy battle.

As the son of a well-known divorce attorney, I seldom could get away from rueful comments. Divorces stick with people. One time, I was traveling up a ski lift. My skis were marked with my last name for identification. I didn't know the guy sitting next me, but I was about to get an introduction...

"Hey, are you related to Howard Thaler?"

I've been asked this question before, often by still-irate ex-husbands who had the misfortune of having their wives represented by my father. So, I waited until the lift was only ten feet above the snow when tentatively I replied: "Yes, I am. He is my father." I always assume that "father" thing evokes a calm image of family and puppies licking a child's face.

I got lucky that time. The skier told me that my father had represented *him* and had really stuck it to his ex. Go dad!

 People who have success in business sometimes show a surprising level of emotion. Maybe it's just the nature of love and marriage; or maybe it's that successful people aren't accustomed to losing. And a divorce—no matter who gets what—is a kind of loss. But a better way to treat a divorce is the same way you'd treat any business trouble: Isolate the problem, resolve it as quickly as possible and move on.

Community Property

The rules of Family Law can wreak havoc on any business. While only nine states are officially community property states, most states subscribe to the underlying philosophy.

Community property refers to the designation of property or assets accumulated during the time of the marriage as being owned by both spouses regardless of which spouse made the purchase.

Is there any separate property? Yes, but only if you inherit or had the dough to begin with—and even that may not help. Let me explain. Money or property inherited belongs to the person who inherited it. And assets you had prior to marriage remain your assets. But, if you commingle your separate assets or if you use a combination of separate property assets and community property assets for anything, your spouse likely will be entitled to a piece of whole pie.

> For example: You inherit money from Aunt Sadie. You use that money for a down payment on a house for you and your wife. Over the years, you make the mortgage payments from monies you earn at your job. And then, suddenly, your wife says she's met someone else and wants a divorce. You used your money to get the house and you used the profits of your labor to pay for it. Too bad. While you would be entitled to a reimbursement or an offset for the down payment, the equity in the property (the amount of the mortgage payments applied to reduce the mortgage) and the increase in value are shared equally.

What's Your Business *Really* Worth?

The same situation applies to the business or to your interest in the business. Just because you started the business and you worked 12-hour days does not mean that your spouse is not entitled to one half of its value. As a result, in the event of a divorce, the business will have to be valued.

The thrill of valuation belongs to forensic accountants, who charge more money than the budget of many third world countries. They evaluate the business and render an opinion as to value. Since both sides usually hire their own experts and since each provides a different opinion, the court often simply splits the difference. Either the other spouse receives half of that value in cold hard cash or in cash equivalents, such as *your* half-interest in the family residence.

This valuation process can take many months. If you have a partnership, whether through a corporation or an LLC/LLP, imagine the excited look on your partner's face when your soon-to-be ex announces he or she intends to park his or her butt at the office for a while to protect a community property interest. Imagine how excited you would be if your partner's spouse does this to *you*.

Imagine the excited looks on your employees' faces when forensic accountants march into the office and announce that they will be reviewing all of your records. Can you say, "IRS" or "tax evasion?" And, yes, the judge can report any unseemly conduct to the proper taxing authorities.

Retirement Plans

Retirement plans and benefits are also shared by your spouse—at least those benefits accumulated during the time of marriage.

Since the money from a retirement plan will not be readily available a qualified domestic relations order (known by the vaguely Roman Empire-sounding acronym *QDRO*) will be prepared and provided to the retirement plan administrator. It will instruct the administrator on the percentage of benefits that you and your ex-spouse will receive when the first one reaches retirement age.

Let's Go Public...The Bad Way

There is one other element of a divorce that is often overlooked. Most of the time, the proceedings and papers filed are open to the public. That means everyone gets to know your business. This can have many unintended consequences.

Just ask Jack Welch, the former CEO of General Electric. During his divorce, it was revealed that GE had provided him with an embarrassingly rich retirement package. Shareholders were furious about the unreported deal. However, the soon-to-be-ex Mrs. Welch was ecstatic—since she was entitled to half. Ultimately, GE was forced to rescind some of the Welches' most lavish benefits.

Hide and Go Seek

Don't make the mistake of thinking you are going to hide assets. First, judges have seen it all; their ability to sniff out fraud can be remarkable. Second, many states require that the parties make a full disclosure of their assets. States such as California require the parties to exchange information and then send a declaration to the court stating that the exchange has been made. Many states allow the property settlement portion of the divorce to be set aside and the nondisclosing party penalized.

> **Translation: If you're caught hiding assets, you'll pay more than you would have if you'd been honest from the start.**

Recently, a lottery winner learned this lesson the hard way. A married woman won the lottery. She didn't tell her husband about the winning ticket but did tell him she wanted a divorce. When it came time to prepare and exchange the asset disclosures, the wife left out her new-found riches. The divorce was finalized and the spouses parted. A few months later, the husband discovered that his ex was spending quite a bit of money. A little research turned up the lottery winnings.

Had the wife disclosed the winnings, she would have been required to give up half. The judge was less than pleased over her deceit and ordered the wife to turn over *all of the lottery money* to the husband.

The lottery-winner isn't the only dim bulb when it comes to dealing with marital assets.

In late 2001, the government of New Zealand, passed a law providing that on February 1, 2002, all couples who had lived together for two years or more were to be considered "married" and all assets were to become community.

The government thought this new rule would create instant families and that many good folks would run out to get married as soon as possible. Wrong. On January 31, 2002 the entire country broke up just to avoid the community property rules. This problem was especially poignant since many small businesses in New Zealand are family-owned and -operated and passed down to the next generation.

Several years later, small businesses in New Zealand are still sorting through the chaos.

Prenuptial Agreements

While I am not advocating a prenuptial agreement for everyone, it is a good idea for some. Like the New Zealand situation, fortunes or items belonging to the "family" often are intended to stay in the family. (I bet Jack Welch's *next* wife will be required to sign an agreement.)

The best reason to make a pre-nup is protect one spouse's interest in a family-owned business. And this kind of agreement doesn't have to be ruthless. It can allow the non-business-owning spouse financial consideration if the marriage ends; but it defines the family business ownership clearly as an asset that predated the marriage. And the agreement can also state that the business ownership can't be sold, broken up, pledged or encumbered (borrowed against) to finance a divorce settlement.

If a prenuptial agreement is your cup of tea, make sure to contact a lawyer who is experienced in family law and prenuptial agreements. Family law is a state-by-state patchwork; and many states have extremely stringent requirements. For example, each party must be represented by an attorney—preferably his and her own. The party who benefits from the agreement may be required to disclose assets and motivations behind the agreement so that the other party understands what he or she is giving up.

Forcing the bride-to-be to sign an agreement scribbled on a cocktail napkin just prior to the marriage ceremony is highly disfavored.

Common Law Marriage

You need to know your rights in the event of a failed marriage and even, wherever possible, take steps to minimize the trauma and the cost. Know the law in your state. Some states recognize *common law marriage*—and this can cause problems for small businesses.

Common law marriage is the legal concept embraced by some states that if you and a person of the opposite sex live together for a certain period of time (usually between five and 10 years) or present yourself as a couple for a lengthy time you are—legally—married. And this kind of marriage comes with all the rights and liabilities that a formal marriage has.

Here is a solution: If you have a business partner or partners, create an agreement executed by all of the partners and their spouses that provides a purchase clause triggered at the time of any marital dissolution. The agreement would state an amount to be paid to the "other" spouse as his or her community property share.

You can all agree to an amount or a formula for calculating an amount. And unless the amount is utterly ridiculous (that is, way too small), chances are the court will support the agreement and deny any challenge.

Make sure that all parties receive advice from counsel as some states might consider such an arrangement as being similar to a prenuptial agreement and can determine the agreement to be void unless many of the same requirements are met.

Palimony

In an age that debates gay marriage and settles for vaguely defined domestic partner relationships, the notion of "palimony" seems quaint. But it does come up in business contexts occasionally.

Actually, palimony—legal rights of a non-married domestic partner—does not exist in any state; but breach of contract exists on every one.

In the famous case of Lee Marvin and Michelle Triola Marvin, Michelle claimed that she and Lee Marvin had entered into a contract wherein she would give up her career to take care of their household in exchange for Lee Marvin taking care of her for the rest of her life. Since that case, the breach of contract theory has been the predominant cause of action in claims for support from non-married parties living together.

Conclusion

Frankly, staying together in a difficult marriage for the sake of the business may make more sense than staying together for the sake of the kids. It is a rare thing for a small business—even a successful one—to survive the divorce of a principal without some damage.

But, sometimes, divorce is inevitable. The best thing a business owner can do is proceed carefully.

No attorney can ever plan for every contingency. But planning as best you can with your attorney for any and all contingencies is of utmost concern. While you cannot see the future, you know the statistics on marriage failures. Many businesses suffer financially for no other reason than neglect as a result of the emotionally charged nature of a divorce. By understanding your rights and obligations, you may not satisfy your emotions, but you will spend less time fighting and more time operating your business.

References

Hamilton, Mary, et al. *What a Woman: A Financial Planning Guide for the Newly Independent*. Silver Lake Publishing (June, 1999).

Richman, Brice L. *J.K. Lasser Pro Guide to Tax and Financial Issues in Divorce*. John Wiley & Sons, Inc. (February, 2002).

Silver Lake Editors. *Family Money*. Silver Lake Publishing (June, 2002).

Ventura, John, and Mary Reed. *Divorce For Dummies*. IDG/For Dummies (May, 1998).

Woodhouse, Violet, et al. *Divorce and Money: How to Make the Best Financial Decisions During Divorce* (6th edition). Nolo Press (October, 2002)

Chapter 19

Nonprofit Organizations

The formula for Utopia on earth remains always the same: to make a necessity of virtue.

—Clifton Fadiman

We have not yet discussed the mysteriously compelling *nonprofit organization.* If you love animals, then you know PETA. If you like mountains, forests and streams, then you know The Sierra Club. If you belong to a church, synagogue or mosque then you a part of a nonprofit organization. Some people speak of "starting a nonprofit" as if it were an industry sector unto itself.

But what does it really mean to be nonprofit?

This chapter will explain what the heck is really going on with nonprofits and what you have to do to become one.

Many nonprofits get their money from their members. That involves setting up a membership program, collecting dues, and providing something special to them for being a member. Because everyone wants to be special, especially if they are giving ridiculous amounts of money to be part of your organization.

The first questions you must ask are these: If you are doing public good, can you make enough revenue *without* soliciting donations? Is there any other financial value in being a nonprofit organization? For example nonprofits often are exempt from paying property taxes. This is something that the people running Kabbalah—a religious nonprofit organization that the singer Madonna has supported—seem to understand. They used the singer's contributions to buy themselves mansions in L.A.

Recently, a referred client called. She headed a dance troop and wanted to form a nonprofit organization for it to operate. I asked her, "Why?" She said she wanted to raise money through donations. Again I said, "Why?" Apparently, the troop needed money and this seemed like a good way to get it. "How about charging for the performances?"

Here's the deal: Nonprofit organizations have plenty of advantages, especially where membership and membership fees are involved. Churches and synagogues are good examples. And they have advantages when services normally billable are going to be performed without remuneration—such as medical or mental health clinics or homeless shelters. While many symphony orchestras are nonprofit, it is because private benefactors or public funds are spent in an effort to show civic culture (and for a few rich folks who need to have their names on a plaque). But there's no inherent reason that an altruistic venture should go through the legal process of becoming a nonprofit.

Another point: soliciting donations is tough work. Most major corporations will not provide grants or even consider requests until the organization has been in business for at least five years.

While cultural and ethnic dancing is important, it pales in comparison to cancer research or the Red Cross or the United Way. There is only so much money to go around—and dance troops just aren't a high priority, especially when they can charge for the work.

So, I told the dancing client to review a prospective business plan that included revenue from performance admission. If the revenue exceeded expenses, then she could forget the nonprofit situation.

What Does *Nonprofit* Mean?

A nonprofit organization is a business, incorporated or not. However, nonprofit does not mean non-income producing. It does not mean that the business runs without money. The term "nonprofit" means that profit is not distributed to the owners or shareholders but rather it is used to service or expand the business.

Consider the three most common types nonprofit businesses:

- religious organizations;

- businesses that operate for the public good such as a homeless shelter or soup kitchen; and

- entities that serve the needs of a specific constituency, such as the American Association of Retired Persons (AARP).

Most nonprofit organizations are designated with 501(c)(3) status under the Internal Revenue Code. However, the exemption is only for income. It does not relieve the business from payroll taxes or workers' compensation.

Property taxes generally apply to most businesses except religious institutions, state taxes may apply, and workplace rules concerning safety remain.

Religious Organizations

No matter your religion, the place you go to worship likely operates in a nonprofit format. The rabbi, priest or minister is paid a salary from which taxes are deducted. And there are other employees from teachers and assistants to clerks and secretaries to janitors and custodial engineers. Individuals or families pay a fee, usually on an annual basis, to be members.

As the saying goes, membership has its privileges. In religious organizations, members may get to vote on salary increases for the minister or serve on committees. Also, members choose the Board of Directors, officers and possibly the "President" of the organization.

In addition to funds raised from membership, religious organizations may solicit additional donations from members or others in the community. This could encompass everything from passing the collection plate on Sundays to bake sales.

Monies given are likely to be "donations" and thus may be tax deductible to the donor. Or the organization may have a "bake sale" or a carnival or a dinner or other related fund raising events.

Public Good Businesses

Schools, universities, hospitals, homeless shelters, and mental health clinics provide benefits to the public. Unlike religious institutions, these organizations do not have members. Instead they may charge fair market value for services (hospitals, schools and universities), or they might charge a lesser amount or nothing at all (clinics and shelters).

> **Either way, these businesses raise money often through private donations from the community.**

Similar to any for-profit business, these organizations traditionally have a board of directors, officers and a chief executive officer or president in charge. Employees receive salaries and taxes are withheld. In fact, all other formalities of a business are followed.

Depending on the type of business and its structure, monies given may be classified as donations subject to a tax deduction for donors

Constituency Businesses

Certain nonprofit organizations exist to assist a certain segment of society. For example, the AARP provides information and assistance to anyone age 55 and older. The National Rifle Association exists to protect gun ownership rights. The community youth theatre offers classes and puts up musicals for theater-goers.

These organizations traditionally operate from membership dues and other contributions. However unlike the religious organizations and public good businesses, contributions, including membership fees likely are not tax deductible.

So You Want to Start a Nonprofit?

Most of the same elements of business apply to nonprofits-offering products and/or services, marketing, client satisfaction, accounting, and acquiring insurance specific to the business. But one thing stands out much more prominently in the nonprofit sector than the private: fund-raising.

Fund-raising is a key element within nonprofits, so important in fact that many choose to hire outside fund-raisers with the job of doing just that: motivating prospective donors to philanthropy.

There are essentially ten elements of a well-rounded nonprofit organization. They are:

- Board

- Facilities

- Finance

- Fund-raising

- Legal

- Marketing/ Public Relations

- MIS (Management Information Systems)

- Planning

- Human Resources
- Staff and Volunteers

Aside from doing your filings (for incorporation) and setting up your taxes (with your trusty accountant), you will want to register with the state agencies (Secretary of State's Office) and get advice from...guess who?

That's right, lawyers

As we discussed in the Business Plan section, knowing where you are going and keeping focus is essential. A nonprofit organization needs a mission statement. All businesses benefit from having one—but nonprofits thrive on them.

A mission statement is especially important for potential donors to understand because, after all, you want them excited about what you are doing. You want them to want to donate...this is how you make your money.

If this all sounds like too much business for your delicate non-materialistic sensibilities, you are not the right person to be running a nonprofit.

The Board

Because most nonprofit organizations are corporations, the Board of Directors is an essential element in starting yours.

There is a difference between nonprofit board members and the senior management of the same organization: The Board of Directors is comprised of a group of individuals who monitor and regulate business, but who are not involved in the everyday running of the business, while senior managers such as CEOs and CFOs actually run the operations and are responsible to the Board.

It is the Board's job to set the bar regarding business practices of the senior management and others involved in the company.

The goal of the Board is to act in the best interest of the nonprofit organization by keeping in line with and continuously working to fulfill their mission statement. This is called the "legal standard of care" and is accomplished through the three Ds—A Duty of Care, a Duty of Loyalty, and a Duty of Obedience. This is an easy-to-remember way to ensure the following:

1. To carry out business in good faith with care and skill a person of prudence would exercise under similar circumstances.

2. To maintain allegiance to the organization, serving not for personal gain, but in the best interest of the organization.

3. To establish the mission of the organization and follow established policy while remaining loyal to said mission.

There are a number of responsibilities designated for the Board of Directors. They should represent various viewpoints or constituencies in the community it serves within its members. As the Board is responsible for ensuring the organization has the money it needs, many members personally make a financial contribution to the organization, organize fundraisers, or even solicit donations themselves.

The following are some typical duties of board members:

• Write bylaws and resolutions to establish rules for the board

• Establish, maintain, and revise policy (goals, objectives, procedure and timetables)

• Monitor policy of the board, personnel, and operations

• Monitor finances and material transactions

• Select, hire, monitor, and fire Executive Director and other senior managers

The board is responsible for major policies and decisions, while the Executive Director should be responsible for more ground level decision-making related to issues that affect the every day operations of the organization such as minor policies, standard operating procedures, and rules of conduct.

The Elements of Small Business

You may decide to pay your board members a "reasonable compensation" for their duties. However, board members are not commonly paid. Sometimes there is crossover—where an individual serves on the board without compensation but provides legal counseling or accounting services for a fee.

For further clarification, you may wish to visit a web site dedicated entirely to Boards of Directors for nonprofit organizations with some great FAQ sections.

The National Center for Nonprofit Boards changed its name in 2002 to BoardSource, but the Web site is the same: (www.ncnb.org). Don't miss their mission statement!

Legal Issues

Taxes are a big issue in nonprofit organizations. There are two IRS forms that are important to remember in the nonprofit sector. If you wish to acquire funds in the form of tax-deductible contributions, you will want to register as a 501(c)(3) charitable organization, but you may be able to acquire deductible donations outside of the (c)(3) realm. The 501(c)(3) has become somewhat of a catchall designation for nonprofits, although the entire 501(c) Tax Code from (1) through (27) deals with nonprofit organizations.

You are not required to incorporate to receive tax-exempt status. This is a common misconception. The benefits of incorporating your nonprofit are the same as those for a for-profit: A corporate veil that can protect directors and members from liability and the guidance you receive from the law regarding corporations.

Organizations that file for 501(c)(3) status should repeat after me: "My organization must serve a charitable, religious, educational, literary or scientific purpose and must be beneficial to the public interest."

If you do not fall within these categories, don't apply for tax exempt status. You won't enjoy the consequences when the IRS demands the back taxes.

As we discussed earlier, organizations that receive exempt status do not pay federal corporate tax and may not pay state or local taxes. But you must register in the state from which you operate. Many states have different laws regarding taxation of its nonprofit organizations. In order to be exempt from the other taxes you may need to file additional applications with those other taxing authorities. Check these sites for additional information: www.irs.gov and www.sec.gov. And *always* remember to file tax returns for the organization. Just because your company is exempt doesn't mean returns don't have to be filed.

Another necessary form includes IRS form 990. This is required as an annual information form, summarizing your organization. It states the names of the Board of Directors, if there were insider transactions, the highest paid salary, and the financial situation of the company. It is important take all these factors into account and make sure your company looks appetizing because this document is public. Anyone can request to see this document, but prospective donors are the ones who will most likely review it before they donate.

Insurance

By now you should have sought legal help regarding start-up of your nonprofit. Even if your organization is a corporation, it is a good idea to take out an insurance policy to protect the organization's liability and that of its Board.

Errors and Omissions coverage for board members and directors is essential, just in case you or other Board members do screw up. Get an agent who has experience with nonprofits. They will assess your needs, and possible risk issues as pertain to your nonprofit. Plus, they can help you outline a strategy to limit exposure and manage your risk.

Human Resources

Human Resources is the section of business that deals with employees. Some common duties of a human resources department are:

- recruiting, interviewing and hiring personnel;

- providing them with a safe workplace;

- setting compensation levels;

- implementing employee grievance policy;

- disciplining employees;

- establishing benefits and retirement programs;

- evaluating employee progress;

- developing job descriptions;

- recruiting interns and volunteers;

- creating and keeping employee records;

- tracking complaints or warnings given;

- conducting exit interviews; and

- issuing bonuses and complying with income tax guidelines.

Although Human Resources is a viable and important element in the nonprofit sector (as well as the for-profit,) chances are the company will be too small to have a department devoted to just that. Most likely, it will be you who addresses all these issues. Or, you can appoint a human resources committee to accomplish the operational and strategic goals set for the year and for the organization in general.

Staff and Volunteers

Because donations come from donors who are most likely interested in philanthropy or another worthy cause, it is logical to receive only a modest salary for the work you do. Other employees also must receive income, but make sure the salaries you set are well within the boundaries that would encourage someone to donate to your cause, not your income.

Running a nonprofit is not a part time job. It is a career. That is why it is important to integrate volunteers into organization. When you sell volunteers on giving their time for free, you might tell them that they may deduct expenses such as gas and oil from their taxes as well as parking, tolls, transportation and lodging and a portion of meals should they have to travel overnight.

Fund-raising

Fund-raising may be the most essential and most complicated aspect of operating a nonprofit organization. The easiest way to get money for your organization is to ask for it. Prospective donors need direction and motivation.

The good news is that once they give, statistically they are more likely to give again. Go to the people with a history of philanthropy before you forge the uncharted waters of unknowns. This will give you a solid base of supporters who know you and who will back you in the future. Also, this will boost your credibility when you seek new prospects.

 Tip: Everyone involved in your nonprofit, no matter what level, should invest in it financially. Don't make anyone break the bank, of course. That would be dumb. Then no one would work for you. But even if they donate a small chunk of change every month, they will feel personally invested in the cause, and the kicker is that everyone will feel more comfortable asking others to donate.

The Capital Campaign

A good place to start is people you do business with, and then local businesses and community leaders. They may or may not give to you, but they may reduce costs of services they provide to you—leaving more money for your mission—or they may direct you to a larger company or corporate headquarters that can give generously to your organization.

> All you have to do is ask. And don't forget what you are doing for them. By giving to philanthropy, companies have the opportunity for more publicity, and good publicity at that.

Many large corporations seek to increase their visibility in positive ways by forming foundations funded by a small percentage of corporate funds and possibly funds from additional fund-raiser event. These foundations then give grants to a number of worthy causes. Once you have made the list, it is likely that your organization is set for life— at least with that foundation.

Most foundations require that the organization be in business for at least five years and that it show an ever increasing stream of revenue and growth. Also, foundations require fairly sophisticated literature that describes in detail what the organization does, why it is needed, how funds are raised, and how funds are spent. In essence a business/marketing plan. In this context, it is often referred to as the "Grant Proposal."

A marketing plan may be implemented before a capital campaign to raise awareness in the community of the nonprofit before asking for donations. The research you do before the campaign can help determine the giving potential of prospects in order to make realistic solicitations.

When executing a capital campaign, you should ask for "major gifts" first. Identify through research those prospects who are capable of donating $25,000 to $100,000…and more. These large amounts donated to the organization make up the bulk of the funds raised during the campaign.

Major gift prospects should be solicited in person. It is always better to meet face to face with them. Doing anything by mail or computer could delay the actual decision-making prospect, and you do not want delays. Set up an appointment with a major prospect and set an amount to ask for. This should not be a shot in the dark. You want to ask for something that they are likely able to give, without ever undershooting. But if you overshoot, they'll merely decline and send you on your way.

I work with a nonprofit organization that specializes in part with educating the families of special needs children. For the annual fund-raiser dinner, the keynote speaker often is a well-known individual who has a special needs child or who has a sibling with special needs. Obviously, the speaker feels more connected to the organization and therefore is more inclined to participate.

Everyone has certain skills at which they excel. Choose wisely the person who will represent the organization with famous individuals or corporations or foundations. Personality does matter. And that person had better know the facts.

Also, if you are concerned with toning down the bluntness of the message, try setting up a meeting with a mutual friend and donor to break the ice. Once you have asked for the gift, let them think about it. It is okay to ask them what level they would be comfortable giving at if you suggest an amount that is too high. You want to close the deal at any level, so you may want to convey the best part of your pitch one more time.

If they decide to donate, thank them graciously for their gift and ask them for contact information of another person who may be interested in giving. If you don't close the deal, try to set up a follow-up appointment.

It is a lot easier to set up a second meeting in person, and if you don't you run the risk of not being able to get them to meet with you again. But pressure or guilt will fail. Remember your friendly motivating skills here.

Always follow up with a note or phone call, and if they do say no, there are always more prospects. Don't get discouraged by rejection. It is bound to happen in fund-raising. Be patient, a good listener, be sincere, and most of all, believe in your cause. Prospects will see that.

Once you have finished your major gift solicitations, you can solicit through other means: mailings, telemarketing, or other fundraising projects, such as silent auctions or benefit dinners. Some charities like to send return address labels as an incentive for you to donate. Generally it is illegal, however, to require that one pay for these "incentive gifts."

Grant Proposals

The grant proposal is part of a process of seeking funds. Think of it as a business plan for your nonprofit. You will share it with others to educate them about your business.

A grant proposal cannot stand alone, however. You need to build a database of potential donors from whom you seek grants. This involves planning, research, outreach, and creation of relationships with these people.

You need to provide information about your organization and, if appropriate, the specific program you intend to add. How you will conduct it, who will be involved, what the expenses will be, and a timeline of the project need to be part of the proposal? Of course, you will not be able to determine exactly that amount of funds needed for the project, but a general outline should be done to ensure a successful outcome of your endeavors. That will also help you see if the project is even feasible, and you can make adjustments to your budget before it is too late and your donors' funds are ill spent!

The Foundation Center has a free proposal writing "short course" posted on its Web site (www.fdncecnter.org/learn/shortcourse.) It gives advice on how to put together a smashing proposal for submission to foundations and other potential donors.

Your proposal should be a product of extremely thorough market research and planning on your part. The Foundation Center's short course elaborates on each of the following:

- The Executive Summary: A general statement of the case you are presenting and a summary of the following proposal.

- The Statement of Need: Why the project is necessary and important to society in general and certain individuals specifically/

- The Project Description: This is where you get to explain the specifics-the inner workings of your nonprofit and how you intend to implement the program and make evaluations.

- The Budget: A financial overview of the nonprofit with explanations of how you arrived at those numbers.

- Organization Information: An overview of the history and structure of your nonprofit, including main activities, target market and services or products.

- Conclusion: A recap of your proposals main points.

Writing a grant proposal will give you solid direction and knowledge when it comes to asking for grants. It will teach you about your own business, cause you to become accountable for furthering your mission, and inform others about all the wonderful thing you are doing to make the world a better place.

Professional Fund-raisers

So now your head is swimming. You are not a good salesman. You are confident and passionate about your project, but something still makes you feel uncomfortable about asking for money—maybe a repressed childhood memory about seeking that increase in allowance. That's okay. And it's fairly common. Hence, the invention of companies that will raise your funds for you. They do it for a fee, of course, and some will simply take a percentage of what they collect.

When choosing an outside fund-raiser, you must remember that this company will represent your business. It is important to take measures necessary to ensure that their behavior is appropriate to your expectations—so as to avoid disputes, less money collected, or even legal action. You can ask other nonprofits in your area whom they have used and do some research on your own.

Some fund-raisers specialize in grants, some specialize in mailers, and some specialize in event planning such as golf tournaments or dinners.

Once you have an idea of what you think will work best for the organization, you can start interviewing the professional fund-raisers. Have them send you literature and a sample contract before you get involved. Find out how they will raise the funds. Find out how much of the contribution actually goes to you, and require them to provide financial reports. Find out what they may be doing besides collecting money, like selling concert tickets or merchandise. Find out how much control you have over how the funds are solicited and if any subcontractors will be used.

The fund-raisers work for you. Make sure you have the ultimate control, but remember that these people are professionals and they are trying to make the most money possible as well. Some states require professional fund-raisers to be licensed or bonded.

It is also a good idea to get a list of references and contact them.

When you sign a contract with a professional fund-raiser, you will want to review it with your lawyer. It should include the following:

- the services to be provided;

- financial responsibility of each party;

- whether subcontractors may be used;

- compensation to be paid and how;

- the contract period; closing and settlement dates;

- cancellations criteria;

- require detailed reporting of results;

- specify ownership of lists.

Remember that you are ultimately responsible for the behavior of the fund-raiser you hire. You should have control over the materials mailed and scripts to be performed during sales calls. Keep in contact with them through out the campaign, track complaints and resolve them immediately, and keep tabs on your money!

You can contact the Better Business Bureau's Wise Giving Alliance (www.give.org) or the American Institute of Philanthropy (www.charitywatch.org) for more detailed information regarding fund-raising standards.

Marketing and Public Relations

If you are the typical philanthropic type, chances are you will give second priority to marketing. But nonprofits are still businesses, and you must do your part to compete for your target demographic in order to make your business successful. In addition to grant proposals designed for specific potential donors, will you need your standard marketing plan, but you must be prepared to answer any and all questions about your organization should opportunity rise.

Your marketing plan should reflect the size and scope of your organization. Do not skimp on design and printing costs. Often, a postcard or advertisement is the first thing that people see of your company. Your goal is to appear as though you are the most professional organization to offer your products or services, especially when the majority of your funds come from those who aren't receiving the benefit of your services.

There are some less obvious ways that a nonprofit can market itself. Press releases, public service announcements, charity benefits, and newsletters are all viable marketing options for nonprofit organizations. It's like marketing incognito…you get to advertise your cause and your programs without people saying "Hey, they're just trying to get my money." Even though you are.

Note that many television and radio stations provide spots for nonprofit organizations and run "calendars" of events on their Internet sites where you can list upcoming events.

Planning

Aside from your marketing plan, you should perform a needs assessment evaluation. There should be an initial evaluation as you start your nonprofit organization and then periodic ongoing evaluations. (Refer to the chapter on Business Plans for a complete explanation of SWOT analysis, and include the needs assessment in your business plan.)

These evaluations can be done by taking surveys of members and current or potential donors, the general public, and of course, personal interviews of employees, senior managers and board members.

Compile the surveys and interviews you have taken into separate "cases." With this information you will be able to gauge motivations levels inside and outside your organization, how current and previous donors and other constituents view you, what you do well or poorly, and how effective your staff, volunteers and board members are.

Performing regular evaluations of your nonprofit, either with a consultant or on your own, should produce the following:

- clear mission and vision statements;

- SWOT analyses and program evaluations;

- well defined client needs and member concerns;

- general priorities and specific goals, objectives and strategies;

- an annual operational plan.

As time goes on, nonprofits should return to evaluations as a tool to create new strategies and monitor progress.

> **What is the difference between a strategic plan and an operational plan, you ask?** An operational plan is more detailed, but should outline procedure and business policy for a one-year period based upon what the strategic plan has outlined. It includes goals and objectives for the year which will further the mission statement of the organization.

Guidelines for action by individuals involved in daily operations, which duties are expected of each responsible party, and the deadlines they can expect to adhere to are all part of the operational plan. Draw up the operational plan at the same time you do your budget. Involve the board as needed.

The strategic plan is a long-term plan which establishes priorities and direction, focuses vision, and ensures that all members are working toward the same goals.

Conclusion

Now you know that nonprofit businesses are not limited to those philanthropic, frugal caretakers that everyone looks at like they're crazy

The Elements of Small Business

because they're taking salaries well below their competency levels. The nonprofit sector is just as competitive and cutthroat as the rest of them, and many fail before they even get off the ground. But if the guidelines of the nonprofit organization match you goals and objectives as a small business owner and entrepreneur, then jump on in.

Nonprofits carry with them a number of philosophies and leadership practices that may not exist on other types of businesses, although most for-profit businesses could gain from studying the nonprofit ethic.

The Duties of Care, Loyalty and Obedience may sound more like the vows you say before joining a convent, but what better way to create a team of solidarity, encouragement and support within your business. When people see the tremendous passion and drive coming from those who represent your business, potential donors will be quickly moved to give, and give generously.

References

Bryson, John M. *Strategic Planning for Public and Nonprofit Organizations: A Guide to Strengthening and Sustaining Organizational Achievement*. Jossey-Bass, Inc. (September, 1995).

Bryson, John M., and Farnum K. Alston. *Creating and Implementing Your Strategic Plan: A Workbook for Public and Nonprofit Organizations*. Jossey-Bass, Inc. (April, 1997).

Carlson, Mim, and The Alliance for Nonprofit Management. *Winning Grants: Step By Step* (2nd edition). John Wiley & Sons, Inc. (June, 2002).

Grobman, Gary M. *NonProfit Handbook* (3rd edition). White Hat Communications (April, 2002).

Karsh, Ellen, and Arlen Sue Fox. *The Only Grant-Writing Book You'll Ever Need*. Carroll & Graf Publishers, Inc. (June, 2003).

Kaye, Judy, Michael Allison and The Support Center for Nonprofit Management. *Strategic Planning for NonProfit Organizations (Nonprofit Law, Finance and Management Series): A Practical Guide and Workbook*. John Wiley & Sons, Inc. (July, 1997).

McLaughlin, Thomas A. *Streetsmart Financial Basics for Nonprofit Managers* (2nd edition). John Wiley & Sons, Inc. (June, 2002).

Riddle, John. *Streetwise Managing a NonProfit: How to Write Winning Grant Proposals, Work with a Board, and Build a Fundraising Program*. Adams Media Corporation (June, 2002).

The Elements of Small Business

Tremore, Judy, and Nancy Burke Smith. *The Everything Grant Writing Book*. Adams Media Corporation (June, 2003).

Wolf, Thomas. *Managing A Nonprofit Organization In The Twenty-First Century* (3rd edition). Simon & Schuster Adult Publishing Group (June, 1999).

Chapter 20

Exit Strategies

You never know where bottom is until you plumb for it.
—Fredrick Laing

The statistics on business failures within the first five years of operations are so astounding that printing them here might result in scaring readers away from ever starting any businesses.

If you're scared off, you won't need this book. So, in the name if better sales, let's move ahead to the point where you either *want* to get out…or *need* to get out.

As any good military planner will say, you need to have an exit strategy before your ever commit resources to any activity. In business, this means you have to think at least a little bit about what the end of your business venture might be. Some common reasons for developing an exit strategy include:

- struggling to make a profit and declaring bankruptcy when the fight gets too difficult,

- making decent profit for a few years and then closing up shop when the marketplace changes away from your business,

- selling out to partners,

- handing the operations over to children or younger family members,

- selling out to a bigger competitor,

- taking money from venture capitalists,

- selling the company to public shareholders (or "going public").

Of course, there are dozens of variations on each of these options. To simplify slightly, I say there are two ways[1] to exit a business:

1) selling out, and

2) shutting down.

In this chapter, we'll consider each of these exits in just enough detail that you can keep some idea of what the light at the end of your business tunnel might be.

Selling Out

Just about anyone who runs a business spends some idle moments thinking about what they'd take to sell their operation. Some start their businesses with a clear goal of growing it up and selling it; others think about selling at the end of a particularly hard day. And many start thinking about selling when friends and family members who work in conventional jobs start retiring.

The first question that you need to ask yourself, if you're serious about selling, is: What does your business have that someone else might want? If you've done any commercial financing, you've generated balance sheets and asset lists for bankers and finance companies. But for the purpose of this exercise, you might think more broadly. The value in your business might include obvious and not-so-obvious assets.

The obvious, tangible assets are the things that your bankers have asked about. They usually include:

---

[1] Of course, you might argue there's a third option: Passing the business on to children or family. I don't really consider that *exiting* a business. But, for a good discussion of family business succession, see Silver Lake Publishing's book *Family Money* (2002).

- inventory;

- equipment;

- real estate;

- contracts, licenses, franchise deals, royalties, etc.;

- accounts receivable;

- cash.

Bankers understand these kinds of assets; likewise, *financial buyers* will understand these kinds of assets. Like bankers, though, financial buyers won't always see the full value of your business—the market share you've carved out, the relationships you've built, the reputation you've established. A person or company that understands those values is a *strategic buyer.*

If you're thinking of selling, it's usually best to look for a strategic buyer. This can be another company already in your market, a similar company that's not in your market but wants to be...or a particularly knowledgeable person or firm that understands your business.

Strategic buyers will look beyond tangible assets to the less obvious, intangible value your business might have. These intangibles can include:

- branding (trademarks and less formal business identity);

- client or customer lists;

- client or customer *relationships*;

- products designs, packaging or patents;

- products in development;

- key personnel.

The Elements of Small Business

As we discussed in the early parts of this book, you can buy a business through a business broker. Obviously, the process can be reversed and you can sell a business through a broker.

> One key advantage to using a business broker: Some owners, who are aggressive about every other aspect of their business, become shy or reticent about selling the business itself. Owners may find the process too...personal; or they may take a "let the buyers come to me" approach. So, the somewhat disinterested broker can be the impersonal boost that a sale needs.

If you're not familiar with business brokers in your area, ask other small business owners. You can also ask any trade or industry groups to which you belong. As a last resort, you can always search on-line or through the Yellow Pages.

However you find a business broker, make sure to ask for references—and *check with the references* that the broker offers. Business brokers are usually not licensed or regulated as closely as insurance agents or real estate brokers; as a result, their experience, knowledge and ability can vary sharply from broker to broker.

Some people compare business brokers to real estate brokers. But the comparison is limited, at best. Selling a business is more complicated, time-consuming and particular than selling a house. Even an expensive house. The sale of a business can involve contract assignments, sharing trade secrets, personnel issues, real estate transfers...or all of these.

There are many opinions about what makes the best business broker. Is it a small operation with local focus? Is it a common-sense industry specialist who understands the details of your operation; or an ambitious financial specialist who prefers the term "investment banker" to "business broker?" There are no right answers to these questions. The best approach is to use your own experience as your guide. What kind of broker would *you* be most likely to trust?

Hiring a Business Broker

Once you've selected a broker, you'll usually be provided with a listing agreement or contract. Read the contract carefully yourself; then send it to your attorney and have him or her review it. Key issues usually include:

- **Price and terms**. How much do you want for the business; and does the purchase have to be in cash? In many small business sales, the owner agrees to some form of deferred payment—often in the form of a private note or an "earn out" arrangement based on the business' revenues. Will you accept that sort of arrangement? Can the broker offer it initially? Or only after consultation with you?

- The broker's **commission or fee**. Is it a fixed amount or a percentage of the sale price? A combination of both? Does the fee or commission increase as the sale price does? Are there any bonuses or "kickers" if the broker makes a sale quickly to reaches other goals?

- **Terms of agency**. How long will the broker *be* the broker? Under what terms or conditions can you fire the broker?

- **Retainers or advances**. Does the broker require any up-front payments? If so, will these payments be used for specific marketing activities? How will they be allies to final fees? If the deal doesn't go through, will advanced payments be returned?

- **Advertisement and marketing**. How will the sale be promoted or publicized? Will an ad in the local newspaper do anything to hurt your day-to-day business? Will an ad in trade journal tip off competitors or scare existing clients? Will you get to review every ad or promotion before it goes out?

- **Broker access**. How often and under what conditions can the broker "show" the business to potential buyers? Are specific times of day better—in terms of not interfering with your regular work? Will you need a specific amount of advanced notice?

Again, there's no right answer to any of these questions. You need to make the arrangement that will get the best price for your business without interrupting or doing damage to ongoing operation.

Generally, though, cash is better than an earn-out—even if you have to accept less in a sale. Broker fees vary dramatically by location and industry; but they usually range between five and 10 percent of the sale price (and should be on the low end of that range, most of the time).

Since selling a business is more complex than selling a house, most broker contracts will give the broker at least six months to try to get a deal done. That's reasonable. Retainers are more problematic; avoid them, if at all possible. Even if the contract calls for a refund, it's very hard to get money you've advanced back. If the only broker you like demands an advance, establish how the money will be used (advertising, other marketing, even research). That way, if there's a dispute later, you can demand proof that the money was spent as it should have been.

Most advertising and marketing in business brokerage is done "blind." That means the broker keeps details of the business private until potential buyers have been vetted and qualified. Make sure that your broker understands this policy and follows it. Loose talk about your business being for sale can make customers nervous.

Access can be a big deal. Many business broker arrangements that end badly do so because the broker claims that the business was not available or "showable" to potential buyers. State clearly from the start when and under what conditions potential buyers can see the business. Intelligent ones will understand that Friday at 8 p.m. is *not* a good time to check out a restaurant.

Assembling Your Information

Once the broker contract has been hammered out, your work has just begun.

Usually, the broker will begin by researching recent sales of similar businesses in your area. This will help support your asking price and establish standard terms—but it will also help identify possible buyers.

In the meantime, the broker will usually give you a list financial and commercial information that will need to prepare. This list will usually include the following items:

- at least three years of tax returns,

- three years of profit and loss statements,

- three years of balance sheets,

- detailed accounts payable and receivable reports,

- list of lenders or financing companies related to current or long-term liabilities—and details on whether these items are assumable or assignable,

- payroll details and employment contracts,

- key customer contracts or distribution agreements,

- complete customer or client list,

- complete vendor list.

If you're well organized, this information can be generated in half an hour from your accounting software and a quick check of a few files. Most small businesses aren't so well organized.

Even if it takes a few days of digging, it's essential that you assemble a standard "package" of this information for potential buyers to review.

You can keep this information for when you meet a potential buyer…or you can give your broker a master copy…but the important thing is to have the basics ready in advance of any negotiation.

Buyers will usually demand it.

The Mechanics of a Sale

As we discussed at the beginning of this book, business transactions can take the form of either an asset sale or a stock sale.

In an asset sale, you sell the things that make up your business but keep the corporate structure of your business and responsibility for paying off any debts, obligations or liabilities.

In a stock sale, you sell the entire business, including assets, liabilities and whatever corporate structure the business takes.

Asset sales are easier—mechanically—to structure than stock sales. And they usually mean a larger sale price. But they leave a considerable amount of work for the seller. After you've agreed on a purchase and sale agreement and sold the assets that constitute the business to the new owner, you usually have to pay off debts, pay out partners, close up shop (sometimes literally) and lay off workers.

> Of course, you also have the option of using your remaining corporate structure to start some sort of new venture. However, since the asset buyer will usually ask you to sign some form of non-compete agreement, your new venture may have to be in an entirely new field.

Stock sales are a little more complicated. In most cases, once you've agreed on the purchase and sale agreement, you will have open an escrow account. An escrow officer will handle the transfer of stock for cash…and make sure that the stock actually represents the complete, unencumbered ownership of the business. This can be a time-consuming process that involves searches for any claims or liens under the Uniform Commercial Code, title searches of any real estate involved and searching public databases of lawsuits or other claims in any places where your business has done business.

In some cases, the background checks can hold up the close of the sale for weeks…or longer. And, in a few cases, the escrow or title agents may require that some of the sale proceeds be held after the close as security against any pending actions.

This process can be a tough one. Complete honesty about any business or legal hassles will help make it go more smoothly. If you know that you've got a skeleton or two out there, you'll be nervous during the escrow period. And you should be. Escrow is designed to dig up skeletons—and it usually does. Therefore, it's usually best to have a lawyer or broker manage the escrow process for you.

The upside to a stock sale is that, once the deal closes, you don't need to worry about business liabilities anymore. In almost every case, they are the new owner's concern. In this litigious age, that's a good thing.

About Real Estate

Real estate is an interesting matter when it comes to selling a business. On the balance sheets, it's an asset; but, in the course of a sale, it can emerge as either a good thing or a bad thing.

Many business owners consider buying real estate—or leasing it for a long term—as a kind of hedge against the ups and downs of their business cycles. But, when it comes to selling a small business, the same "assets" can seem like liabilities.

A Southern California chain of frozen yogurt stores was a good example of this kind of shift. Its owners had signed a number of long-term leases for stores in pricy, high-traffic neighborhoods. They considered these contracts to be assets; the deals locked them into desirable locations for 10 years or more at fixed, below-market rates.

Then, several years sooner than any of the owners expected, a larger frozen yogurt chain approached them about selling. The offer was attractive—with one exception. The larger buyer didn't want the long-term leases on commercial space (it had its own stores in many of the locations). Suddenly, the real estate switched from being a good thing to being an unwanted drag on the deal.

The owners of the smaller chain agreed to sell the assets of their company to their larger competitor. But they agreed to keep all responsibility for the long-term leases on several dozen locations.

They made money from their sale—but they had to sublet or buy out the leases they kept. That took time and ate into the profits they made from the sale.

Real estate *can* be a good hedge. But, if you buy a building or lease a lot of retail space, it's a good idea to establish a separate entity (corporation, LLC or real estate trust) for owning or controlling those assets. That way, you can keep the real estate apart from the other business operations; and, if you get rid of the business, you can either get rid of the real estate, too, or keep it and be a landlord, etc.

Shutting Down

If you keep your tangible assets separate—or don't *have* many tangible assets—and sales have declining for several years while your mind has turned to thoughts of golf and shuffleboard, you might consider simply shutting down the business.

Dissolving a business can be easy or difficult, depending on the form of the business and how many debts you have.

If the form of your business is a sole proprietorship and you don't have significant debt or bills due, all you need to do is stop doing business, pay off your vendors and move on to the next thing.

> If you've borrowed money from the bank or a commercial finance company, you're still responsible for that debt. But, since you've borrowed the money as a sole proprietor, the lenders don't usually care how you make the payments—as long as you make them. So, you can move on to a traditional job and pay those debts. Or you can set up a new business and pay them.

If the form of your business is a corporation, LLC/LLP or limited partnership, shutting down is a little more complex.

To begin, you'll need to get the written authorization to shut down from all partners or members. Once you have this, you will usually have to file a notice of termination with the Department of Corporations, Secretary of State or similar agency in the state where the business is domiciled …and anywhere it has facilities or does significant business.

You may also have to publish a notice of intent to terminate in a local newspaper or journal of record. And you'll need to give notice of termination to any person or company with whom you have a contract or legal agreement.

It can take anywhere from two weeks to six months to get the final termination paperwork back from the states. The time lag is designed to do two things:

1) give the state time to make sure that you've paid all appropriate taxes and fees;

2) give the public—and, more specifically, your vendors or creditors—the chance to make any legal of financial claims they have against your business.

Once you've filed all your termination paperwork, paid off all your vendors and creditors and paid all of your taxes, you can distribute the business' assets among the owners. If you're the only owner, that's easy. If there are partners, you will have draw up a letter or more formal contract that explains how the assets are being distributed and that all owners agree to the deal.

Just as you should use a lawyer to draft your corporation or LLC filings—especially if you have partners—you should use one to help with the termination. Many states make the termination process slow and complicated, in order to keep fees flowing as long as possible. A good corporate counsel can let you know where the snares lie.

Once everything has been distributed and all contracts have been ended, you'll have to sent a final notice to the state. In some cases, you may have to post a bond or pledge some other form of financial security against taxes or fees which might come to light in the future. But, if no tax issues exist, you will receive a letter indicating that the termination (it may be called a "dissolution") is complete.

Be aware: If labilities surface after the corporation, LLC or limited partnership has been dissolved, members may be held responsible for these issues—usually, up to a share of the liability equal to their ownership percentage in the dissolved entity.

Bankruptcy

Some businesses end up adrift in a sea of red ink that even Moses couldn't part. In these cases, selling out is not an option and neither is a simple dissolution. Instead, bankruptcy may be the best choice.

Probably no other word in the business language has such a pejorative meaning as *bankruptcy*. Yet, the number of business failures in the 1990s and 2000s has resulted in a record number of bankruptcies.

Unlike most of the court battles you might have, bankruptcy is controlled by federal statutes and by the federal judiciary. However, the rules are not uniform in each state. In fact, the states have certain rights to set parameters for qualifications.

Bankruptcy rules are organized into categories called chapters. Each treats debts and obligations—and how they're paid—differently.

When you choose to declare bankruptcy and you have few assets and own no property, then you may not need an attorney other than for the assistance with the filing. The papers necessary to commence a bankruptcy can be quite voluminous and cover topics that may not be well-understood by the lay person. However, if you own a business, a home, or shares in a corporation, then an attorney is essential.

Chapter 7

Bankruptcy is available to businesses and to individuals. The most widely used form of bankruptcy for both is liquidation under Chapter 7. This section provides for the liquidation of your assets or your company's assets. You start with filing a whole lot of papers [Form 20-1] that provide a list of all assets and all debts, including receivable income and payable expenses. In theory, since the reason for filing a bankruptcy is a lack of money, chances are there will not be an issue with having more assets than liabilities.

Note that your creditors will receive notice of the bankruptcy and will have the right to question you or even make objections. However, upon filing the bankruptcy, all collections cease. If your home is being foreclosed on or is about to be foreclosed on, all proceedings are halted, at least temporarily.

Once filed, all of what you have or your business has is called the "bankruptcy estate." While a judge oversees the estate, the administration of it is handled primarily by a "trustee." The trustee is an attorney who is appointed by the judge to administer the estate, or put simply, the trustee is charged with gathering your assets, if any, and distributing them to your creditors. By hiring a reputable attorney who specializes in bankruptcy, he or she likely will know the trustee and his or her propensities. Your attorney also will have some knowledge of the judge and the best ways to make the process go smoothly.

Generally, four to six weeks after the initial filing, you will be required to appear at a 341(a) hearing. At this hearing, which your attorney will attend, the trustee asks questions about the information contained in your paperwork. While the questions vary between a business bankruptcy and an individual bankruptcy, the crux of the questions centers on your assets and how you concluded that they were valueless or lacked any substantial value.

 By the way, acting distraught or forlorn at bankruptcy hearings won't help. The trustee does not get paid by you or the court. Instead, the trustee is entitled to a percentage of monies he recovers for the creditors. For example, when a "secret" Swiss bank account is discovered and turned over to your creditors, the trustee gets his slice of the pie. The best way to act is quietly and professionally.

If you file as an individual but operate a corporation or LLC, then the fun really begins. While the corporation is not your personal asset, the shares of the corporation that you hold *are*. Thus, they are subject to the bankruptcy. If your business is in the same financial condition as your personal finances, then the shares of stock have little or no value. However, if your personal finances are in the dumpster but the business is making money, the trustee has the authority to sell your shares of the business in order to pay off your creditors.

If you have partners in the LLC or corporation, the value of their equity can be affected by your personal bankruptcy. If you try to hide your filing from them, you're probably violating your fiduciary duty to the business. Don't do that. It will only add to your problems.

Once again, a good lawyer with experience in bankruptcy is essential here. For example, if the business is performing well, your attorney might argue that your personal abilities provide the value to the business and therefore a sale of your shares would not create much value for creditors. Or, if permits are required for the operation of the business, your attorney might point out that the time and expense of transferring the permits would make the business difficult to sell and, again, not create much value.

At the 341(a) hearing, your creditors have the right to ask questions about your assets and their valuation. Typically, arms length creditors and unsecured creditors such as credit card companies will not send any representatives. But secured creditors may be more inclined to ask questions. While your attorney has little ability to object at this stage, the trustee will not allow the questioning to progress too far unless certain information comes to light such as hidden or unreported assets.

Also, creditors have a right to take your deposition known as a "2002 examination." That process involves questioning of you under oath by an attorney for one or more of your creditors about the veracity of the documents you filed and any assets you undervalued or failed to report. A 2002 examination is not relevant unless the creditor believes you have not been truthful—so, it's usually a pretty nasty exchange.

Then there is the possibility of a lawsuit. While judgments, current and potential liabilities are subject to discharge in bankruptcy, *intentional wrongdoing* is different. For example, if before filing the bankruptcy, you intentionally misrepresented something—committed a fraud—the filing will not save you. If no lawsuit has been filed prior to the bankruptcy filing, one can be filed within the bankruptcy court. The suit will proceed like any other suit, except that the case is heard by the judge without a jury.

Ultimately, you or your company will be discharged from Chapter 7 bankruptcy and the debts and creditors will go bye-bye. And then you begin again with Chapter One of this book. So remember not to abuse it or make too many dog ears.

Chapters 11 and 13

Okay. So what happened to Chapters 1 through 6 and 8 through 10? Who knows?

Actually, these other Chapters (really, they're sections of the bankruptcy law) are reserved for local governments and other particular legal entities. Most of them do not have anything to do with ordinary businesses or individuals.

Chapter 11 provides a way to continue doing business for businesses that believe they can be successful—if only their creditors will give them a break.

Before you undertake this filing, make every attempt to work out deals with your creditors. Many will prefer to give you more time or even forgive part of your debt, in order to avoid dealing with a bankruptcy. As most bankruptcy lawyers will tell you, you have the most leverage to re-negotiate with creditors *before* you file. Once you're in the system, neither you nor your creditors are in charge. The trustee is.

And you're spending your time and scarce money dealing with process, rather than earning your way out of trouble. In addition to filing all of the applicable paperwork, you will be required, either individually or in behalf of your business, a plan to pay your creditors on which they will agree. Simply said, you can't suggest a plan to pay 50 cents on the dollar and then expect the trustee or the judge to force that solution down the throats of the creditors.

Don't be confused by the Chapter 11 filings of large public companies where the companies seem to have control over the creditors. In their cases, millions of dollars are at stake and tens of thousands of jobs depend on a viable plan...and liquidation of the assets may not yield enough money to pay all the creditors. So the creditors have an interest in working with the debtor company.

In a small business, you won't have so many employees and many may have been laid off long before you file. Most of your debts likely include leasing companies who have enabled you to finance certain items but have a lien on them. While the leasing companies have little desire to foreclose on the goods, at least they have that option.

The trustee will take of this into account when he or she assembles a plan that splits the difference between what you can afford and what your creditors are likely to accept. If that doesn't work—if the creditors don't agree to the plan—then you will be forced into a Chapter 7 liquidation whether you like it or not.

Chapter 13 is a bankruptcy for individuals only—businesses need not apply. Like Chapter 11, Chapter 13 provides time to pay creditors. However, they must be paid and you'll usually have only three to five years in which to do it.

Chapter 13 is especially popular where Chapter 7 is not possible. For example, if you are employed but don't have the cash necessary to pay your monthly debt service, Chapter 13 provides a longer timetable in which to make payments. The payments are then made to the court via the trustee and distributed among your creditors.

Don't File Unless You Have To

A client who owned a flower shop called me. The business was not incorporated and was running into cash flow problems. She and her husband had accumulated credit card debt in the tens of thousands of dollars and could not keep up with the payments. They wanted to file a Chapter 7 bankruptcy. But they had a problem: They owned a house with equity well over $250,000. Since their total debt fell below the equity in the house, thus resulting in more assets than liabilities. They weren't *eligible* for a Chapter 7 filing. They could have taken their chances on a Chapter 13 filing, gambling that the creditors wouldn't push them to sell their residence. But, since they had so much equity in the house, this wasn't a good bet either.

After talking with the husband and wife for a while, I realized that they hadn't even tried to ask their creditors for extended terms.

Granted, those phone calls can be tough ones to make—admitting that you're short of cash and are going to need some weeks or months to pay your bills—but they're a lot easier that sitting through bankruptcy hearings. And most creditors are used to customers in cash crunches. What they usually want is good information about how much time you'll need and how you're going to get out of the bind.

Why file for a bankruptcy if you don't have to? Before you bail out, consult an attorney who specializes in bankruptcy and *has experience in business*. Maybe the lawyer can make the hard calls. If your creditors understand your dire financial condition, they may be willing to enter into an arrangement to extend payments or even suspend them for a period of time. **You'll never know if you don't ask.**

The Paper Chase

If bankruptcy is inevitable, get ready to do a lot of paperwork. If you thought tax return forms were difficult, wait until you see the Bankruptcy Petition (for simplicity's sake, in this section, I'll reference a Chapter 7 filing—it's the most common).

The cover sheet and second page contains the names of the parties, the chapter under which you are filing, the name of the attorney (though you're not *required* to have one), and other basic information. Then come the schedules. The pages, similar to that which you might file with a tax return, contain the specific information about your assets and liabilities.

First, a "Summary of Schedules" is created. It tells the trustee what is to come. Schedules include lists of the following: real property, personal property, exempt property, secured creditor claims, unsecured creditor claims, contracts and leases, co-debtors, current income, and current expenditures.

Real property is any land you own, whether its use is for business or residence. You are required to provide a description, your interest including whether the property is community, the value of the property and the amount of any secured claim. If you lease your home and/or your office, then this page will be left open.

Personal property has a broad definition. First, it starts with the cash you have including any money you have in your bank accounts. It also includes any deposits you made to utility companies to get your utilities started. Remember those deposits and the curse words you muttered when you realized you had to pay them? Then comes household goods—books, pictures, antiques, records, tapes, and even that Carly Simon CD must be accounted for in terms of their total value. Have any furs not painted by PETA or any jewelry? They must be declared.

How about insurance policies or annuities? Or stocks and bonds? Or retirement plans? These must be disclosed as well. (Though most recognized retirement plan dollars are exempt.)

And then there is alimony and inheritances— which I include in the same section since if you are paying alimony you will need an inheritance.

Own any intellectual property? Did you write a hit song or an award winning script? Have any crops or any barnyard animals? Have any machinery or any farming equipment?

And there is the "E" answer: all of the above. In this case, you put down the value of anything not covered by the specific categories.

The next section concerns *exempt property*. Your lawyer will advise you on the specifics. In most cases, you are allowed to stay alive. And you are allowed to make a living. So, cash on hand used to pay for necessary expenses often is exempted. Your average household goods are exempt as is your clothing, and as we said above, retirement savings are generally exempt.

Next are the *secured claims*. If the bankruptcy is filed on a corporation, then the secured claims likely will include any business equipment subject to a lease, regardless of whether the lease results in ownership. If the bankruptcy is personal, then secured creditors might include department store merchandise purchased with the department store card. Unlike the typical Visa or Mastercard purchase, the store credit card provides in the fine print that the store has a lien on any items purchased with that card. In the event of a bankruptcy, Circuit City can actually try to recover the big screen TV you bought for that Super Bowl Party.

Then come the *unsecured claims*. They are the "all others" of whom you owe money. Major credit card debt is the most common. Also, if someone has a court judgment, that judgment should be included—and can be discharged.

Following the creditors are executory *contracts and leases*. And then there are the *co-debtors*. If you have partners, this is where you get to give their names and information. Just think how much they will appreciate the gesture.

Once you have covered all that you have, it becomes time for the income and expenses.

> A word to the wise: if you claim to have $5,000 per month in expenses, it helps to show approximately $5,000 in income. While showing too much income obviously makes no sense, showing too little is equally troubling, especially if the mortgage or lease/rent payment is more than you claim to make.

The next section is the "Statement of Financial Affairs." In addition to business or employment income, you are asked to list individually and verify everything you totaled on the Summary of Schedules.

Then you are asked about your intentions, especially concerning the secured debts. "Winning the lottery" is not what the trustee will be looking for. This schedule will inform the court and the trustee as to whether you intend to give up certain secured property or attempt to keep it. Many individuals who have a house, try to keep it. That is acceptable so long as you inform the mortgage company, the trustee and the court.

Finally, a proof of service by mail containing names and addresses of all of the creditors must be provided to show the court and the trustee that you have informed everyone about the bankruptcy so that they can come to the 341(a) hearing and make you feel like a deadbeat.

Don't feel bad. When you get to the hearing, there will be a slew of other deadbeats, many in far worse financial condition than you. Your lawyer will walk you through the process and will deal with any problem creditors. And just think: Once discharged, you can return to the start of this book and begin the process all over again.

Conclusion

The *grande finale* of your business can come in many forms: sale, dissolution or even bankruptcy. Each has its complexities and challenges. I hope you've done well enough with business during its run that the exit is worth the effort.

No matter which of these exit strategies you choose, your attorney and accountant will be critical in making yours a smooth exit. Generally, any exit will require some manner of final accounting of how the business has done—for a buyer, tax man or bankruptcy trustee.

As in any major business transaction, make sure to read all of the relevant documents carefully. I'm always amazed at how many business people don't do this. If you're off to Sun City, you don't want to have to worry about old problems finding you.

And, if you're on to your next adventure, see you back at Chapter One.

References

Caher, James P., and John M. Caher. *Personal Bankruptcy For Dummies*. IDG/John Wiley & Sons, Inc. (February, 2003).

Debtor, David G. *Bankruptcy and Related Law in a Nutshell* (6th edition). West/Wadsworth Publishing (January, 2002).

Delaney, Kevin J. *Strategic Bankruptcy: How Corporations and Creditors Use Chapter 11 to Their Advantage* (reprint edition). University of California Press (January, 1999).

Elias, Stephen. *How to File for Chapter 7 Bankruptcy* (10th edition). Nolo Press (September, 2002).

Newton, Grant W. *Corporate Bankruptcy: Tools, Strategies, and Alternatives*. John Wiley & Sons, Inc. (January, 2003).

Onaitis, Susan. *Negotiate Like the Big Guys: How Small and Mid-Sized Companies Can Balance the Power in Dealing with Corporate Giants*. Silver Lake Publishing (October, 1999).

Silver Lake Editors. *Family Money*. Silver Lake Publishing (September, 2002).

Epilogue

Parting Glances

Do what you can, with what you have, where you are.

—Theodore Roosevelt

So now you know the whole story. It's lonely at the top. It's tiresome. It's difficult. And the buck stops with you. But you make the rules, you choose the road (even the one less traveled), and you reap the benefits of the blood, sweat, and tears.

The fact is there is no trick or magic formula to learn. Just be smart. Don't be governed by emotion and recognize that you have certain costs associated with your success. Plan for them and budget for them. And recognize that you have certain limitations. But you can turn to experts for advice. The earlier you consult the lawyers or accountants or other experts, the better you will feel, the faster the problem will get solved and the cheaper the solution will be.

Remember: no one ever said, "I did too much research" or "I observed too much how others operated their businesses." Watch, listen and learn. And one day the neophytes will be learning from you.

Good luck!

Appendix

Business Forms and Reports

The following list is a recap of the essential business forms, reports and government documents described in this book.

Because some of these are long (and others change periodically), I've posted them on Silver Lake Publishing's Internet Web site at http:\\www.silverlakepub.com\thaler.

1. Sample registration form for fictitious business name [Form 3-1]

2. Sample Articles of Incorporation [Form 3-2]

3. Sample shareholder's certificate [Form 3-3]

4. Sample operating agreement for Limited Liability Company (LLC) [Form 3-4]

5. Sample operating agreement for Limited Liability Partnership (LLP) [Form 3-5]

5. IRS Form SS-4 [Form 3-6]

6. IRS Form 2553 [Form 3-7]

7. Sample Employment Agreement for operating or managing partner [Form 4-1]

8. Sample "Buy-Sell" Agreement among partners [Form 4-2]

9. Sample company description from business plan [Form 7-1]

10. Sample catalogue sheet [Form 8-1]

11. Sample company brochure [Form 8-2]

12. Form of an unlawful detainer action [Form 9-1]

13. Sample balance sheet [Form 12-1]

14. Sample sources of income and expense report [Form 12-2]

15. Sample profit and loss statement [Form 12-3]

16. Sample cash flow statement [Form 12-4]

17. Sample employment application [From 14-1]

18. Sample employment contract [Form 14-2]

19. IRS Form W-4 [Form 14-3]

20. IRS Form W-2 [Form 14-4]

21. Sample nondisclosure agreement [Form 16-1]

22. Sample non-competition agreement [Form 16-2]

23. Sample list of assets and liabilities for bankruptcy proceeding [Form 20-1]

Index

The Elements of Small Business

Notes

_____

_____

_____

_____

_____

_____

_____

_____

_____

_____

_____

_____

_____

_____

_____

_____

_____

_____

_____

_____

_____

_____

_____

_____

_____

_____

_____

Notes

The Elements of Small Business

_____

_____

_____

_____

_____

_____

_____

_____

_____

Notes

365

The Elements of Small Business

_____

_____

_____

_____

_____

_____

_____

_____

_____

_____

_____

_____

_____

_____

_____

_____

_____

_____

_____

_____

The Elements of Small Business

_____

_____

_____

_____

_____

_____

_____

_____

_____